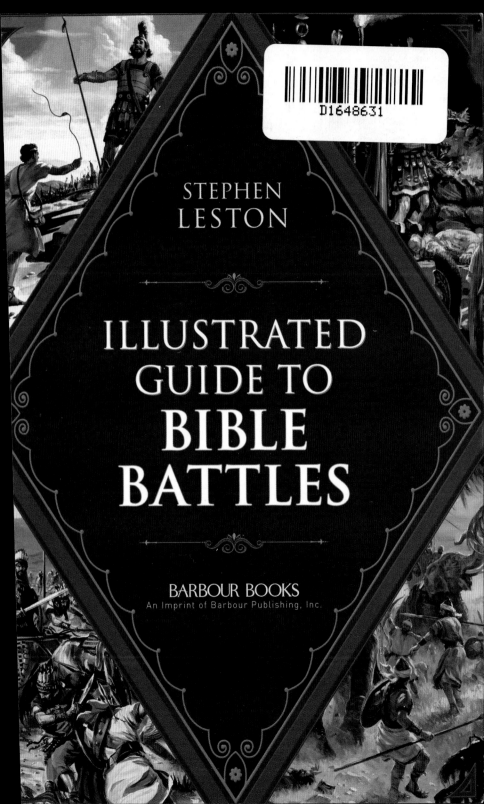

STEPHEN
LESTON

ILLUSTRATED
GUIDE TO
BIBLE
BATTLES

BARBOUR BOOKS
An Imprint of Barbour Publishing, Inc.

PHOTO CREDITS:

All "Location" maps: Hudson, Christopher D. *Bible Atlas & Companion*. Uhrichsville, OH: Barbour, 2008.

Pages 7, 9, 10, 11, 12, 16 (top), 16 (bottom credit: Dbachmann), 19 (all), 21 (bottom), 23 (bottom), 24 (credit: Wolfgang Sauber), 25, 36 (credit: Rama), 37 (top), 52 (credit: Wolfgang Sauber), 55 (all), 57 (credit: Anthiok), 57 (bottom), 58, 61, 62, 64 (top), 65 (credit: Remi Jouan), 66, 67 (credit: Rémih), 69, 72 (credit: Dbachmann), 73 (top, credit: Beivushtang), 74, 76, 77, 78, 79, 81 (top, credit: Plegadis), 81, 82, 83, 89 (all) (credit: Avishai Teicher), 91 (all), 98 (credit: Luis García), 99 (top), 100 (credit: Ekeidar), 101 (bottom), 102, 104 (credit: Водник at ru.wikipedia), 107 (top, credit: Ori~), 108, 111 (top, credit: E. Rehfeld), 111 (bottom, credit: Ldud), 117 (top, credit: Ori~), 117 (bottom, credit: Marie-Lan Nguyen), 119 (top, credit: Yuval Mendelson), 119, 120, 121, 125, 127 (bottom), 128, 141 (credit: Ealdgyth), 143 (top, credit: Ori~), 143 (bottom, credit: Steven G. Johnson), 144, 145 (bottom), 152, 153, 154, 158, 166 (credit: Olaf Tausch), 169 (top), 172 (credit: Khruner), 173 (top, credit: Gordio), 175, 176, 181 (top), 185 (top), 188 (credit: Nemo), 192, 196 (credit: Mike Peel), 200, 202, 203 (credit: Horsch, Willy), 206 (top), 209, 212, 213, 214, 215, 216, 220, 232, 233, 239 (credit: Gugganij), 225 (bottom, credit: Audioscience/Shutterstock.com), 240, 241, 242 (credit: Jniemenmaa), 244 (credit: Rapsak), 245, 246 (credit: FollowTheMedia), 247 (top, credit: Manfred Heyde), 250, 251 (top, credit: Steerpike), 251, 252 (source: Godot13), 254 (source: דגולי׳א), 255 (source: Wolfgang Sauber), 256 (credit: Ingeborg Simon), 257, 260 (credit: Kalogeropoulos), 261, 264, 266, 268, and 273: COMMONS WIKIMEDIA (licenses use: CC-BY, CC-BY-SA, GFDL, GPL/LGPL)

Page 275 TheBiblePeople.com

All other images: SHUTTERSTOCK

Published by Barbour Books, an imprint of Barbour Publishing, Inc., P.O. Box 719, Uhrichsville, Ohio 44683 www.barbourbooks.com

ecpa Member of the Evangelical Christian Publishers Association

Our mission is to publish and distribute inspirational products offering exceptional value and biblical encouragement to the masses.

Printed in the United States of America.

TABLE OF CONTENTS

To my wife, Heather: You are the one who completes me—the one God designed to partner with me through life on this earth. I could not have a better gift or friend.

To Anna, Amber, Alyssa, and Andrew: I cannot tell you how much I love you and how much you have honored your mother and me with the way you live. May you always remember that the battle belongs to the Lord—He is in control (Joshua 1:9).

To my church: You give me the support to pursue what I love—helping people understand and order their lives according to the Word of God. Together may we stand faithful.

INTRODUCTION

War can be brutal—regardless of the motive behind it. The Bible tells the story of faithful Abraham leading a righteous war in an effort to save his family members. It also recounts the wars of power-hungry, selfish leaders. Whether motivated by righteousness or greed, the battles recorded in the Bible reveal how God uses the results of war to advance His mission for humanity: salvation.

The study of the Bible's battles reveals that God is not a spectator regarding human events. He does not sit idly by and speculate who the winners and losers will be. He does not grow anxious as the war drums grow louder and wonder how the attacking armies will change the course of history.

God is all-powerful and all-knowing. There were times in biblical history when He ordained war in order to bring about His judgment or plan. And there were times in history when wars resulted from human, sinful greed; but God did not wring His hands and hope for the best in those situations. God knew the outcome of each war before it began. He masterfully used the outcome to bring about the story of salvation and guide human history to its ultimate end.

Each chapter of this book contains an introduction to the time period as well as big-picture themes found in this era of biblical history. You'll also find overviews of over ninety of the Bible's battles.

My prayer for you as you read this book is that you will be struck by the majesty and power of God. I pray that you'll see His grace at work in spite of sinful people and that you'll enjoy discovering how a holy God can overcome the most sinful situations to accomplish His plan. This is God's world, and even though evil people seek to use painful means to carry out their ends, God never surrenders control. May you find hope in the wisdom of God, peace in the rule of God, and strength in the power of the God. God never changes. This is and always will be His world.

Stephen Leston

ACKNOWLEDGEMENTS

It takes the efforts of a number of people to complete a book with this many details. I am grateful to the individuals who worked hard to build outlines, check facts, and make contributions within each chapter.

I would like to extend special thanks to Karen Engle, who helped develop the manuscript. I'm grateful to Ben Irwin, who brought his editorial talents to the manuscript. Thank you to Mary Larsen, who helped ensure all the *i*'s were dotted and the *t*'s were crossed. Also, hats off to Andy Sloan, who performed a final, scholarly review and helped confirm the many details in this book.

Thanks also to Kelly McIntosh, Paul Muckley, and the team at Barbour Publishing, who had the vision for this title. I'm grateful to be associated with it.

Thank you to my lovely daughter Anna, who helped with some of the research. I am so proud of you, Anna. And most importantly, thanks to Heather, my beautiful wife, who allowed me to take the extra evenings and weekends in order to create this resource.

Chapter 1

FROM ABRAHAM TO THE PROMISED LAND

"And I will give to you and to your offspring after you the land of your sojourn-ings, all the land of Canaan, for an everlasting possession, and I will be their God."

(Genesis 17:8)

INTRODUCTION

Since the fall of Adam and Eve, one thing has marked humanity: war. It would be fair to say that the Old Testament cannot be truly understood without refer-ence to violent conflict, since it was an inescapable part of ancient Israelite life. From Cain killing Abel to the conquest of Canaan to David's rule and beyond, the pages of the Bible are filled with bloodshed. Sadly, God's people did not always emerge victo-rious in the battles they fought. Sometimes the enemy was more powerful. One thing is for certain: every battle that Israel won was only because of God's intervention. The people of Israel were called to trust God's sovereignty and let Him take care of the nations; when the Israelites trusted in themselves and chose to fight on their own, without God's authorization or direction, they experienced defeat.

God's redemptive plan to establish His King to rule and reign in a specific place would be carried out through the formation of the nation that became known as Israel. The conquest of Canaan was intimately connected to this plan since the land had been promised to Israel, through Abraham, as an everlasting possession. As God formed His chosen people and built them into a formidable nation, He

Spring in northern Israel

sought to establish them on a specific piece of property that He had designated for them. Considering the location of this piece of property—the sole land bridge connecting Eurasia with Africa, with no detour between sea and desert—it is no wonder that the powers of the ancient world did not hesitate to fight, often brutally, to take hold of this strategic area. Any people trying to establish themselves in this part of the world were destined to live under almost unrelenting pressure from neighboring nations—not to mention peoples who already lived in the land. Thus war was inevitable for Israel.

However, at the beginning of their escape from Egypt, the Israelites received this exhortation from Moses: "The LORD will fight for you, and you have only to be silent" (Exodus 14:14). The people of Israel were reminded that the promised land they were headed to belonged to God and that He would fight for their possession of it. It was the one place on earth over which God asserted direct ownership. God told them, "The land shall not be sold in perpetuity, for the land is mine. For you are strangers and sojourners with me" (Leviticus 25:23). Once in the land, Israel found itself at the center of a major geopolitical conflict, one that has repercussions to this day. God insisted that any nation that could tempt Israel with idol worship and pagan practices had to be destroyed—completely. God's people were to be set apart, a light to the nations that surrounded them. There was no room for the Israelites to be half obedient.

Some have said that the study of history is really just the study of war. Ultimately, war is a sad reality resulting from the deep poison common to all humans: sin. The manifestation of sin—hatred, selfishness, and pride—is war's fuel. Psalm 2 explains that nations rage because they refuse to submit to the Lord and the King He has chosen to rule over us. The kings of the earth want to hold the power and the glory that belong only to Jesus.

Knowing war was an inevitable reality for Israel, God established rules for His children for how they were to conduct themselves in battle. God expected His people to act and fight differently than the other armies that pillaged and plundered as they conquered. The soldiers of the armies of godless nations would kill mercilessly, rape women, enslave children, and destroy natural resources. God wanted the Israelites to approach war in a manner that reflected the integrity of their Creator. Deuteronomy 20:1–20 provides some of the rules that God established to govern war as fought by the Israelites:

Ancient charioteer

- The people of Israel were not to fear their enemies, no matter how powerful they seemed, for the God who rescued them from slavery was with them (verse 1).
- The priest was to remind people before the battle not to be afraid because God would fight the battle for them (verses 2–4).
- The Israelites were to completely destroy everything that had breath, to protect themselves from being influenced by the city's detestable practices of idol worship (verses 16–18).
- When attacking a city for a long time, the Israelites were forbidden from destroying its trees. They were allowed to eat from the trees but could not cut them down (verses 19–20).
- When attacking a city outside the promised land, they were allowed to take the women, children, livestock, and everything else in the city as plunder (verse 14).

View of the promised land from Mount Nebo in Jordan

Warfare in the Middle East during the time of the Old Testament had developed into a sophisticated art and science. Military structures and strategies made up the landscape of the nations. Throughout this region there was a basic military structure in place for almost all the armies. Most military units had the same five divisions: horsemen, spearmen, archers, slingers, and swordsmen.

FROM ABRAHAM TO THE PROMISED LAND

Horsemen: Soldiers riding horses or chariots armed with spears, swords, or bows operated as mobilized infantry. They could chase a retreating force or attack a scattering army. Sometimes they would utilize horses as a weapon to knock people down, or use the speed of their horses to press against opponents, forcing them into compromising positions.

Spearmen: Spearmen could launch spears from horses or atop hills or high places with the accuracy of modern-day missiles. Their powerful weapons could take out soldiers as well as their horses.

Archers: Archers would often launch volleys of arrows from a distance as an enemy force approached, thus slowing their advance. In order to protect against an archer attack, the advancing enemy soldiers would huddle together and put their shields over their heads to serve as collective armor. While this was effective in protecting the advancing army, it slowed them down enough to allow a unit to get into position to counterattack.

Slingers: Slingers were able to launch rocks at high velocity from their slings. They would exploit the weaknesses in their enemies' armor by targeting uncovered spaces on bodies. For example, a slinger could launch a stone right between the eyes of a heavily armored person, like David did with Goliath, thereby killing him.

Swordsmen: Hand-to-hand infantry soldiers would engage in one-on-one battles using their swords to slay the enemy. These strong warriors had the ability to wield heavy weapons for long periods of time in the heat of battle.

The rocky, dusty terrain and unfavorable climate of ancient Israel made fighting in the region difficult. Some places were so hot that many of the soldiers fought without armor. Heatstroke threatened lives almost as much as any weapon of war. In addition, maintaining horses proved to be quite challenging. Battles were often fought in valleys since these spaces typically provided shade as well as cover and concealment. Often, opposing forces would stand on either side of a valley and taunt each other before sending their troops into the valley to fight. Many tactical advances that were developed in this region are still used today.

As we examine the battles of the Bible, it is important to keep in mind that the biblical authors did not record these stories to celebrate war, to glory in death, or to promote violence as a way of life. These events were recorded because they are true, and there is much we can learn from them. When humans oppose God's plan for this world, there will be conflict. God loves and protects His children, but He will punish those who oppose Him. Justice will prevail. Yet He is a merciful God; all those who cry for mercy will find it in Him.

Desert in Israel

The War of Kings
GENESIS 14

Gezer
Jericho
nnah
Salem (Jerusalem)
Bethlehem
Adullam
Hazazon-
tamar?
(En-gedi)
Mamre
Hebron
Kiriath
Dead Sea
Sodom?
Gomorrah?
NEGEV
Bela (Zoar)
Admah?
Zeboiim?
Bozrah

LOCATION

The Valley of Siddim was the battleground for the cities of the Jordan plain, whose residents revolted against the Elamite Empire and its Mesopotamian allies. The traditional view holds that the Valley of Siddim was at the south end of the Dead Sea. Special mention is made in Genesis 14:10 of the slime (or tar) pits present in the valley; these slime pits evidently played an important part in the outcome of the battle.

KEY PLAYERS

- Abram (Abraham): a faithful man called by God to leave his native land of Mesopotamia for a promised new land, family, and inheritance in Canaan
- Lot: Abraham's nephew who lived in the city of Sodom at the time of the battle
- Chedorlaomer: the king of Elam (east of Babylon) during the time of Abraham

WEAPONS AND WARRIORS

There were five branches of military common in the Middle East at this time: horsemen, spearmen, swordsmen, archers, and slingers. When Abram entered the battle, he did so with 318 men who were not divided into these standard military divisions. Instead, he organized small guerilla forces to strike from several points, attacking at night. Abram's men probably fought with spears and slings, light infantry weapons, and a lot of faith—compared with the heavily armored men they were up against.

Ancient bronze spearhead

Battle Synopsis

The Battle of Siddim, also called the War of Kings, is the first specific account of military engagement in the Bible. In the days before the destruction of Sodom and Gomorrah, the Elamite Empire, under King Chedorlaomer, controlled the land of Canaan, including the plain of the Jordan River. Five kings of the cities of the plain revolted against Chedorlaomer. In response, Chedorlaomer assembled forces from three other cities that supported his rule. Together these four kings overwhelmed the five kings of the Jordan. Those who escaped fled to the mountains. Some of the people of Sodom and Gomorrah—including Abram's nephew Lot—were taken captive (Genesis 14:1–9). Abram immediately armed 318 of his trained servants and set off to pursue Chedorlaomer and free Lot, catching up with Chedorlaomer in the city of Dan. Abram showed great military wisdom by attacking Chedorlaomer from multiple sides at night.

After the battle, Melchizedek (king of Salem) blesses Abram

Outcome

Short-Term

Abram and his men defeated Chedorlaomer and the other Mesopotamian kings, recovered all the captives, including Lot, and even retrieved the goods that were stolen (Genesis 14:13–17).

Long-Term

The people of Sodom and Gomorrah did not learn from Abram's righteous example, nor did they trust God after He delivered them. Instead, they lived a depraved lifestyle and were eventually judged by God.

God's Role

Though not explicitly stated, Abram was victorious solely because of God's involvement. There would have been no way for Abram to defeat four kings and their massive armies with only 318 lightly armed men. Abram's approach suggested he had great faith in God and in his men. After the victory, Abram refused the spoils because he would not allow anyone to say that a man had made him rich (Genesis 14:23); the credit for his success and wealth belonged to God alone. Later God told Abram that He was Abram's shield (Genesis 15:1); no earthly army could overcome His power.

Military Heroes and Villains: Abraham

The War of Kings is one of the earliest recorded battles in history. When we examine it, we discover something very important about Abram (Abraham): he maximized his resources and fought strategically.

Abram found the Mesopotamian army at Dan. They were likely coming back to Mesopotamia with prisoners of war and the spoil. Abram then decided on a strategy, which revolved around three key tactics:

Tactic 1: Attacking at night for maximum confusion
Tactic 2: Dividing his force and attacking from several directions
Tactic 3: Keeping the enemy on the move

The strategy resulted in a surprise that scared the enemy into fleeing for their lives. Abram's men chased the Mesopotamian army for fifty miles or more, all the way to the north of Damascus. What is most interesting to note is that Abram's primary objective was to rescue Lot, not to destroy the Mesopotamian army. Indeed, Abram succeeded in recovering Lot and all the plunder and captives the Mesopotamians had taken during the siege. Abram then marched home a victor.

Is Abram a war hero? Indeed he is. In fact, Abram showed a military cunning that has inspired military commanders throughout history. To take 318 lightly armed men up against armed horsemen, spearmen, archers, slingers, and swordsmen was

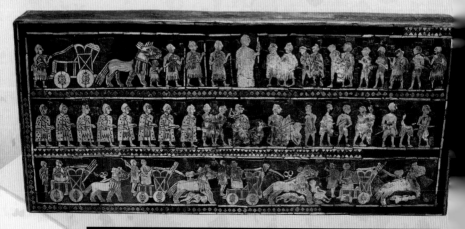

Approximately 4,500 years old, this ancient Sumerian artifact known as the Standard of Ur depicts ancient battle weapons and infantry.

a complicated task, to say the least. By attacking at night and splitting his forces, Abram caused maximum confusion among the enemy. As a result, when Abram pursued the Mesopotamian army, he managed to gain the upper hand. By keeping the enemy's military force on the move, Abram prevented them from harnessing their forces and determining the strengths and weaknesses of Abram's own force.

Abram proved he was a skilled leader and a cunning commander who understood how to maximize his strengths.

Abraham's Departure, József Molnár (1821–1899)

Simeon, Levi, and the Shechemites
GENESIS 34

LOCATION

After Jacob reconciled with Esau, he settled in the city of Shechem. This was a Canaanite city inhabited by the Hivites. According to Genesis 33:18, Jacob camped near the city and eventually purchased land—the land on which he had set up his tent—from the sons of Hamor. He built an altar to the Lord and called it El-Elohe-Israel, or "God, the God of Israel." Shechem lay north of Bethel and Shiloh on the road going from Jerusalem to the northern districts. It was located between two historically significant mountains: Gerizim and Ebal.

KEY PLAYERS

- Hamor: Shechem's father, a Hivite; the city of Shechem's first ancestor (Judges 9:28)
- Shechem: Hamor's son and prince of the land
- Simeon and Levi: Jacob's sons and Dinah's brothers who destroy the city of Shechem
- Dinah: the daughter of Jacob and the tragic victim in this account
- Jacob: Isaac's son who moved his family to Shechem

WEAPONS AND WARRIORS

Because of the nature of this campaign, the first weapon used was deception. Simeon and Levi tricked the males of the family of Hamor into getting circumcised. Weak and still healing from the procedure, the men were hardly in a position to defend themselves. During the attack on Shechem, all Simeon and Levi needed were swords.

Simeon and Levi Slay the Shechemites, Gerard Hoet (1648–1733)

BATTLE SYNOPSIS

Dinah, Leah and Jacob's daughter, left her home to visit the women of Shechem. When Hamor's son Shechem, the prince of the land, saw Dinah, he forced himself on her and raped her. He then asked his father to persuade Jacob to give him Dinah as his wife.

Hamor approached Jacob and reasoned that if the two of them agreed not only to a marriage between Dinah and Shechem but also to widespread intermarriage between the families of Hamor and Jacob, then they would all dwell in the land together in peace and prosperity. Jacob's sons were outraged at what had happened to their sister. So they handled the negotiations with Hamor—with evil intent. They said they would consent to intermarriage only if all the men of the city agreed to undergo circumcision.

Hamor and Shechem eagerly agreed, and the men of Shechem were circumcised. Three days later, while the men of the city were still recovering, Simeon and Levi, Dinah's full brothers, descended on the city with their swords. They massacred all the men, including Hamor and his son Shechem. They removed Dinah from Shechem's house, looted the city completely, and captured the women and captured the women and children.

Seduction of Dinah,
James Tissot (1836–1902)

OUTCOME

SHORT-TERM

Later, just before his death, Jacob prophesied that the tribes of Simeon and Levi would be divided and scattered among Israel as a consequence for their ancestors' violent actions (Genesis 49:5–7).

LONG-TERM

After the Israelites conquered Canaan, the Levites were given towns to live in within the lands belonging to other tribes (Joshua 14:1–4; 21:1–42). Simeon's tribe dwindled in size and was eventually absorbed into the tribe of Judah (Joshua 19:1–9).

GOD'S ROLE

Dinah's rape was a horrible crime. Sin of this depth is wretched in God's sight, and He certainly does not endorse this kind of action. Equally, God does not want His children to take justice into their own hands. Levi and Simeon showed no concern for God's righteousness, and their resulting crime was just as heinous as the one committed by Shechem. Worse yet, it disgraced God's covenant of circumcision. God did not allow this sin that resulted from Levi and Simeon's hard hearts to go unpunished.

FROM ABRAHAM TO THE PROMISED LAND

Pharaoh's Pursuit of the Israelites

EXODUS 14

LOCATION

Before the Israelites crossed the Red Sea, God told them to encamp in Pi-hahiroth while awaiting an attack by Pharaoh. This area, situated between Baal-zephon and Migdol, was a very difficult location to be in if facing an attack. Because the Israelites were camped by the Red Sea, there was no way to escape. God placed the Israelites in this situation so it would be clear that their only hope of survival was through His miraculous intervention.

KEY PLAYERS

- Pharaoh: the king of Egypt who rebelled against God's command to set the people of Israel free
- Moses: God's appointed leader who led the Israelites away from Egyptian oppression and to the edge of the promised land
- Egyptians: people of an ancient Near Eastern power known for oppressing the Israelites
- Israelites: descendants of Abraham; God's chosen people, who were promised the land of Canaan

WEAPONS AND WARRIORS

The Egyptian army was outfitted with advanced weaponry—including six hundred specialized chariots (along with other chariot units)—making them the most sophisticated military technology of the time. Their fighting force included highly skilled archers who could launch arrows from moving chariots. Egyptian soldiers wore light armor and carried copper-tipped spears. The Israelites, by contrast, were unarmed; their few heavy goods, such as tools and tents, were carried on the backs of donkeys. The Israelites were no match for the well-equipped and fast-moving Egyptian army.

Papyrus showing Egyptian use of bows

FROM ABRAHAM TO THE PROMISED LAND

14

Pyramids, Egypt

Red Sea, Egypt

THE ILLUSTRATED GUIDE TO BIBLE BATTLES

Battle Synopsis

After many plagues and the death of Pharaoh's firstborn son, the king of Egypt finally released the nation of Israel. However, after the Israelites left, God hardened Pharaoh's heart. Pharaoh and his leaders realized they had lost all their slaves and decided to force the Israelites back to Egypt. Pharaoh sent his entire military force after the Israelites.

The Israelites saw the approaching army and became terrified; they were trapped against the Red Sea. The advancing Egyptian army blocked their only escape. The Red Sea was on one side, and mountains were on the other. Thinking their flight from Egypt had been for nothing, they cried out to the Lord for help. Already they reasoned that life had been better for them in Egypt. Moses didn't know what exactly God would do, but he knew God had to help. "The LORD will fight for you," Moses told the people. "You have only to be silent" (Exodus 14:14). The Israelites' role was limited to remaining calm. God commanded Moses to lift up his staff and stretch out his hand over the water of the Red Sea—and the sea parted.

God sent a specially commissioned angel and a pillar of cloud to come between the Israelites and the Egyptians, protecting the Israelites all of them had made their way to the other side. The pillar acted as a source of light by night for the Israelites but as darkness to their enemies. When the Egyptian army arrived at the water's edge, it was still parted, so they entered with the intent to chase down and destroy the Israelites. As soon as the Israelites reached the other side safely, God commanded Moses to once again stretch out his hand over the sea. The walls of water came crashing down, killing every Egyptian soldier.

OUTCOME

SHORT-TERM

God made His name known to the Egyptians and to the whole world, revealing Himself as the great and powerful Deliverer (Exodus 14:17–18; Joshua 2:10).

LONG-TERM

Centuries later, after the fall of Jerusalem, some Jews insisted on going to Egypt. The prophet Jeremiah warned them not to go (Jeremiah 42–43).

GOD'S ROLE

God alone delivered the Israelites out of Egypt; He orchestrated events to bring about the salvation of His people and the destruction of their enemies. Moses followed God's specific instructions, which led to the parting of the waters. Then God caused the water to retreat back over the Egyptians. This miraculous event shows clearly that God fought for Israel.

Egyptian Infantry

The Egyptian infantry developed expertise in using chariots, which enabled them to attack with speed and force. Their tactics were simple yet deadly. Two men rode on each chariot; one would drive it while the other would fight. Spears were used for close combat as the troops got closer and closer to the enemy, while volleys of arrows peppered the enemy during the approach. The infantry's armor consisted of leather tunics with metal scales sewn onto them. This provided pro-

tection as well as maximum flexibility of movement. The Egyptians of this period did not use heavier armor because most of their fighting occurred in extreme heat. For this reason, many of the foot soldiers would not wear any armor at all. Between the speed of their horses and skill of their soldiers, the Egyptians perfected the art of mobilized infantry. The approaching sound of the horses would instill fear in the opposing army. The Egyptians' skilled handling of bows, spears, and swords made them a formidable force.

During this time, a sword called the khopesh came into use. A combination blade and hook, the khopesh was a very sophisticated weapon. The soldier would be able to pull down the shield of his opponent using the hook and quickly stab him in the face or throat using the blade. The Egyptians became skilled at disarming their opponents with this weapon, allowing them to kill with ease.

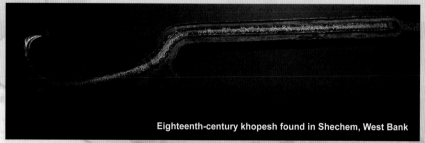

Eighteenth-century khopesh found in Shechem, West Bank

Most of Egypt's soldiers were farmers recruited by local governors. The farmers were called to fight whenever Pharaoh needed them. Because Egypt was surrounded by deserts and seas that formed natural barriers to invading armies, the Egyptians were able to protect themselves by relying on a greater reserve force than those of other countries of their size and power.

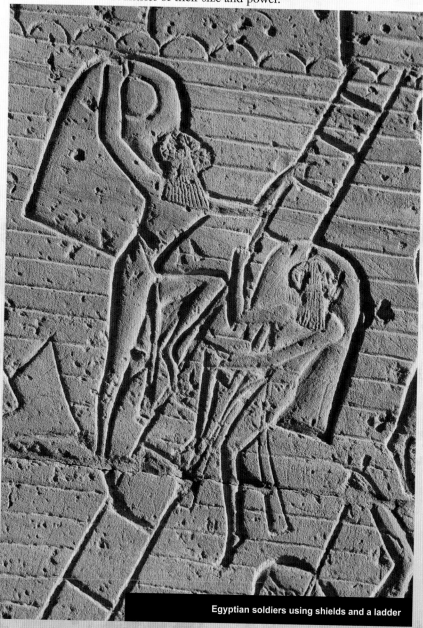

Egyptian soldiers using shields and a ladder

The Israelites' Defeat of the Amalekites
Exodus 17:8-15; Deuteronomy 25:17-18

Location

The location of Israel's first official battle was a place called Rephidim. The name *Rephidim* likely means "rests" or "stays"— that is, resting places. Rephidim was a stopping point for the Israelites as they made their way from Egypt to Sinai. Here they gained their first victory after leaving Egypt. It was also at Rephidim that they complained about not having any water. In response, God provided water from a rock. Because of the people's murmuring, the place became known as Massah and Meribah, which mean "testing" and "quarreling."

Key Players

- Moses: God's appointed leader who led the Israelites away from Egyptian oppression and to the edge of the promised land
- Joshua: Moses' second-in-command, who led the Israelites into the promised land after Moses' death
- Hur: Moses and Aaron's companion
- Aaron: Moses' older brother, who spoke for Moses to Pharaoh; the first high priest of the tabernacle
- Israelites: descendants of Abraham; God's chosen people, who were promised the land of Canaan
- Amalekites: people of a nomadic nation who came to have a history of hostility toward Israel

Weapons and Warriors

This is an interesting battle because the only weapon described in detail is the "staff of God" that Moses carried (Exodus 17:9). Moses used this staff in his encounters with Pharaoh (Exodus 4:1–5). When Moses held his staff out over the Red Sea, it parted (Exodus 14:26–27). The power was not in the staff itself but came from God. He was moving among the Israelites, and the staff served as nothing more than a sign of His power and presence.

Battle Synopsis

The Israelites were a long way south of the land of Canaan, and they were heading away from it. The Amalekites who lived in the Negev and in the Sinai Peninsula attacked the people of Israel without any provocation. When Moses saw the Amalekites, he knew his people would have to fight, so he sent Joshua out with some of the appointed fighting men to meet the enemy in battle. Meanwhile, Moses made his way to the top of a nearby hill overlooking the scene of combat. As the battle raged, Moses stood there with his staff in hand. Whenever Moses held his staff in the air, the Israelites below gained the upper hand. Whenever Moses let his staff down, the Amalekites would start to prevail. Therefore, Moses kept his staff in the air—with the help of Aaron and Hur, who supported his weakening arms—until the Israelites triumphed over the Amalekites.

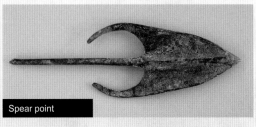

Spear point

Outcome

Short-term

The Israelites won the battle but did not completely destroy the Amalekites. Nevertheless, their victory allowed them to continue moving through the desert.

Long-term

Because the Amalekites were not annihilated, the people of Israel were destined to face them in battle again. Centuries later, King Saul's failure to destroy the Amalekites cost him his throne.

God's Role

God played a central role in this battle. Israel's army would not have been able to triumph over the Amalekites apart from His intervention. They needed the mighty power of the Lord. Over two hundred times in the Old Testament, God is referred to as the "Lord of hosts." This title refers to the power of God over all creation. He alone is the Lord of creation and holds power over all things. This also means that God is the Commander over the army of heaven and is able to conquer any foe. Because He is the Lord of hosts, God was able to give the Israelites the victory over the Amalekites.

Moses, Aaron, and Hur
Millais (1829–1896)

FROM ABRAHAM TO THE PROMISED LAND

The Amalekites' Victory at Hormah
NUMBERS 14:28-45

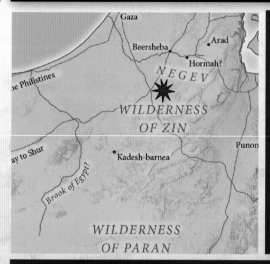

LOCATION

After an attempt—unsanctioned by God—to enter the promised land, the Israelites were routed by Amalekites and Canaanites in a place called Hormah, which means "destruction." The precise location of Hormah remains a mystery, though it was situated somewhere in the southernmost region of the promised land

KEY PLAYERS

- Moses: God's appointed leader who led the Israelites away from Egyptian oppression and to the edge of the promised land
- Israelites: descendants of Abraham; God's chosen people, who were promised the land of Canaan
- Amalekites: people of a nomadic nation with a history of hostility toward Israel
- Canaanites: descendants of Canaan, the son of Ham, who included the Sidonians, Hittites, Jebusites, Amorites, Girgashites, Hivites, Arkites, Sinites, Arvadites, Zemarites, and Hamathites
- Twelve spies: the Israelite men—including Joshua and Caleb, the only two who trusted God and proposed entering the land—who entered Canaan at Moses' command

WEAPONS AND WARRIORS

The Israelites went up against a portion of the Canaanites and Amalekites. The enemy would have been armed with swords, spears, and slings—along with archers and horsemen capable to move as light infantry. The army of Israel was probably armed with swords, spears, slings, and archers—but missing one key weapon: the power of the Lord. Without God on their side, they were a weak and feeble fighting force, unable to stand against their enemies.

BATTLE SYNOPSIS

This battle should never have been fought. God had brought the Israelites to the doorstep of the promised land. But when ten of the twelve spies came back with a terrifying report of the land's occupants, the people were too afraid to enter the land, doubting God's protection and provision. As a result, God outlined a series of consequences, which included death without entering the land for those who were too fearful to trust in Him. The people were saddened by the news and decided to take matters into their own hands. So they mounted an attack by invading the southern portion of Canaan, but they were trounced by the Canaanites and Amalekites. They were unable to right their previous error by fighting under their own power. God refused to bless their efforts.

The Spies Return from Canaan
Detail from facade of Duomo, Milan

OUTCOME

SHORT-TERM

Because of the Israelites' disobedience and lack of faith in God, the Israelites were defeated. Many people died because of their rebellion.

LONG-TERM

The Israelites' failure to trust God resulted in God delaying their entrance into the promised land. Every adult—with the exception of Caleb and Joshua (Numbers 14:30)—would die before the next generation would be allowed to enter the land sworn to their ancestors.

GOD'S ROLE

Some may struggle to see the hand of God in this defeat, but He was fully present in it. The key to every Israelite victory was their willingness to trust God as their provider and protector. Whenever they lost sight of this, they suffered defeat and failure. The Israelites needed to learn the importance of relying on God at all times as they engaged in the battles for the promised land.

Replica of an ancient sling

On the Way to Canaan
NUMBERS 21:1-3

LOCATION

The Israelites were traveling by way of Atharim, a route likely located in the area just south of the Dead Sea. When the Canaanites took some of the Israelites as captives, the people made a vow to the Lord to destroy the cities that these Canaanites inhabited. God gave His people the victory, and the area was named Hormah, which means "destruction."

KEY PLAYERS

- King of Arad: a Canaanite king who lived in the Negev
- Israelites: descendants of Abraham; God's chosen people, who were promised the land of Canaan
- Moses: God's appointed leader who led the Israelites away from Egyptian oppression and to the edge of the promised land
- Canaanites: descendants of Canaan, the son of Ham, that included the Sidonians, Hittites, Jebusites, Amorites, Girgashites, Hivites, Arkites, Sinites, Arvadites, Zemarites, and Hamathites

WEAPONS AND WARRIORS

The dominant weapons of the age were bows, spears, swords, slings, and cavalry. Warfare remained fairly consistent throughout this period of history. Archers were used from a distance to disorient an opposing force. Horsemen using spears and swords were next in line. Foot soldiers came in last and engaged in hand-to-hand combat. Both the Israelites and the Canaanites would have utilized similar strategies in fighting. The only difference is that when the Israelites trusted God and followed His direction, they had His power on their side. This was an advantage no opposing army could match.

BATTLE SYNOPSIS

The nation of Israel was moving toward the promised land. As they did so, the Canaanite king of Arad attempted to stop them. He attacked the people and took some of them captive. In response, the Israelites sought the Lord. They made a vow to God that if He would give them victory, they would destroy the enemy's cities. God was on their side, and the Israelites went on to defeat the Canaanites. After they had destroyed the Canaanite cities as promised, they named the place where they were victorious Hormah.

The Negev, Israel

OUTCOME

SHORT-TERM

The Israelites named the battleground where they destroyed the city of Arad and its confederacy Hormah, designating it as a place of destruction.

LONG-TERM

This battle served as a sign to the Canaanites that the people of Israel were a force to be reckoned with. Later, just before the siege of Jericho, Rahab the prostitute told Israelite spies that the Canaanites were terrified of Israel (Joshua 2:8–9).

GOD'S ROLE

One thing is clear from Israel's history: without God, they would have been utterly unable to defeat their enemies. God proved time and time again that He was their protector. When some of the Israelites were taken captive, God was the only One to whom they could turn. When they made a vow to the Lord, He heard their cries and responded by giving them power to overcome their enemies.

Ancient horseman with bow and arrow

FROM ABRAHAM TO THE PROMISED LAND

The Challenge of the Midianites
NUMBERS 31:1-11

LOCATION

Midianite territory was located east of the Gulf of Aqaba in western Arabia. The Midianites had expanded their land to include the Sinai Peninsula. Archaeological digs have discovered a rather extensive walled city as well as a fairly sophisticated irrigation system in this area.

KEY PLAYERS

- Phinehas: the grandson of Aaron
- Moses: God's appointed leader who led the Israelites away from Egyptian oppression and to the edge of the promised land
- Midianites: descendants of Midian, the son of the Hebrew patriarch Abraham by his second wife, Keturah
- Evi, Rekem, Zur, Hur, and Reba: kings of Midian
- Balaam: the diviner who was killed by the Israelites

WEAPONS AND WARRIORS

This battle was initiated by God when He called the Israelites to take a thousand men from each of their twelve tribes (twelve thousand men total) and arm them. This constituted a huge strike force with which to attack the Midianites.

Bronze age spearhead

Battle Synopsis

Following the exodus, the Midianites viewed the Israelites as a military threat and joined the Moabites to stand in the way of God's people (see Numbers 22:1–7; 25:1–9). In response, God commanded Moses to annihilate the Midianites. He instructed Moses to take a thousand men from every tribe, as well as Phinehas, the son of Eleazar the priest. Since this was God's battle, He wanted Phinehas to carry the sacred articles and instruments set aside for worship. The Israelites attacked the Midianites and slew them; all five of their kings were put to death. The warriors spared only the women who were virgins. They killed the rest of the females and all the men and boys, took spoils from the land of Midian, and burned all the cities.

Five Kings of Midian Slain by Israel
Gerard Hoet (1648–1733)

Outcome

Short-Term

As a result of this tragic episode, the law concerning marriage with captives was enacted (Deuteronomy 21:10–14).

Long-Term

The Midianites did not go away. They survived to create even more trouble for Israel.

God's Role

This was God's battle. The Midianites made clear that they intended to annihilate the Israelites. God initiated the battle to protect His people, and He blessed them with the power to overcome the Midianites. By sending Phinehas, the son of Eleazar the priest, into battle, God made clear that He was the general in charge of this holy mission; therefore, if His people would trust Him and follow His lead, they would be victorious. Through this victory, God assured His people of His presence with them and showed them that everything He had promised would come to pass.

Military Heroes and Villains: Moses

One important aspect of any wartime operation is the chain of command. The chain of command, in a military context, is the line of responsibility and authority along which directives are given. When examining the events of the exodus, it's worth noting that God fought for the Israelites every step of the way. Through Moses, God told the Israelites where to go when they left Egypt; He told them where to stop, where to camp, and what to do when Egyptian forces came upon them. Moses simply followed orders.

The command structure seen from Exodus through Deuteronomy is unique yet sound. Israel's commander in chief was God Himself. He formed the overall strategy and gave tactical instruction to Moses. Moses served as a good colonel,

Moses leads the Hebrews through the Red Sea. Renata Sedmakova / Shutterstock.com

following God's instruction to the letter on every occasion except one (Numbers 20:8–12).

Moses' military mind certainly enabled him to serve his role as well as he did. He was the adopted grandson of Egypt's king and had likely been trained and educated with other young Egyptian men. Much of their education would have been in military combat, which included practical experience in hand-to-hand fighting. Military understanding, strategic wisdom, and an obedient spirit when given instructions prepared Moses to skillfully lead his people under God's command.

With each circumstance Moses faced, he was required to obey his military Commander. At the same time, each circumstance affirmed Moses' competency in military maneuver. The Bible shows that Moses was proficient in a variety of secondary military activities. He successfully managed logistics, including the quick departure of millions of Israelites from Egypt. He armed his people, trained them well, and helped them to repel an attack from the Amalekites. Moses showed military intelligence by sending spies into the land that Israel was to conquer. He conducted diplomatic negotiations with the king of Egypt before the exodus and sent conciliatory messages to the rulers of the Edomites and the Amorites. It is very likely that he maneuvered his army with the use of hand signals.

Moses critically managed the people and demonstrated expert knowledge about the terrain. He had the ability to follow God's commands because he had the experience of being raised in Egypt and (in all likelihood) serving in a military capacity. In other words, Moses understood chain of command.

FROM ABRAHAM TO THE PROMISED LAND

Things to Think About

- What can we learn from these stories about how God protects His people?

- What happens when God's way is challenged or ignored?

- What can we learn about the holiness and justice of God from the battles recorded in the first five books of the Old Testament?

- What can we learn about God's love for His children from these battles?

Chapter 2

BATTLES OF THE CONQUEST AND THE ERA OF JUDGES

"Be strong and courageous, for you shall cause this people to inherit the land that I swore to their fathers to give them. Only be strong and very courageous, being careful to do according to all the law that Moses my servant commanded you. Do not turn from it to the right hand or to the left, that you may have good success wherever you go."

(Joshua 1:6–7)

INTRODUCTION

A s Joshua prepared to embark on taking the promised land, there were no doubt many obstacles that could have caused him to second-guess God's instruction. The enemy was strong, and the potential for a protracted war and many deaths was very real. However, just before Joshua was about to begin the campaign, God spoke to him. God wanted Joshua to understand something very important.

God had made a promise to Joshua's ancestor Abraham: He was going to give Abraham's descendants, the Israelites, the land of Canaan. God knew taking this land would not be easy. The Israelites would face enemies who would seek to kill them, deceive them, and draw them away from the Lord. These pressures would be great and would constantly surround them. Yet God told Joshua to act courageously, move forward in faith, and follow the law of the Lord. Joshua was instructed to consecrate the people—to set them apart for the Lord—before they crossed the Jordan to take the land. Each battle would be the Lord's battle. Joshua and the people needed to place their confidence in God before beginning their journey (Joshua 1:1–8).

View of the Golan Heights in the summer, northern Israel

The conquest of Canaan raises difficult questions for students of the Bible. How could God send the Israelites into this land to eliminate the people already dwelling there? Answering this complex question is difficult because doing so requires the impossible: entering into the mind of God. Yet scripture provides some insight that may help us make sense of the stories in this part of the Bible. In Genesis 15:12–16, we read how God caused Abram to fall into a deep sleep. While Abram slept, God spoke to him, reaffirming an earlier promise that the patriarch would have many offspring who would become a great nation. This nation, Israel, would one day be taken into captivity in Egypt, but after four hundred years its people would be released and eventually brought into the promised land. There was a reason why God allowed so much time to pass before giving the Israelites the land: God said, "The iniquity of the Amorites is not yet complete" (Genesis 15:16). The Amorites were living in rebellion against God, practicing all kinds of evil—even sacrificing their own children to their gods (see Deuteronomy 18:9–10)—and faced punishment for their sin. God was waiting patiently before bringing final judgment on the Amorites for their rebelliousness.

View of the landscape in Galilee, Israel

When the Israelites entered the land, they were not acting on their own behalf. They were not waging war simply to destroy other people so they could take over property that was not theirs to take. That would be self-serving genocide. God used the Israelites as a tool of judgment upon people who had been given plenty of time to repent but failed to do so.

Because this is God's world, He rules it by the authority of His own will (Psalm 2). "The earth is the LORD's and the fullness thereof" (Psalm 24:1). Yet this one parcel of land had a special connection to Him. God claimed special ownership over the whole land of Canaan, going so far as prohibiting the Israelites from permanently transferring ownership of their land—because it all belonged to God (Leviticus 25:23).

The conquest of the promised land demonstrates that God should be feared and trusted. When the Canaanites did not fear God, judgment followed. When the Israelites did not trust God, they were unsuccessful. Taking the land was not a strategy that Joshua or the rest of the Israelites came up with; it was God's plan.

The conquest unpacks the glory, holiness, wrath, mercy, and kindness of God and shows God's faithfulness in keeping His promises to the nation of Israel—and to the entire world.

View of the Judaean desert

The Battle of Jericho

JOSHUA 5:13-6:27

LOCATION

Jericho, one of the oldest cities in the world, was the very first city the Israelites attacked as they began their conquest of the promised land. The city is located near the Jordan River in what is today known as the West Bank of Israel. Water springs that surround the city and produce a vast, fertile oasis with a massive grove of palm trees gave Jericho its nickname—"the city of palm trees" (Deuteronomy 34:3). Because the city is situated more than 800 feet below sea level, Jericho's inhabitants throughout the centuries have enjoyed a very mild climate.

KEY PLAYERS

- Joshua: Moses' second-in-command, who led the Israelites into the promised land after Moses' death
- Commander of the army of the Lord: the commander of God's heavenly army, who brought a message to Joshua
- Rahab: a prostitute in Jericho who harbored two Israelite spies
- The priests: men who led the Israelites in the battle of Jericho by blowing horns or carrying the ark of the covenant

WEAPONS AND WARRIORS

As with every other battle during Israel's conquest, the outcome of this one depended not on human weaponry but on God. His presence, represented by the ark of the covenant, led the Israelites. Other unusual weapons in this battle included the rams' horns that the priests blew and the people's shouting voices.

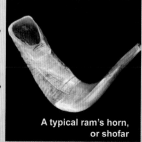

A typical ram's horn, or shofar

BATTLE SYNOPSIS

Joshua led the Israelites across the Jordan River into Canaan, where they approached the city of Jericho. There God spoke to Joshua, telling him exactly what to do, and Joshua obeyed. As commanded by God, Joshua had the Israelites march around the city once every day for six days. Seven priests carried rams' horns in front of the ark of the covenant. On the seventh day, the Israelite army marched around the city seven times; on the seventh time around the city, the priests blew their rams' horns while all the Israelites shouted loudly. At this point, the walls of the city miraculously collapsed; the Israelites charged into the city and captured it. Jericho was completely destroyed; no man, woman, child, or animal was spared except the family of Rahab, who had earlier hid two of Joshua's spies and saved their lives.

The Walls of Jericho Fall Down
Gustave Doré (1832–1883)

OUTCOME

SHORT-TERM

The Israelites experienced their first victory in the land of Canaan. Jericho was completely destroyed. Joshua declared a curse on anyone who would try to rebuild the city (Joshua 6:26).

LONG-TERM

Because one of Israel's fighters, Achan, had kept plunder against God's command—plunder that was supposed to be dedicated to God—thirty-six Israelites died in the next battle against Ai (Joshua 7).

GOD'S ROLE

Before the battle of Jericho, God had reminded Joshua that the fight was His. God had told Joshua to be strong in Him and to be careful not to deviate from the law of the Lord in any way (Joshua 1:1–9). Joshua could expect success in his mission because God was going to provide the victory. God sent the commander of His heavenly army with a message for Joshua before the battle. This messenger appeared as a man with a "drawn sword in his hand" (Joshua 5:13). Joshua inquired as to which side the man was fighting for. The man replied that he was on the Lord's side. One common interpretation of this event is that the mysterious messenger was a preincarnate manifestation of Jesus.

Defeat at Ai
JOSHUA 7

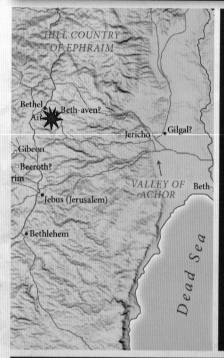

HILL COUNTRY
OF EPHRAIM

Bethel
Ai? Beth-aven?

Jericho Gilgal?

Gibeon

Beeroth?
rim

VALLEY OF Beth-
ACHOR

Jebus (Jerusalem)

Bethlehem

Dead Sea

LOCATION

The second place targeted by the conquering Israelites was the royal Canaanite city of Ai. The ruins of Ai are commonly thought to be the modern-day archaeological site et-Tell. Ai was located two miles east of Bethel; Abram had built an altar between Ai and Bethel when he surveyed the promised land. The battle of Ai was one the Israelites would not soon forget; it was here the children of God learned that they could not simply capture a city and take over the promised land in their own power. They had to trust God, rely on His power, and follow His ways.

KEY PLAYERS

- Joshua: Moses' second-in-command, who led the Israelites into the promised land after Moses' death
- Achan: an Israelite who angered God by keeping plunder from the destruction of Jericho that should have been devoted to God

WEAPONS AND WARRIORS

Joshua sent spies to gather intelligence on Ai. The spies reported that because it was a small city, there was no need to bring the entire Israelite army into this battle. Thus Joshua sent a small force of about three thousand men, most likely comprised of swordsmen, slingers, and spearmen.

Battle Synopsis

After the success of Jericho, Joshua sent spies to the next city in his sights, the city of Ai. Unfortunately, he implemented a battle plan of action without first consulting the Lord. The spies reported Ai was small; they advised Joshua not to send the entire army into battle. So Joshua sent a mere three thousand soldiers, who were promptly defeated by the defenders of Ai. Why did God's people endure such a humiliating defeat so early in their campaign? After the battle of Jericho, a man named Achan had angered God by violating His command to consecrate all of Jericho's silver and gold. None of it was to be taken by any soldier (Joshua 6:18–19). Achan ignored God's command, taking silver and gold for himself and hiding it in his tent. As a result of Achan's sin, God allowed the Israelites to suffer defeat. They would not enjoy victory as long as Achan's sin remained unpunished. One man's sin had devastating consequences for the whole nation.

Modern Bedouin tent, Israel. Achan likely would have hid Jericho's silver and gold in a similar structure.

Outcome

Short-Term

Because of Achan's sin, the Israelites were weak and unable to serve the Lord. They lost the battle, along with thirty-six men.

Long-Term

The people of Israel had to address the sin—by killing Achan's entire family—before they could advance their conquest of the promised land.

God's Role

God said the reason for Israel's defeat was because Achan kept plunder from Jericho against His command. No one sins in a vacuum; sin affects not only the person who sins but the entire community as well. God viewed Israel as a single unit and held the whole nation responsible for the sin of one man. God also affirmed the promised land was His gift to His children. However, to receive the blessing of living in the land, they had to follow His instructions. They were not to add or subtract anything from the word of the Lord. Because each battle belonged to the Lord, everyone needed be set apart for Him alone.

Fortress ruins, Israel

Victory at Ai

JOSHUA 8:1-29

HILL COUNTRY
OF EPHRAIM

Bethel Beth-aven?
Ai Beth-aven?
Jericho Gilgal?
Gibeon
Beeroth?
rim VALLEY OF Beth-jes
ACHOR
Jebus (Jerusalem)
Bethlehem
Dead Sea
Ad

LOCATION

The second place targeted by the conquering Israelites was the royal Canaanite city of Ai. The ruins of Ai are commonly thought to be the modern-day archaeological site et-Tell. Ai was located two miles east of Bethel; Abram had built an altar between Ai and Bethel when he surveyed the promised land. This second battle at Ai was one the Israelites would not soon forget; it was here the children of God learned that they could not simply capture a city and take over the promised land in their own power. They had to trust God, rely on His power, and follow His ways.

KEY PLAYERS

- Joshua: Moses' second-in-command, who led the Israelites into the promised land after Moses' death

WEAPONS AND WARRIORS

When the Israelites were in the desert, they fought as tribal warriors, using hand-to-hand combat. By the time the Israelite army began its conquest of Canaan, it had morphed into a highly organized fighting force. Typical weapons for Israel were swords, spears, slings, and long-range bows.

Bronze Age spear tip mold

Battle Synopsis

God's plan for the battle of Ai was for Joshua to take thirty thousand men into battle. The soldiers surrounded the city in ambush fashion. Joshua then took five thousand of the thirty thousand soldiers and approached Ai. When the soldiers of Ai saw the approaching five thousand men, they came out of the city to attack. Since Israel had unsuccessfully charged the city once already, the soldiers of Ai were overconfident, thinking they could chase down the Israelite warriors as they had before. But when the men of Ai left the city to pursue Joshua and his five thousand soldiers, the other Israelite fighters entered Ai and burned it to the ground. When the soldiers of Ai saw the smoke from their city, they turned back toward Ai—but they were trapped on either side by thirty thousand Israelite soldiers. Every inhabitant of Ai was killed. This time God allowed the Israelites to take the gold and silver for themselves.

Joshua Burns the Town of Ai
Gustave Doré (1832–1883)

Outcome

Short-term

Ai was totally defeated and burned to the ground; Israel's victory was complete.

Long-term

With this defeat, the Israelites learned they had to do things God's way if they wanted to succeed. The nation moved one step closer to inhabiting the promised land.

God's Role

As a result of their victory at Ai, the Israelites learned that the battle truly did belong to the Lord. He set up the tactical methods for war. He gave the plans, directed men, and set boundaries for besieging a city. The people had learned in their earlier defeat at Ai that consequences for disobedience were grave; this time they witnessed victorious results for following God's instructions. God was patiently helping Joshua and the people learn what it meant to live under God's authority and for His glory and purpose alone.

Joshua's Defeat of the Southern Kings
JOSHUA 10:1-43

LOCATION

The Israelites' defeat of the southern kings of Canaan occurred in the city of Gibeon, located about halfway between Jerusalem and Bethel, along the foothills of the Cisjordan (modern-day West Bank). The area's hilly, wooded, and sparsely settled terrain gave the Israelites ample cover. With an elevation of about 2,400 feet, Gibeon towered over other cities, making it easy to defend. Archaeological digs have affirmed this region was rich in natural resources. Wine cellars were discovered, indicating a wine-led economy, along with a very sophisticated water system. Gibeon was a thriving commercial city that made it a leading community in Canaan.

KEY PLAYERS

- Joshua: Moses' second-in-command, who led the Israelites into the promised land after Moses' death
- Adoni-zedek: the Amorite king of Jerusalem who gathered other Amorite kings together to fight against Joshua and his men
- The Gibeonites: a group of Hivites who misled Joshua into making a treaty with them

WEAPONS AND WARRIORS

Joshua's entire army, including his best fighting men, fought in this battle. The conflict took place in a wooded, hilly region that provided great cover and concealment. God supplied unique weapons for this battle. According to Joshua 10, God demonstrated His power by making the sun stand still, providing time for Joshua to finish the battle. In addition, God hurled down hailstones from heaven; as a result, more Amorites died from the hail than from the Israelite army's weapons.

Battle Synopsis

The fall of Ai had caused no small alarm among the kings of the southern cities of Canaan. When Joshua formed an alliance with the Gibeonites, the local kings became even more afraid. As a result, the Amorite ruler of Jerusalem, Adoni-zedek, persuaded several other Amorite kings in the region to form an alliance and make war against the Gibeonites. The Gibeonites had tricked Joshua into signing a treaty with their nation, obligating Israel to protect them. So they sent word to Joshua that war was on the horizon. Joshua marched his people to defend the Gibeonites. This was a true act of leadership; Joshua and his warriors had to trudge up several thousand feet of mountainside. Then Joshua had to harness his troops for war—under the cover of night, so as to not tip off the enemy. Joshua surprised the enemy, who was unable to fight back.

God directly intervened in two powerful ways during this battle. First, He poured down hailstones from heaven, killing more Amorites than the Israelite soldiers killed with their weapons. Second, God made the sun stand still at Joshua's request, giving Joshua time to finish the battle. The five enemy kings fled and hid in a cave in Makkedah. Joshua had his men roll large stones in front of the mouth of the cave, and he kept the kings as prisoners until he had time to deal with them. Later he struck down all five kings and hung their bodies from trees until sunset. In one battle the Israelites were able to defeat the armies of the kings of five key cities—Jerusalem, Hebron, Jarmuth, Lachish, and Eglon.

Outcome

Short-Term

The Israelites defeated the Amorite army; however, a few Amorites survived and escaped (Joshua 10:20).

Long-Term

Less than a century later, Solomon forced the remaining Amorites into slavery (1 Kings 9:20–21).

God's Role

God had promised to deliver Joshua's enemies into Joshua's hand (Joshua 10:8). Joshua did not sit idly by, expecting God to work without his participation. Instead, Israel's leader went to great effort to cooperate with God's work. At the same time, God was actively involved in the victory. He sent a massive storm of heavy hail. He allowed the sun to stand still until the battle was over. The Amorite gods could not compete with the one true God.

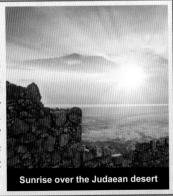

Sunrise over the Judaean desert

Military Heroes and Villains: Joshua

God chose Joshua, a remarkable man who served as Moses' second-in-command, to lead the Israelites into the promised land after the death of Moses. Joshua's strategic and tactical principles, as well as his leadership and personal conduct, reveal his expertise as a military commander.

With impressive strategy, Joshua invaded the land of Canaan from the east, avoiding a major trade route stretching north–south along the Mediterranean: the Via Maris. By doing so, he kept the Israelites from becoming entangled with the people and military of Egypt, who regularly used this trade route. Joshua established a base of operations east of the Jordan River. This protected the rear flank of his army, and it ensured safe passage if he needed to retreat. Finally, Joshua understood the value of good reconnaissance before a battle, which is why he made use of spies.

On a tactical level, Joshua masterfully invaded from the middle of Canaan, which allowed him to attack one side before focusing on another. This gave him maximum flexibility, yet he was also able to avoid overreaching and attacking too wide a margin. Joshua made use of high ground whenever possible; he knew when to go on the offensive and when to set ambushes. Joshua skillfully utilized the land for concealment and cover. He understood how to turn the terrain into an advantage.

Jordan River

Most importantly, Joshua understood what it meant to trust in God. He knew the battle did not ultimately depend on his strategic or tactical abilities but on his willingness to trust the one true Commander of armies. When Joshua forgot this and relied too much on his own abilities, he was quick to repent. He wanted to follow God wholeheartedly, and this was the key to all his military victories. Joshua ended his time as Israel's leader with a call to the nation to follow his example: to love and serve God. Joshua did not ask to be venerated but begged the Israelites to stay faithful to the One who had given them the land in the first place (Joshua 24:14–15).

The Israelites Cross the Jordan River
Gustave Doré (1832–1883)

BATTLES OF THE CONQUEST AND THE ERA OF JUDGES

Joshua's Defeat of the Northern Kings
JOSHUA 11:1-23

LOCATION

Joshua's next conquest was in northern Canaan. The battle occurred at the waters of Merom. The location of Merom most likely corresponds to the modern-day city of Meirun, in the Upper Galilee region of northern Israel. Even though no hard archaeological evidence proves these two cities are connected, tradition and extra-biblical literature have suggested they are. This region is mentioned in the Talmud as including shepherding villages because of its altitude and climate. In addition, this region was well suited for growing and harvesting olives, making it renowned for its olive oil.

KEY PLAYERS

- Joshua: Moses' second-in-command, who led the Israelites into the promised land after Moses' death
- King Jabin: the king of the Canaanite city of Hazor
- The Anakim: a tribe of exceptionally large and strong people who were feared by the Israelites when the twelve spies who initially surveyed the land of Canaan reported about them (Numbers 13:27–33)

WEAPONS AND WARRIORS

The use of chariots is mentioned for the first time in the book of Joshua during the battle against the northern kings of Canaan. These iron-wheeled, mobile firing platforms brought shock value as they cut a terrible swathe through the ranks of their enemy. Chariots were used to charge the enemy and generate fear. At one point in this battle, Joshua burned the Canaanites' chariots (Joshua 11:7–9).

Battle Synopsis

After the southern campaign, Joshua turned his attention northward. He made his way from Gilgal to the Upper Galilee region. The kings of the north formed a strong coalition; Israel was outmanned and militarily incapable of standing against the weapons of the northern coalition. Without divine intervention, there would be no victory. The alliance was led by Jabin, king of the Canaanite city of Hazor, and included the kings of Madon, Achshaph, and Shimron, as well as many other kings. The Canaanites advanced to meet Joshua "with all their troops, a great horde, in number like the sand that is on the seashore, with very many horses and chariots" (Joshua 11:4).

At the waters of Merom, the Canaanites assembled and set up camp. Not only were they better trained and equipped than the Israelites, but they had the military

Galilee, Israel

advantage of large chariots, which could attack with devastating effect. Yet God gave Joshua wisdom to deal with the odds against him. To defeat his enemies, Joshua resorted to unconventional tactics. The Israelites approached the Canaanite camp in secret, while the Canaanites were making preparations for war, and attacked them by surprise, catching the Canaanites completely off guard. Joshua's forces "hamstrung their horses and burned their chariots" (Joshua 11:9) and destroyed the most effective branch of the Canaanite army. The Canaanites were scattered and pursued by the Israelites, who cut them down and "left none remaining" (Joshua 11:8).

After this, Joshua turned his attention toward Hazor, the most significant city or "head" of the northern kingdoms (Joshua 11:10). The Israelites seized the city, massacred the people, killed its king, and burned the city to the ground. Finally, to complete the work of the conquest, the Israelites plundered the surrounding cities and slaughtered their inhabitants, "but none of the cities that stood on mounds did Israel burn, except Hazor alone" (Joshua 11:13).

Horses and charioteers fighting in an ancient Middle Eastern battle

SHORT-TERM

The destruction of Hazor was complete, as was God's judgment. However, the Israelites did not successfully annihilate the Anakim. A few Anakites remained in Israelite territory in the cities of Gaza, Gath, and Ashdod (Joshua 11:22).

LONG-TERM

The people of Israel finally possessed the inheritance promised to Abraham's descendants in Genesis 12:7. The victory at the waters of Merom gave them a permanent foothold in Galilee.

GOD'S ROLE

When Moses led the people from Egypt to the doorstep of Canaan, the people were afraid to attack because of the Anakim, giant people who lived in Canaan. The Israelites had forgotten that God was on their side and that their success was entirely dependent on Him. Forty years later, the children of those fearful Israelites stood face-to-face with the same enemy and found that God was stronger. God gave His people the ability to defeat the Anakim. The Israelites possessed the land, not because they were stronger than their enemies, but because God fought for them and was faithful to keep His promise.

Ancient Egyptian relief showing chariots similar to what would have been used during Joshua's day

BATTLES OF THE CONQUEST AND THE ERA OF JUDGES

Israel's Continuing Conquest

JUDGES 1:1-11

Taanach
Beth-shan
Ibleam
Shamir?
Thebez
Pirathon
Shechem
Shiloh
Bethel
Shaalbim Mizpah
Gezer
Aijalon
Ramah
Jericho
on
Zorah
Jebus (Jerusalem)
Bethlehem
Hebron

LOCATION

Israel's next battles were initiated by the tribes of Judah and Simeon. Simeon was located at the southern end of Israel, while Judah was directly north of it. There are three key places named in this battle: Bezek, Jerusalem, and the Negev (or Negeb). The city of Bezek was located twelve miles northeast of Shechem, in Manasseh's territory. Jerusalem was in the northern part of Judah. The Negev, a dry desert area, extended south from Judah to the Gulf of Aqaba.

KEY PLAYERS

- Canaanites: one of the many regional tribal groups or "nations" driven out of the promised land by the Israelites
- Tribe of Judah: the largest and strongest tribe of the twelve tribes of Israel
- Tribe of Simeon: one of the smaller tribes of Israel
- Adoni-bezek: the Canaanite king of Bezek, whose name means "lord of Bezek"
- Perizzites: a tribal group—whose background and origins are unknown—who lived in Canaan from the time of Abraham

WEAPONS AND WARRIORS

Following Joshua's death, the tribe of Judah took the lead in spearheading the war with the Canaanites. Judah's leadership proved to be wise, and the Lord blessed this tribe just as their ancestor Jacob had foretold during the blessing of his sons before his death (Genesis 49:8–12).

Ancient shield

Battle Synopsis

After Joshua's death, the Israelites sought the Lord for what to do next. God told them that the tribe of Judah was to lead them into battle. There were still cities that needed to be conquered. The warriors of Judah asked the Simeonites to come alongside them. Together the men of Judah and Simeon went north to the central part of Israel and struck down ten thousand Canaanites and Perizzites at Bezek. One of the Canaanite kings, Adoni-bezek, was known for conquering cities and taking their kings as captives; he would cut off their thumbs and big toes and force them to serve him. He had done this with seventy different kings. The men of Judah and Simeon captured Adoni-bezek and returned the favor by doing the same thing to him. The Israelites then attacked Jerusalem and burned the city before advancing against the Canaanites in Hebron and Debir.

Outcome

Short-term

Israel continued to make progress in its conquest of Canaanite cities. Yet the Israelites did not finish the job as thoroughly as they had been commanded.

Long-term

Because the Israelites did not clear the land completely, a remnant of Canaanites was able to stay in the land. This remnant became a source of tension for years to come.

God's Role

God had promised to give the land of Canaan to His people. The Israelites' mission was guaranteed to succeed—not because of who Israel was, but because of who God is. God promised success, and He was faithful to keep His promise. However, the Israelites did not follow God's plan exactly as instructed. At times they left people alive or did not destroy cities that were supposed to be destroyed. Nevertheless, God was merciful and faithful; He gave the Israelites the land He had promised to their ancestors. God provided the Israelite army with the strength they needed to stand against some very powerful kings in their battles against the Canaanites.

Battles of the Judges (Cycles)

JUDGES 3:1-31; 4:1-24; 6:1-7:25; 10:6-11:40

LOCATION

The Israelites did not clear the land completely; thus they faced several enemies who continued to dwell in the promised land. The presence of the Canaanites threatened the balance of power by isolating Israelite settlements from one another. Some Canaanites were scattered among the woodland of Harosheth-hagoyim (Judges 4:2, 13, 16). This area skirted the northern fringe of the Jezreel Valley, along the narrow pass that connected the valley to the northern Mediterranean coast, and along the roads that linked the Galilee region with the Sea of Galilee and the Jordan Valley.

KEY PLAYERS

- Othniel: Caleb's younger brother and Israel's first judge
- Ehud: a left-handed Israelite judge from the tribe of Benjamin
- Deborah: a prophet and the only female judge mentioned in the Bible
- Barak: a military general and commander of Deborah's army
- Sisera: the commander of King Jabin's Canaanite army
- Gideon: an Israelite judge from the tribe of Manasseh
- Jephthah: an Israelite judge from the tribe of Manasseh

WEAPONS AND WARRIORS

The primary strength of the Canaanite kings in these battles was in their fortified towns. Their main military armament was the war chariot; Sisera alone boasted nine hundred chariots (Judges 4:3). Barak led a force of ten thousand men, but Sisera's army had the advantage. Ehud fought with a two-edged sword, while Gideon's army of three hundred went into battle with trumpets, clay jars, and torches.

Oil lamp, similar to the clay jars Gideon's men may have used in this battle

Battle Synopsis

The Israelites found themselves caught in a debilitating cycle of sin, which they repeated over and over again: they would serve the Lord, fall into idolatry, become enslaved to other nations, and finally cry out to God for help. God responded each time by providing a judge to defeat Israel's oppressors, after which the people of Israel would serve the Lord once again.

Outcome

Short-Term

God brought deliverance to His people through human judges (leaders), but the Israelites' faithfulness to Him didn't outlive each judge.

Long-Term

Israel went from being a reasonably strong federation to a weak confederation, which ultimately led to a change in regime.

God's Role

God's hand and presence were evident throughout this tragic period of Israel's history. When the Israelites were fighting Jabin and his powerful army, God sent a rainstorm to incapacitate Jabin's chariots. When Gideon fought the Midianites, God allowed the enemy to become so disoriented that they ended up killing each other. In spite of Israel's continuing cycle of sin, God revealed Himself as the true Lord of hosts—the God of the armies. No nation could stand before Him.

Haifa Bay, modern-day Israel, fed by the Kishon River

BATTLES OF THE CONQUEST AND THE ERA OF JUDGES

THE CYCLE OF SIN IN JUDGES

The people in the book of Judges found themselves caught up in a cycle of sin and salvation.

Judges 3:1–11: The Israelites angered God by intermarrying with the people of Canaan who were still in the land and by worshipping the Canaanite gods. God allowed Israel to fall into the hands of Cushan-rishathaim, the king of Mesopotamia. Then God raised up Othniel as His people's judge or deliverer. Othniel, Caleb's younger brother, successfully rescued the Israelites from oppression.

Judges 3:12–30: Israel again turned from God. God permitted Eglon, the king of Moab, to gather an army—made of Moabites, Ammonites, and Amalekites—and promptly defeated Israel. When the Israelites cried for help, God raised up another judge, Ehud, to deliver them. Ehud deceived Eglon and stabbed him in the gut. After escaping, Ehud led the Israelites in a victorious battle against the Moabites.

Judges 3:31: God raised up Shamgar, who killed six hundred Philistines.

Judges 4:1–24: The Israelites turned away from God again, and the Lord gave them over to Jabin, king of Canaan. Jabin's fearsome army, commanded by Sisera, included nine hundred iron chariots; Israel had no hope of matching such a force. God raised up Deborah, the only female judge mentioned in the Bible. Deborah recruited Barak to lead ten thousand troops in an effort to draw out the Canaanite army so the Israelites could defeat them. A heavy rainstorm caused the Kishon River to overflow, and Sisera's nine hundred iron chariots were stuck in the resulting mire. Thus the battle miraculously switched in favor of the Israelites (Judges 5:19–22). Sisera, forced to escape on foot, ended up being murdered by a woman when he sought refuge in her tent. Thus God delivered Israel.

Judges 6:1–7:25: The people of Israel sinned again, and God allowed the Midianites to oppress them. This time when the Israelites cried out to God, He chose Gideon to free them. God shrunk Gideon's army from thirty-two thousand men down to three hundred; the Israelite army was sorely outnumbered. Gideon orchestrated a night attack from three different directions, which took the Midianites completely by surprise, causing chaos and disorientation in the darkness. God allowed the Midianites to be defeated.

Judges 10:6–11:40: The people began serving foreign gods, so God turned them over to the Philistines and the Ammonites. God raised up Jephthah to deliver Israel. Before going into battle, Jephthah promised that if God gave him victory, he would sacrifice the first thing he saw coming out of his house after returning home. Jephthah assumed it would be an animal. After leading the Gileadite army to victory over twenty Ammonite towns, Jephthah returned to his home at Mizpah. The first thing that came out of his house was his young daughter. Jephthah kept his vow and sacrificed his daughter.

Judges 13:1–16:31: Because the Israelites rebelled against the Lord again, God allowed for the Philistines to oppress them for forty years. God raised up Samson, a judge who had miraculous strength. The Spirit of the Lord was with him. Sadly, Samson yielded to the temptation of women, so God removed His Spirit and Samson's strength. The Philistines captured Samson and gouged out his eyes. Finally, Samson called out to God for help. God restored his strength, and he delivered the nation from the Philistines.

Jephthah's Daughter Comes Out to Meet Her Father
Gustave Doré (1832–1883)

BATTLES OF THE CONQUEST AND THE ERA OF JUDGES

Canaanite Infantry

The Canaanites were a strong fighting force during the Bronze Age (ca. 3300–1200 BC). They were the early forgers of iron chariots and had developed a rather sizable mobile force toward the end of the Bronze Age. Canaanite chariots were larger and heavier than Egyptian chariots. They were designed with six-spoked wheels along with an advanced wheel design that took the weight of the chariot off the horse. This allowed their chariots to move faster, even though they were made from heavier metal than Egyptian chariots. The newly engineered design included a larger platform to fit both driver and warrior. It also allowed for greater movement.

Canaanite infantry was well armed and well protected. Chain mail body armor, shields that were easy to maneuver, and sickle swords were standard issue. The sickle sword, also called a *khopesh*, evolved from battle-axes. It was a sword with a hook on the end. Sickle swords allowed a soldier to slice his opponent or wrap the sword around the enemy's leg and trip him. This sword was a multipurpose weapon that gave the Canaanite infantryman a huge advantage in face-to-face combat. Warriors were often equipped with bronze belts, spears, and leaf-shaped daggers with wooden handles. Blunt stone pommels—large, rounded stones fastened to handles to create maces—were also used by the Canaanite military.

Handle from a Bronze Age sword

Canaanite tactics were fairly simple. They used their chariot force to strike first, while the enemy marched in columns. On each chariot stood a bowman who fired arrows at the enemy to disrupt their columns. Next the Canaanite infantry would appear from behind the chariots to attack the scattered enemy.

Chariots gave the Canaanites their biggest military advantage. If they were stopped, the entire battle strategy of the Canaanites would be foiled. The sheer power of these chariots, their ability to scatter an opposing force, and the speed at which they could flank an enemy made the task of stopping the Canaanites rather difficult for most nations.

Ancient chain mail armor,
similar to what the Canaanites may have used

BATTLES OF THE CONQUEST AND THE ERA OF JUDGES

The Rise and Fall of Abimelech

JUDGES 8:29–9:57

LOCATION

Shechem, the first capital of the northern kingdom of Israel after it split from Judah (1 Kings 12:25), was located in the tribe of Ephraim, on the road leading from Jerusalem to the northern territories, and north of Bethel and Shiloh. Abram built an altar to the Lord at Shechem because the Lord had blessed him and promised to bring descendants through him (Genesis 12:6–7). Abimelech, Gideon's son by a Shechemite concubine, established himself as the city's king (Judges 9:6). Shechem was the location of a battle for control over this portion of central Israel.

KEY PLAYERS

- Shechemites: Israelites who lived in Shechem, a city in Ephraim near the border with Manasseh
- Abimelech: Gideon's son who was proclaimed king of Shechem after his father's death
- Gaal: Ebed's son who boasted he could defeat Abimelech

WEAPONS AND WARRIORS

This battle was fought by traditional hand-to-hand combat; rocks and fire were used as well. When the people of the town of Thebez barricaded themselves in a tall fortress, they threw rocks on the opposing force.

Millstones in Tabgha, Israel

Battle Synopsis

Gideon's son Abimelech ruled as king over the Shechemites, even though he had no right to do so. The Israelites who lived in Shechem maintained a link with the Canaanite founders of the city; Abimelech's mother was likely a Canaanite. After ruling three years, God sent an evil spirit to stir up discord between Abimelech and the Shechemite leaders. The Shechemites began to set ambushes on mountain roads, hoping to disrupt trade routes that profited Abimelech. Eventually, another leader, Gaal, declared he could remove Abimelech; because the men of Shechem no longer trusted Abimelech, they followed Gaal.

Abimelech retaliated by setting an ambush outside the gate of Shechem; as the people left the city for their daily work, Abimelech attacked them. The people retreated, and Abimelech set fire to the tower in which they took refuge. About a thousand Shechemites died. Abimelech then besieged the nearby city of Thebez, and everyone in the city shut themselves in a tower. A woman threw a millstone down on Abimelech's head. Abimelech died after begging his armor-bearer to stab him lest he be killed by a woman.

Modern-day Shechem

Outcome

Short-Term

God repaid Abimelech for his wickedness by allowing him to be killed.

Long-Term

This was the first time that an area within Israel was led by a monarch of sorts. Abimelech was in some ways a preview of what was to come when the Israelites would request a king to rule over them.

God's Role

Evidence of God's providence permeated this civil strife. When Abimelech took over as ruler, he killed all but one of Gideon's other sons (Judges 9:5–6). This was an outrage, and Abimelech's sin did not go unpunished by God. Justice was eventually served for the rest of Gideon's family. God's hand was also present in protecting the nation as it dealt with infighting. He kept the Canaanites from taking advantage of an internal conflict when they could have done so by attacking at this vulnerable moment in Israel's history.

The Death of Abimelech
Gustave Doré (1832–1883)

BATTLES OF THE CONQUEST AND THE ERA OF JUDGES

Jephthah's Defeat of Ephraim
JUDGES 12:1-6

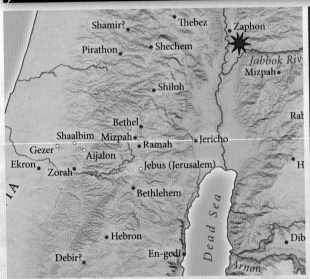

LOCATION

The location of this fight was Zaphon, a region in Israel. Zaphon was situated near Succoth and Beth-nimrah on the east side of the Jordan River, in territory belonging to the tribe of Gad and near its boundary with Manasseh..

KEY PLAYERS

- Jephthah: an Israelite judge from the tribe of Manasseh who led the Gileadites against the Ephraimites
- Gileadites: descendants of Manasseh, through Gilead
- Ephraimites: descendants of Ephraim, one of the tribes of Israel that, together with the tribe of Manasseh, formed the house of Joseph

WEAPONS AND WARRIORS

Jephthah, a fearsome warrior, was gifted in the art of battle. When his attempt to negotiate with the Ephraimites to prevent bloodshed failed, Jephthah gathered all the men of Gilead and fought with Ephraim. An unforseen weapon, a dialectical difference in the pronunciation of the word *Shibboleth*, revealed the true background of Ephraimites trying to hide their identity.

BATTLE SYNOPSIS

When the Ammonites were making war against Israel, the elders of Gilead in Manasseh asked Jephthah to command their army (see Judges 11). The king of Ammon had hoped to take land he thought belonged to him. Jephthah sent a message, charging that the Ammonite king had no legal claim to the land. The king ignored Jephthah's message, and so war broke out. In the end, Jephthah triumphed, but his troubles were hardly over. The tribe of Ephraim heard of the battle and became jealous because they had not taken part in the war. In retaliation, the Ephraimites threatened to burn Jephthah's house with him inside. Jephthah claimed that he did ask for help, but Ephraim had not answered his plea. Jephthah tried to discourage the Ephraimites from needless bloodshed, but it was to no avail. War broke out between the two tribes. Jephthah struck first and was victorious; forty-two thousand men from the tribe of Ephraim died.

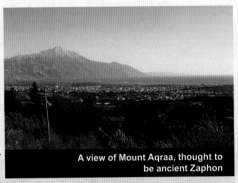

A view of Mount Aqraa, thought to be ancient Zaphon

OUTCOME

SHORT-TERM

Instead of thanking Jephthah for delivering them from the Ammonite threat, the Ephraimites jealously determined to destroy him.

LONG-TERM

This battle increased tension among the tribes and contributed to the overall instability of the nation.

GOD'S ROLE

At first it appeared as if God had no involvement in this civil war between two Israelite tribes. However, God was involved, though behind the scenes. Jephthah clearly gave credit to God for his victory over the Ammonites. The people of Ephraim, however, were not moved by his testimony. They had lost sight of God and wanted to be part of the battle for their own honor and position. It was always God who gave victory; therefore, God's glory was the only thing that mattered. Jephthah was only victorious because he knew this and trusted God.

War with the Tribe of Benjamin

JUDGES 19-21

Bethel · Rimmon?

Mizpah ·

B E N J A M I N

Kiriath-jearim · Gibeah

· Jebus (Jerusalem)

· Bethlehem

LOCATION

Just north of Jerusalem a city called Gibeah lay within the tribe of Benjamin. The city's name means "a hill"—an appropriate name since Gibeah was located on a high ridge 3.5 miles north of Jerusalem. Saul would proclaim this city the first capital of Israel's united kingdom. Archaeologists uncovered a large fortified building at Gibeah and identified it as a fortress from the time of King Saul.

KEY PLAYERS

- Israelites: descendants of Jacob; God's chosen people, who were promised the land of Canaan
- Benjaminites: descendants of Benjamin, one of the twelve tribes of Israel
- The traveling Levite: a descendant of Levi who became the center of the controversy in Gibeah
- The Levite's concubine: a woman who was murdered by the men of Gibeah

WEAPONS AND WARRIORS

The Benjaminites boasted twenty-six thousand swordsmen, plus seven hundred chosen men who were good with slingshots (Judges 20:15–16; 1 Chronicles 12:2). They were brave and skilled archers (1 Chronicles 8:40; 2 Chronicles 14:8), as well as excellent swordsmen. Many warriors of the tribe of Benjamin were taught to fight left-handed, which put their opponents at a tactical disadvantage. The Israelite army was made up of four hundred thousand soldiers.

Sling bullet

Battle Synopsis

The battle of Gibeah was triggered by an incident of gross inhospitality. A concubine belonging to a man from the tribe of Levi was raped to death by a rowdy mob in a town belonging to the tribe of Benjamin. When the Levite found his dead concubine at the door, he butchered her into twelve pieces and sent one piece to each of the tribes of Israel as a summons.

The outraged tribes sought vengeance. Even though they sought God's direction before the battle, the people of Israel paid dearly in their battle against the Benjaminites. It was only after suffering defeat twice that they fasted and prayed, and then they were given success. In the final battle, only six hundred men of Benjamin survived. Even women and children of Benjamin were killed. The tribe was driven to the point of extinction. The Israelites, however, thought the tribe should not be completely wiped out, and they devised a plan. The men from a town in Manasseh, Jabesh-gilead, had refused to take part in the war against Benjamin, so the Israelites struck them down. Their virgin daughters were then given to the surviving men of Benjamin. Though the whole episode serves to summarize just how far the Israelites had wandered from God during the time of the judges, this action had the effect of saving the tribe of Benjamin from extinction.

Outcome

Short-term

Benjamin, weakened from civil war with the rest of Israel, temporarily became the smallest of all the tribes; however, it later produced Israel's first king, Saul.

Long-term

Following the end of the united kingdom of Israel in 930 BC, only the tribe of Judah retained its complete integrity.

God's Role

God directed the order of the battles and eventually gave Israel the victory. He delivered the tribe of Benjamin into the other tribes' hands. Concerned for purity and justice, God did not allow sin to go unchecked in Israel. Yet sin was rampant in the whole kingdom, not only in the tribe of Benjamin. The rest of the people of Israel had become prideful. God allowed the whole nation to struggle in its effort to punish the tribe of Benjamin. God was not just concerned about the outcome of the battle but also about the hearts of those who fought in it.

The Benjaminites Take the Virgins of Jabesh-Gilead
Gustave Doré (1832–1883)

Battle with the Philistines at Aphek
1 SAMUEL 4:1-18

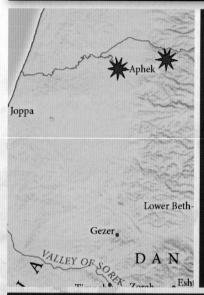

LOCATION

The cities of Aphek and Ebenezer, located in central Israel within Ephraim, were staging areas for a battle between Israel and the Philistines. *Aphek* means "fortress" or "stronghold"; accordingly, this city served as a Philistine fortress. Aphek was a highly strategic site, located at the headwaters of the Yarkon River, which blocked traffic on the coast; this forced invading nations to attack through a narrow space between the river and a mountain. Ebenezer was less than a day's journey by foot from Shiloh, near Aphek, near the western entrance of the pass of Beth-horon.

KEY PLAYERS

- Israelites: descendants of Jacob; God's chosen people, who were promised the land of Canaan
- Philistines: an aggressive, warmongering sea people who occupied part of southwest Canaan between the Mediterranean Sea and the Jordan River; Israel's main enemy before the Assyrian invasion in the eighth century BC
- Eli: the high priest of Israel

WEAPONS AND WARRIORS

The Philistines were a very strong fighting force, known for their innovative use of iron in developing war materials. Archaeologists have discovered carvings of Philistine soldiers in Egypt that show their soldiers dressed for battle in feathered helmets, breastplates, and short skirts with wide hems and tassels. The Philistines often carried small, round shields and straight swords. Goliath, a giant Philistine, wore bronze armor on his legs, along with a heavy bronze coat of mail (1 Samuel 17:5–6).

Battle Synopsis

The author of the book of Samuel recorded that the Philistines were camped at Aphek, while the Israelites were stationed at Ebenezer. The Philistines consistently sought to dislodge the people of Israel from the land. During the first battle, the Philistines defeated Israel and killed four thousand men, at which point the Israelites decided to bring the ark of the covenant from Shiloh into battle, like a good-luck charm. The Philistines defeated the Israelites again, this time killing thirty thousand and capturing the sacred chest.

Eli and his two sons, Hophni and Phinehas, died that day. As soon as a messenger from the battlefield "mentioned the ark of God, Eli fell over backward from his seat by the side of the gate, and his neck was broken and he died" (1 Samuel 4:18).

Outcome

Short-Term

The ark's removal from Israel signaled estrangement between God and His people. The Israelites wrongly believed they had power to coerce God into doing their will simply because they possessed the ark.

Long-Term

God removed Israel's leadership to make room for Samuel, a prophet and judge, to guide the nation.

God's Role

God was not only in charge when things went well for Israel; He was also in charge when things appeared to be failing. In this instance, God allowed the Philistines to triumph for several reasons. First, God used the Philistine army to bring judgment on the house of Eli. Eli and his sons had been given positions of authority but had used those positions for sinful purposes. Second, God used the Philistines to teach the Israelites that the ark of the covenant was not to be a good-luck charm. Success in battle was ensured not by possessing the ark but by remaining faithful to the God of the ark. Third, when the Philistines took control of the ark, they learned their idols were nothing compared to Israel's God. God allowed His glory to be made known to everyone through this battle.

Samuel and the Philistines

1 SAMUEL 7:3-17

LOCATION

Samuel repelled the Philistines at the city of Mizpah. Many other notable events occurred in this city, according to the Old Testament. It was where the nation of Israel gathered to address the sin of the men of Benjamin (Judges 20). It was also where Saul was chosen to be king of Israel (1 Samuel 10:17–24). Tell en-Nasbeh, about eight miles north of Jerusalem, is likely the site of the biblical city of Mizpah.

KEY PLAYERS

- Israelites: descendants of Jacob; God's chosen people, who were promised the land of Canaan
- Philistines: an aggressive, warmongering sea people who occupied part of southwest Canaan between the Mediterranean Sea and the Jordan River; Israel's main enemy before the Assyrian invasion in the eighth century BC

WEAPONS AND WARRIORS

Weapons during this time in Israel's history were the same as in the preceding period of the judges. Swords, spears, slings, and bows made up the main part of the nation's arsenal. The Philistines, on the other hand, were master ironworkers. They were able to take the basic weaponry of the time and improve it. Their weapons were sharper, stronger, and overall more powerful than the tools of the Bronze Age. This advantage made the Philistines a force to be reckoned with.

Iron ax blade, early Iron Age

BATTLE SYNOPSIS

Psalm 34:6 states that when people humble themselves before the Lord, He will save them. That's precisely what happened when the Israelites gathered at Mizpah to repent of their idol worship—to fast, pray, and sacrifice to the Lord. When the Philistines heard about the Israelite gathering at Mizpah, they mustered their forces for war. Just as Samuel was offering a burnt offering, God sent a powerful noise that threw the Philistine army into confusion, giving the Israelites the opportunity to defeat them. To remind the people that it was God who had delivered them from the Philistines, "Samuel took a stone and set it up between Mizpah and Shen" (1 Samuel 7:12). He named the stone Ebenezer, or "stone of help." Samuel knew the people of Israel needed to remember how this victory occurred.

Near Tell en-Nasbeh, Israel

OUTCOME

SHORT-TERM

The Philistines were subdued. Cities that had been conquered by the Philistines were restored, and peace was established between the Israelites and the Amorites.

LONG-TERM

The people of Israel allowed Samuel to judge them "all the days of his life" (1 Samuel 7:15). He moved from city to city and judged the Israelites every place he went. This promoted a sense of unity among the tribes.

GOD'S ROLE

The people of Israel had fallen into idol worship. Samuel called them to repent, and they did so. In battle, Israelite soldiers were no match against the Philistines, who were far more powerful and had many more weapons. But Israel had God. When the people repented, God rescued Israel from the Philistines' attack. He did so by making a loud, thundering noise in the heavens. The Israelites heard the same noise, but only the Philistines became confused and overwhelmed by it.

BATTLES OF THE CONQUEST AND THE ERA OF JUDGES

Military Heroes and Villains: Philistines

Ashdod ruins, Israel

The Philistines were descendants of the Casluhim (Genesis 10:14; 1 Chronicles 1:12), an ancient, non-Semitic people. Known as a seafaring people, the Philistines appeared in the land of Canaan at the start of the twelfth century BC, coming from Crete. These people inhabited the Mediterranean coast of Canaan and quickly became Israel's main enemy after the time of the judges.

The Philistines were a formidable fighting force; they made their way into Canaan and subdued it, using their iron weapons, their imposing size, and their superior fighting skills to defeat their enemies. Small, circular shields used in combat allowed them to be faster and more agile in battle than others. Their

Iron shield

Yarkon River near modern-day Tel Aviv, Israe

swords were stronger than most, enabling them to kill with speed and ease. The Philistines were pagan in their worship, and thus many in Israel referred to them as the "uncircumcised" (Judges 15:18; 1 Samuel 14:6; 2 Samuel 1:20).

The Philistine people were also master ironworkers. Their skill was so highly regarded that even people from Israel turned to them to have their tools sharpened (1 Samuel 13:20). Apparently one of the military tactics the Philistine army used to keep the Israelites in subjugation was to kill their blacksmiths. If the Israelites had no blacksmiths, they could not make swords or other weapons to use in battle against the Philistines.

Saul fought hard against the Philistines, but he was not faithful to God in battle. Saul violated God's direct command often, which made his leadership erratic (1 Samuel 13). God allowed the Philistines to emerge as a constant threat; their size, weapons, and fierceness continually terrorized the people of Israel (1 Samuel 17:21–25).

Over time the Philistines assimilated into Canaanite culture and disappeared from biblical records, especially as Assyria and Babylon emerged as superpowers. One living legacy of the Philistines still present today is the name *Palestine*, a derivative of the term *Philistine*.

The Bible describes the Philistines as having ruled the five city-states of Gaza, Ashkelon, Ashdod, Ekron, and Gath (Joshua 13:2–3). Their territory extended from Gaza in the south to the Yarkon River in the north, but with no fixed border to the east.

BATTLES OF THE CONQUEST AND THE ERA OF JUDGES

Military Heroes and Villains: Amalekites

The Amalekites were descendants of Amalek, who was the son of Esau's son Eliphaz and his concubine Timna (Genesis 36:12). This made the Amalekites distant relatives of the Israelites. However, the Amalekites were the first enemy the people of Israel encountered after fleeing Egypt and crossing the Red Sea. Newly freed from slavery, the Israelites had moved from the wilderness of Sin and were camped at Rephidim when the Amalekites attacked them, and struck down those who lagged behind (Deuteronomy 25:17–18). The Amalekites refused to allow the Israelites to pass in peace. Joshua then led the army of Israel in a battle against the Amalekites, and emerged triumphantly (Exodus 17:8–16).

The Amalekites were a nomadic people. Rather than setting up a single place to live, the Amalekites followed their livestock and dwelt in various regions depending on the time of the year. As their animals wandered from pasture to pasture, the Amalekites moved with them. Their weapons would have been typical of nomadic people from the time—weaponry designed for hand-to-hand combat. Swords, spears, slings, and bows were the mainstays of their arsenal.

The people of Israel later avenged the Amalekites' attack against their ancestors; however, the Israelites failed to completely eradicate their enemies as instructed.

According to 1 Samuel 15, God had called Saul to thoroughly destroy the Amalekites; but some of the Amalekites obviously survived. As a result, the Amalekites continued to be a thorn in Israel's side for many years.

The name *Amalek* evolved to be associated with hatred against the Jewish people. Interestingly, the Bible presents the Persian leader Haman, whose mission was to annihilate all Jews, as descending from the lineage of Agag, king of the Amalekites (Esther 3:1).

The Victory of Joshua over the Amalekites
Nicolas Poussin (1594–1665)

Things to Think About

The battles of the conquest of Canaan and the era of the judges teach us about God, faith, obedience, and holiness. It is important to read these accounts not just for the action that takes place but so we can learn how to relate to and depend on God. Here are some questions to reflect on:

- What does the conquest of Canaan teach you about your faith?

- Why did God allow the Israelites to fail in their quests at times?

- What can we learn about God's character from these accounts?

- Why is God concerned about His holiness?

- What can we learn about obedience from these stories?

- Try to find at least five examples of God keeping His promises to Israel.

Wall relief of Philistine captives

BATTLES OF THE CONQUEST AND THE ERA OF JUDGES

Samuel, mosaic in front of the church on the Mount of Beatitudes

Chapter 3

BATTLES OF THE UNITED KINGDOM: FROM SAUL TO DAVID

But the people refused to obey the voice of Samuel. And they said, "No! But there shall be a king over us, that we also may be like all the nations, and that our king may judge us and go out before us and fight our battles."

(1 Samuel 8:19–20)

INTRODUCTION

The people of Israel had been fighting since the day they entered the promised land. Because they had failed to drive out all the inhabitants as the Lord had commanded, they were forced to repel constant attacks. The Israelites decided they needed a king like all the other nations—a military leader who would protect them. Even though God was their King and had promised to provide for them, the people persisted in crying out for a king. And so the Lord gave them what they asked for. Israel's people were given a king to match their hearts' desire. He was tall, strong, and appeared to be a fighter. The Israelites were ready to rally behind their new king, a man named Saul, and anticipated great success.

God's presence never left Israel, despite the fact that He was supposed to be Israel's only King. God's continued protection of His people from annihilation reveals a great truth: Even though the people of Israel rallied around a human king who proved unfaithful to God, God remained in control and never stopped

David and Saul
Nikolai Zagorsky (1849–1893)

being faithful to His children. His faithfulness was not something that could be thwarted by human rebellion.

Ultimately, God rejected Saul's family as the kingly line for the nation. Instead, God raised up His choice for king—someone who would walk by faith and trust in Him alone. God raised up David. Centuries later the apostle Paul wrote, "And we know that for those who love God all things work together for good, for those who are called according to his purpose" (Romans 8:28). David's life reflected this truth; he was a man called by God, a man who loved God with his whole heart. David's story and the battles he fought were examples of how God uses all things, even His enemies, to carry out His plan.

Long before Saul was anointed Israel's first king, the fledgling nation faced many threats. Chief among them was the Philistines, a formidable force that sought to control the region. This violent nation had mustered their forces with such strength that the people of Israel grew increasingly terrified. The Philistines (including some giants among them) were skilled warriors; they were heavily armored and able to kill with ease. They boasted weapons made of bronze and iron, and they were talented silversmiths as well. Man to man, Israel did not fare well against the Philistines. In addition, the Philistines apparently made it a practice to kill the metalworkers in Israel, thus thwarting their efforts to develop more effective weapons.

Saul Tries to Kill David
Gustave Doré (1832–1883)

The Philistine threat was one reason the people of Israel cried out for a king. The Ammonites represented yet another threat, this one from the east. They constantly tempted the Israelites with their pagan worship.

Saul's major task was to unite the Israelites into a single fighting force to ward off their enemies. But while Saul enjoyed some success in doing so, the people consistently forgot who their Chief Commander was. Rather than trusting in God's power to lead them, the people of Israel trusted in themselves and their own capabilities. When faced with their biggest challenge—stronger enemy armies—the Israelites tried to develop a more powerful army than what they thought God could provide. Time and time again, their own strength proved insufficient. Whatever success they achieved in battle was only because of God's strength and power.

God blessed Israel in unique ways during the early days of their kingdom. The nation did not face any threats from outside nations; all their threats came from within the land of Canaan. Egypt, Assyria, and other nations showed little interest in conquering Israelite territory during this period. Israel's only real military threat came from the Philistines, who proved a constant source of pain to the fledgling nation. Even though Saul spent his entire reign at war, the nation was able to establish itself with some internal economic growth. During Saul's reign, and David's as well, the nation expanded and became stabler. As a result, the kings of the united monarchy managed to increase the territory under Israelite control.

This period in Israel's military history was marked by several key lessons:

1. Success in life comes by trusting God, not by trusting in oneself.
2. God prefers obedience to any religious sacrifice.
3. When things seem to be going wrong, God is still orchestrating His plan, making sure it will come to pass.
4. It is better to turn to God all the time than to ignore Him.
5. God is merciful, even to His enemies.

More of the historical portion of the Old Testament is dedicated to this period in Israel's history than to any other time period. Israel's history is clearly important to God; we should consider it important, too. Each success or loss included in scripture reveals what happened to those who trusted in God and what happened to those who did not. The lessons learned by those who fought the Lord's battles and were obedient and victorious—or disobedient and defeated—should inform our lives today. God is to be trusted all the time, especially when things look impossible. It is through the impossible that God's glory is most clearly seen.

Saul's Battle to Save Jabesh-Gilead
1 SAMUEL 11:1-11

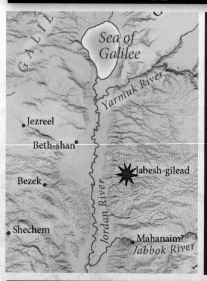

LOCATION

Jabesh-gilead was situated twenty miles or so south of the Sea of Galilee on the east side of the Jordan River, in what was known as the Jordan River Valley. In biblical history, all inhabitants of this city were put to death by Israel's army, with the exception of four hundred virgins (Judges 21:8–12). These women became wives of the men of the tribe of Benjamin. Years later, when the Ammonites attempted to conquer Jabesh-gilead, Saul (himself a Benjaminite) responded decisively.

KEY PLAYERS

- Nahash: the king of the Ammonites during the reign of Saul
- Saul: the son of Kish from the tribe of Benjamin; God's chosen leader to rule the scattered nation of Israel as its first king
- Men of Jabesh: inhabitants of a town east of the Jordan, between the Dead Sea and the Sea of Galilee.
- Ammonites: a Semitic people, closely related to the Israelites, tracing their ancestry to Lot's son Ben-ammi

WEAPONS AND WARRIORS

This was a battle of sheer force. When Saul learned of the situation in Jabesh-gilead, he called the people to arms. According to scripture, three hundred thousand men of Israel and thirty thousand men of Judah answered the call. Saul divided them into three divisions and launched his attack on multiple fronts against the Ammonites. The plan succeeded; the Israelite army routed the enemy completely.

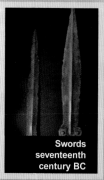

Swords seventeenth century BC

BATTLE SYNOPSIS

Trying to take advantage of the Philistine threat to Israel, Nahash, the Ammonite king, besieged Jabesh-gilead.

The men of Jabesh-gilead sought some form of peace treaty with Nahash. But Nahash's price for surrender was that every man had to have his right eye plucked out. When Saul heard about Jabesh-gilead's plight, the Spirit of God gripped him and his anger burned. Saul took a pair of oxen and cut them into pieces. He sent messengers carrying the pieces of oxen throughout Israel to warn the people that the same thing would happen to their oxen if they did not come to the city's

defense. Saul gathered three hundred thousand men from Israel and thirty thousand men from Judah. The next day, he divided his troops into three companies. In a predawn strike, they entered the Ammonite camp and struck down the Ammonites until the day grew hot. "And those who survived were scattered, so that no two of them were left together" (1 Samuel 11:11).

OUTCOME

SHORT-TERM

The Israelite army slaughtered the Ammonites and scattered the few who were left. Saul had already been anointed as king, but it wasn't until after this battle that the entire nation embraced him as their rightful leader and king (1 Samuel 10:24–27; 11:12–15).

LONG-TERM

The Ammonites remained on the scene during the reign of David, Israel's greatest king. David tried to be friendly to the Ammonites, a kindness they did not return (2 Samuel 10; 1 Chronicles 19).

GOD'S ROLE

This victory—and Saul's emergence as a leader for his people—was only possible because the Spirit of the Lord came upon Saul. The Ammonites had threatened the people of Jabesh-gilead; in response, Saul was able to unify the nation and rally to the city's defense. In his own power, he would have accomplished nothing. God alone gave Saul the ability to unite the country for this battle.

The Battle at Michmash Pass
1 SAMUEL 13:16–14:23

LOCATION

Michmash was a town of Benjamin, about seven miles northeast of Jerusalem. The area straddled the eastern branch of the watershed road, the north–south artery of the Cisjordan Mountains, and flanked its western branch. *Michmash* means "hidden place," and the town's location proved to be strategic for Israel on this occasion. Jewish exiles returning from Babylon reinhabited this city (Nehemiah 11:31). Michmash also served as Jonathan Maccabaeus's residence and seat of government (see the Maccabean Revolt, chapter 10). The Philistines established a fortified base at Michmash. By pushing to the eastern side of the plateau in Judah, they were able to block the Israelites from the mountains where they had previously staged their military campaigns. If the Philistines had continued to control this region, the emerging army of Israel may have suffered a crippling defeat.

KEY PLAYERS

- Saul: the son of Kish from the tribe of Benjamin; God's chosen leader to rule the scattered nation of Israel as its first king
- Jonathan: King Saul's son; David's close friend
- The Philistines: an aggressive, warmongering sea people who occupied part of southwest Canaan between the Mediterranean Sea and the Jordan River; Israel's main enemy before the Assyrian invasion in the eighth century BC

WEAPONS AND WARRIORS

There certainly was no stockpile of weapons in Israel. The Philistines had imposed an embargo on iron to keep the Israelites from accumulating weapons. As a result, Saul's army was limited to fighting with bows, arrows, and slingshots. Only Saul and Jonathan had swords or spears in hand. The Philistines, on the other hand, possessed three thousand chariots and six thousand mounted cavalry—not to mention a massive army to challenge Saul's six hundred ill-equipped soldiers.

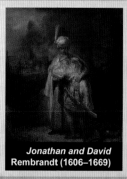

Jonathan and David
Rembrandt (1606–1669)

BATTLE SYNOPSIS

Jonathan had defeated a small Philistine garrison at Geba. After the attack, the Philistines mobilized a great army at Michmash. When the men of Israel heard the Philistines were coming, they fled in terror; thus Saul's army of three thousand dwindled to a skeleton crew of six hundred (1 Samuel 13:1–15).

Jonathan took his armor-bearer on a secret patrol north toward Michmash. Jonathan told his associate that they would reveal themselves to the Philistines. If the Philistines said, "Wait until we come to you," the pair would not advance; if the Philistines said, "Come up to us," they would attack (1 Samuel 14:9–10). When the Philistines saw Jonathan in the ravine, they said, "Come up to us." This was Jonathan's sign that the battle was the Lord's. Jonathan charged the Philistines and killed them with his sword. His armor-bearer followed behind him, killing the few remaining wounded Philistines. Their actions threw the camp into disarray, and the Philistines began killing each other in the confusion. When Saul saw what was happening, he entered the battle and pursued his enemy to victory. This battle marked the beginning of Saul's wars with the Philistines.

OUTCOME

SHORT-TERM

Two men who obeyed the Lord, Jonathan and his armor-bearer, set off a chain reaction that led to the defeat of the Philistines.

LONG-TERM

Eventually, God gave Saul's reign over to David because of Saul's disobedience and rash behavior—which included binding his army under an oath not to eat anything until their enemies had been defeated (1 Samuel 14:24). This foolish bravado nearly cost Jonathan his life. What God wanted first and foremost from Saul was heartfelt obedience, not religious ritual or compulsive behavior.

GOD'S ROLE

Jonathan sought and trusted in God's leading and protection; thus God gave Israel an improbable victory. In contrast, Saul only attacked when victory was almost certain. From the first time the Israelites entered the land, God told His people not to be afraid and to trust in His power and ability to conquer their enemies—regardless of size or weaponry. One man trusting in God's power was stronger than a vast army of heavily armed warriors.

Valley stream in the desert near Jerusalem, Israel

Military Heroes and Villains: Saul

I srael's first king started out well enough, but eventually his reign spiraled out of control. Soon Saul found himself out of favor with God. How could this happen to someone who had been close with the Lord?

For years Israel had been loosely ruled by "judges," or leaders, who presided over domestic issues and led them in battles against the peoples who oppressed them. Because of the constant threat from Israel's main enemy, the Philistines, the people pressed Samuel to appoint a king to rule over them (1 Samuel 8:5). They thought that if they were ruled like the other nations—with a king—things would improve. Samuel warned them against such thinking, but God gave them what they asked for: a king after their own hearts. At the time, Saul had not been pursuing kingship; God chose him as the one who aptly fulfilled the expectations of the people. Saul, the son of Kish from the tribe of Benjamin, was a tall, strong, and capable fighter. Even though Samuel anointed him king, Saul did not fully step into the role until the Ammonites attacked Jabesh-gilead. That's when Saul truly emerged as a leader. Under the power of God's Spirit, Saul rallied the troops to attack the Ammonites. After the victory, the people rallied around him as their king.

However, the Philistines mounted another attack against Israel, and Saul grew afraid. Samuel had told Saul to wait seven days for him to come and offer a sacrifice to the Lord before the battle (1 Samuel 10:8). Samuel was late in arriving, so Saul offered the sacrifice in place of Samuel—the first in a number of very serious mistakes (1 Samuel 13:8–14). Saul demonstrated more fear of the Philistines than he did for the commands of God, and God was angry (see also 1 Samuel 15:22–23). Samuel rebuked Saul and told him God had rejected his kingship. Eventually God removed His Spirit from Saul. Saul's final years were dreadfully tragic; he was tormented by an evil spirit and endured spells of manic depression.

David and Saul
Ernst Josephson (1851–1906)

Saul died at the battle of Mount Gilboa, taking his own life by falling on his sword, and eventually was buried in Zela in the region of Benjamin (1 Samuel 31; 2 Samuel 21:14).

THE ILLUSTRATED GUIDE TO BIBLE BATTLES

Death of King Saul, Elie Marcuse (1817–1902)

BATTLES OF THE UNITED KINGDOM: FROM SAUL TO DAVID

Battle against the Amalekites

1 SAMUEL 15

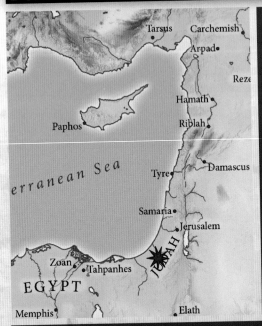

LOCATION

This battle occurred in the "city of Amalek" (1 Samuel 15:5). Amalek was not necessarily a city as we would think of it; it was probably more like a fortified camp. The Amalekite settlement was situated between Havilah and Shur, north of Egypt. The center of the Amalekite camp was on the Sinai Peninsula. This may have been in the vicinity of Kadesh-barnea. It was a desert region that both Abraham and Moses had previously passed through.

KEY PLAYERS

- Saul: the son of Kish from the tribe of Benjamin; God's chosen leader to rule the scattered nation of Israel as its first king
- Jonathan: King Saul's son; David's close friend
- Amalekites: people of a nomadic nation with a history of hostility toward Israel
- King Agag: an Amalekite king who was taken alive by King Saul after the Israelites destroyed the Amalekites

WEAPONS AND WARRIORS

Saul gathered his army in Telaim. There were two hundred thousand footmen, who fought hand to hand in battle, and ten thousand men of Judah. This battle would have been fought primarily with swords, spears, slings, and bows.

Saul's Anger at David
Antoni Brodowski (1784–1832)

BATTLE SYNOPSIS

This battle was one that God wanted the Israelites to fight. The Amalekites had attacked the children of Israel in the wilderness (Exodus 17:8–15). God never forgot Amalek's cruelty, and He eventually called on Saul to take his army and wipe out the evil nation. According to scripture, God did not want a single Amalekite person or animal left alive (1 Samuel 15:3). He used Israel as a tool of divine destruction on this nation.

La mort d'Agag
Gustave Doré (1832–1883)

Saul and his army made their way to the region where the Amalekites dwelt. The first thing Saul did was to advise the Kenites to leave the area, for God did not want them to die in this battle. The Kenites acquiesced and fled. Israel's army attacked and killed almost every one of the Amalekites, but Saul disobediently left the king alive and kept some of the choice animals, supposedly for a sacrifice. When he arrived, Samuel confronted Saul, telling him that the Lord was displeased with the notion of sacrifice at the expense of disobedience. Rebellion in the eyes of God was the same as witchcraft.

OUTCOME

SHORT-TERM

Israel won the battle, but because Saul did not fully obey God's command, the Lord regretted that He had made Saul king over Israel.

LONG-TERM

Saul proved that obedience to the Lord was not his first priority. As a result, God did not allow the kingship to remain with Saul's family line. God would form a new line with a new king who was not a descendant of Saul.

GOD'S ROLE

This battle was not a response to an enemy attack. When Saul received the order to attack, God intended to use him as His agent of justice against the Amalekites. It was not the first time God said retribution was coming to the Amalekites. In Exodus 17:14–16; Numbers 24:20; Exodus 17:14–16; and Deuteronomy 25:17–19, we read that God had promised to avenge the Amalekites' sin.

God is a God of justice; and when it comes, as it always does, it will come in full. Saul's failure to fully carry out God's instructions was counted against him. Saul was given a period of probation, but he failed to repent. As a result, God left Saul with a miserable sense that he was reigning without authority. Saul would no longer be an instrument of deliverance and blessing to Israel.

The Battle of Socoh
1 SAMUEL 17

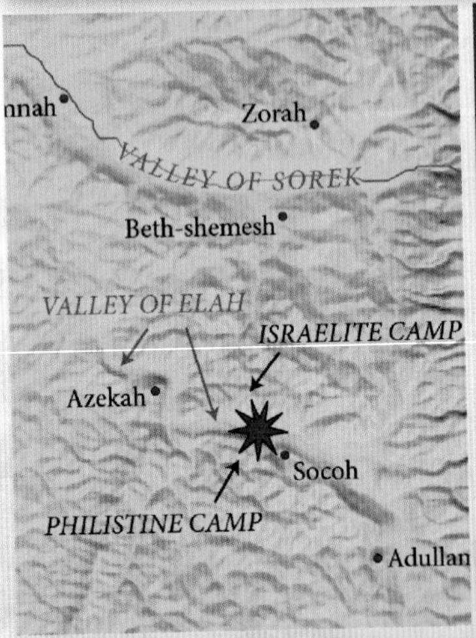

LOCATION

The Valley of Elah derived its name from the Elah tree, a type of oak tree. There was also a brook nearby called the Brook of Elah, famous for the five stones that David took for his battle with Goliath. The Valley of Elah was located on the western side of Judah's low hills. This battle occurred after the Philistines tried to push along the valley toward the heart of Judah. King Saul blocked them, facing off against the Philistines at Socoh in the center of the valley.

Map labels: nnah · Zorah · VALLEY OF SOREK · Beth-shemesh · VALLEY OF ELAH · ISRAELITE CAMP · Azekah · Socoh · PHILISTINE CAMP · Adullam

KEY PLAYERS

- Saul: the son of Kish from the tribe of Benjamin; God's chosen leader to rule the scattered nation of Israel as its first king
- David: the second king of Israel's united kingdom and—according to the New Testament Gospels of Matthew and Luke—an ancestor of Jesus
- Goliath: a giant Philistine warrior of Gath; a spearman whose strength made him an almost invincible hand-to-hand warrior

WEAPONS AND WARRIORS

Initially, Saul garbed David with Saul's own coat of mail and helmet of bronze, as well as with a sword strapped on to the armor. These weapons were suitable for a worldly warrior but not for a soldier of the Lord. Instead, David fought with his shepherd's staff in hand, along with five smooth stones, his shepherd's bag, and his sling. For protection, Goliath wore a bronze helmet on his head, a coat of mail that weighed "five thousands shekels of bronze" (1 Samuel 17:5), and bronze armor on his legs. He carried a bronze javelin, a spear—whose head alone "weighed six hundred shekels of iron" (1 Samuel 17:7)—and a shield. Additionally, he was accompanied by a shield-bearer who traveled in front of him.

BATTLE SYNOPSIS

The Philistines gathered their armies for battle with Israel once again—assembling at Socoh, near the Philistine border. The Philistines camped on one side of the valley, and Saul and the Israelites camped on the other. A shepherd boy named David was bringing food to his brothers, who were soldiers fighting for Israel. David heard the taunts of the champion Philistine giant, Goliath, and became angry. David, who was passionate for God's honor, knew Goliath was a mere man who had no power over the Most High God. Though King Saul attempted to dissuade him, David was determined to slay Goliath (1 Samuel 17:32–37). Armed with only a sling, five stones, and his staff, David approached the giant man. Goliath insulted David, but David responded, "You come to me with a sword and with a spear and with a jav-elin, but I come to you in the name of the LORD of hosts, the God of the armies of Israel, whom you have defied" (1 Samuel 17:45). They drew near each other, and David launched one stone at Goliath's forehead and killed him. The men of Israel and Judah then chased the Philistines out of the region "as far as Gath and the gates of Ekron" (1 Samuel 17:52).

Spring in the Valley of Elah, Israel

OUTCOME

SHORT-TERM

David's popularity increased with the people of Israel, but so did Saul's jealousy and paranoia.

LONG-TERM

Saul's jealousy eventually resulted in his death, along with that of his son—not to mention David's ascent to the throne of Israel (1 Samuel 31; 2 Samuel 2).

GOD'S ROLE

God was directing David's steps long before his battle with Goliath. God allowed David to spend many years protecting his sheep from lions and bears (both of which were symbols for God's enemies). This training proved invaluable, given what David was to face on the battlefield. Furthermore, the Spirit of the Lord was upon David (1 Samuel 16:13), who understood that God was in control and worthy to be trusted. In David, God gave Israel a new king who knew he needed to trust in God alone—not in swords and spears—to deliver His children and conquer His enemies.

David and Goliath
Caravaggio (1571–1610)

Saul's and David's Victories

1 SAMUEL 14:47-48; 18:1-19:8; 2 SAMUEL 23:8-39

God enabled both Saul and David to experience victory over enemies. First Samuel 14:47 states that Saul fought against all the enemies surrounding the nation of Israel. Specifically, there were two groups of people mentioned in 1 Samuel 14 concerning the victories of Saul. The first were those living in the promised land who boasted a racial connection with the Jewish nation:

- Moabites, from the line of Lot
- Ammonites, from the line of Lot
- Edomites, from the line of Esau

The Moabites, Ammonites, and Edomites were all hostile to Israel, even though they traced their lineage through Abraham, just as the Israelites did. God allowed Saul to experience victory over these tribes. Saul defeated each of them, as well as two other Gentile enemies who fought against the Israelites:

- The kings of Zobah, located in Syria
- The Philistines, a group that likely originated from Crete and later migrated to Canaan

David enjoyed even greater triumph over Israel's enemies than his predecessor, Saul. Saul realized that David would be the one who would take the throne after he died; knowing this caused him to fear David. As a result, Saul hatched a plan

Woodcut of David pouring out water, with his mighty men
Julius Schnorr von Carolsfeld (1794–1872)

to have David killed. First, he offered his daughter Michal to David in marriage. David did not have the resources to pay the bride price; in lieu of paying any money for the marriage, Saul required David to bring him the foreskins of one hundred Philistines. David succeeded—and then some—by overcoming two hundred Philistines.

Though David ultimately relied on God for victory, he also benefited from the military prowess of at least thirty special soldiers, known as "David's mighty men." Many of these warriors joined David when he was still a fugitive from Saul; they remained by his side throughout his forty-year reign. Three of the mighty men that formed David's inner circle and served David wholeheartedly were Josheb-basshebeth, Eleazar, and Shammah.

Michal Watches David Dance before the Ark of the Covenant, Francesco Salviati (1510–1563)

BATTLES OF THE UNITED KINGDOM: FROM SAUL TO DAVID

David's Strike on the Philistines
1 SAMUEL 18:28-19:10

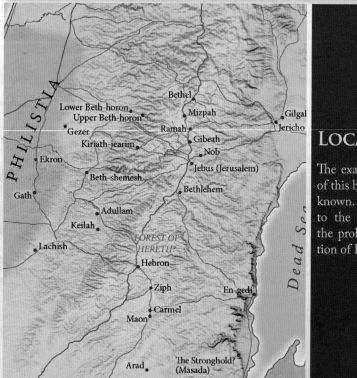

LOCATION

The exact location of this battle is not known. The map to the left shows the probable location of Philistia.

KEY PLAYERS

- Saul: the son of Kish from the tribe of Benjamin; God's chosen leader to rule the scattered nation of Israel as its first king
- David: the second king of Israel's united kingdom and—according to the New Testament Gospels of Matthew and Luke—an ancestor of Jesus
- Jonathan: King Saul's son; David's close friend

WEAPONS AND WARRIORS

The Philistines were fierce warriors. They were well trained to use their weapons with lethal skill. One particular weapon the Philistines boasted was their ox-drawn wagon. The wagon, or chariot, carried a warrior armed with a broad sword and a round shield. The warrior was able to move through a crowd, stand above others, and attack with power at close range.

Battle Synopsis

This battle, in a real sense, was not only between David and the Philistines but also between David and Saul. While God allowed David to weaken the Philistine forces, a wider rift developed between David and Saul. The more victorious David was, the angrier Saul became. In this particular battle, war broke out; David struck the Philistines with great force, causing them to flee.

Outcome

Short-Term

David was victorious over the Philistines, but Saul's jealousy reached a tipping point. David fled for his life and spent the next several years as a fugitive.

Long-Term

David was able to establish his position not only with the people of Israel but also with respect to the Philistines. Eventually, David was anointed as king over Israel, replacing Saul.

God's Role

God had promised He would give the land of Canaan to the Israelites and that He would protect them. Even though the people sinned by trusting a human king instead of God, God still kept His end of the bargain. He prepared David not only as a shepherd and a fighter but, most importantly, as a man after God's own heart. David was the right man at the right time to provide protection from Israel's enemies.

King David

BATTLES OF THE UNITED KINGDOM: FROM SAUL TO DAVID

David's Attack of the Philistines at Keilah
1 SAMUEL 23:1-29

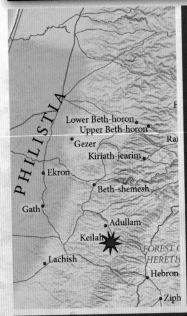

LOCATION

David and his men, who had been in the forest of Hereth (1 Samuel 22:5), attacked the Philistines at the city of Keilah, located southwest of Jerusalem in Judah. Keilah was described as a town with gates, bars, and threshing floors. Even though David saved the town from Philistine invasion, the people were willing to surrender David to Saul. When Saul came looking for David, David was able to escape to the wilderness of Ziph, southeast of Keilah. Centuries later, Keilah was one of the towns that contributed to the rebuilding of the walls of Jerusalem (Nehemiah 3:17–18).

KEY PLAYERS

- Saul: the son of Kish from the tribe of Benjamin; God's chosen leader to rule the scattered nation of Israel as its first king
- David: the second king of Israel's united kingdom and—according to the New Testament Gospels of Matthew and Luke—an ancestor of Jesus

WEAPONS AND WARRIORS

The two forces in this battle were David and his men, and the Philistine army. In addition, David had an ephod at his disposal. An *ephod* was the vest worn by the Israelite high priest. The sacred lots, known as the Urim and Thummim, were contained within the vest. The Israelites used these objects to inquire of God. This is likely how David determined whether God wanted him to fight each battle.

High priest wearing the ephod

BATTLE SYNOPSIS

The Philistines attacked the city of Keilah, and word soon reached David. Saul, still king of Israel, appeared either not to know or not to care. When David heard of the situation, he inquired of the Lord twice to find out if he should travel to Keilah and defend the city. The first time David sought God's leading, the Lord told him to go, but his men were afraid to take on the Philistines. When David sought the Lord a second time, God promised He would give David's men success against the Philistines. True to God's word, David and his men triumphed in battle.

Mountains of Judah

OUTCOME

SHORT-TERM

After this battle, God distracted Saul with the Philistines, and David and all his men were able to escape Saul's jealous grasp (1 Samuel 23:26–29). God protected David, His sovereign choice for Israel's next king.

LONG-TERM

David fled to the wilderness, while Saul spent his remaining days seeking to kill him. Saul eventually died in battle, and David was finally crowned king of Israel.

GOD'S ROLE

David first approached the Lord to see if he should fight; and then he sought the Lord a second time on behalf of his men. God was faithful to answer and promised David success. God also allowed David to flee the city when Saul was pursuing him and protected him from Saul's wrath. Even though David was not yet king, God allowed him to fulfill some of the duties of the king. Through David, God was providing for the people of Israel even in the midst of their unfaithfulness to Him. Saul did not trust God and became fearful as a result.

King David

David's Strategic Movements

1 SAMUEL 26-27

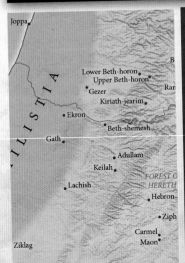

LOCATION

Three different locations were key to this part of David's story. The first was the wilderness of Ziph, located south of Jerusalem and west of the Dead Sea. This was a barren area not far from where David hid while fleeing from Saul. The second place was Gath, a Philistine stronghold on the southwest side of Canaan. The third was Ziklag, the city where David settled for a time after he persuaded the Philistines to let him live among them. Ziklag, located at the southern tip of Israel, belonged to the kings of Judah from the time of David.

KEY PLAYERS

- David: the second king of Israel's united kingdom and—according to the New Testament Gospels of Matthew and Luke—an ancestor of Jesus
- Amalekites, Geshurites, Girzites: peoples whom David attacked from his base at Ziglag
- Achish: a Philistine king of Gath

WEAPONS AND WARRIORS

Rather than killing Saul while he slept, David used psychological warfare and stole Saul's water and spear. Saul knew David could have killed him if he had wanted to. David also employed conventional warfare against the Girzites, Amalekites, and the Geshurites, three groups who inhabited land in the general vicinity of Ziklag. This was a war of spears, slings, arrows, and swords—weapons ideal for hand-to-hand combat.

Ancient arrowhead

BATTLE SYNOPSIS

Saul found the area in the wilderness where David was hiding and set up camp for the night. God caused the men in Saul's army to fall into a deep sleep. While they were sleeping, David snuck into Saul's camp. But instead of killing him, David took Saul's spear and water. David believed Saul was worthy of respect, regardless of his vendetta against David. Saul, realizing that David had shown unexpected kindness by sparing his life, expressed great remorse. But David couldn't trust Saul. Therefore, David fled to the one place he knew Saul could not catch him: Philistine territory. David raided the Geshurites, Girzites, and Amalekites, and told the Philistines' leader, King Achish, that he was attacking Israel. Thus, Achish allowed David to take refuge among the Philistines.

Blanche Garde, Tel Tzafit (Gath), Israel

OUTCOME

SHORT-TERM

David was able to hide from Saul by deceiving the leader of the Philistines. Every time he conquered a city belonging to the Geshurites, Girzites, or Amalekites, David would claim he had conquered an Israelite city instead.

LONG-TERM

God allowed David to raid Geshurite cities of old and thereby continue the work that should have been finished by the first generation of Israelites who entered the land.

GOD'S ROLE

God used David to show His power and mercy to the nation of Israel. God made the men of Saul's army fall into a deep sleep so that David could sneak into Saul's camp. David's decision to spare Saul's life reflected God's own mercy. God also allowed David to find favor in the eyes of the Philistine leader, who gave David a safe place to live. David, who did more than any other leader to undermine the rule of the Philistines, actually lived among them and found refuge in their presence—more evidence of God's power.

David Spareth Saul's Life
Richard Dadd (1817–1886)

David's Victory over the Amalekites

1 SAMUEL 30

LOCATION

This battle took place in Amalekite territory. Since the Amalekites were a nomadic people, their territory was quite large and included the Negeb (Negev) and the Sinai Peninsula.

KEY PLAYERS

- David: the second king of Israel's united kingdom and—according to the New Testament Gospels of Matthew and Luke—an ancestor of Jesus
- Amalekites: people of a nomadic nation with a history of hostility toward Israel

WEAPONS AND WARRIORS

David's army consisted of six hundred men, two hundred of whom stayed behind because they were too exhausted to cross the brook Besor. David brought his hand-to-hand fighting force, armed with spears, bows, swords, and slings. The battle began with a surprise assault on the enemy camp at night.

Moon over the Negev (Negeb), Israel

Battle Synopsis

The Philistines had gathered to go to war with the Israelites. David and his soldiers from Ziklag tried to join the battle, but the Philistine leader did not trust David since he was an Israelite. When David and his soldiers returned home, they discovered that Ziklag was burned to the ground and that all their wives, children, and livestock had been taken. David's men turned against him, blaming him for the disaster that had befallen them. David asked Abiathar the priest to bring him the ephod. He then inquired of the Lord through the Urim and Thummim (Exodus 28:30) to determine what to do. God told David to seek out those who attacked Ziklag. David found a sick Egyptian who was with the Amalekites. This Egyptian showed David where their camp was. David raided the camp by surprise at night and rescued all the people and livestock that had been taken from Ziklag.

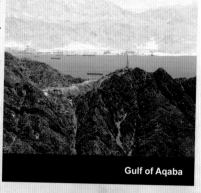

Gulf of Aqaba

Outcome

Short-Term

David's victory was complete. He sent some of the spoils to the elders of Judah who lived in numerous cities, mending relationships that had been strained by his time among the Philistines.

Long-Term

After Saul's death, David returned to the land of Judah, where he became king.

God's Role

The providence of God—His unseen hand in the events of life that assures and achieves His greater plans and purposes—can be seen in 1 Samuel 30. Though David pretended to be disappointed at being rejected by the Philistines and sent back to Ziklag, this event made it possible for David and his men to attack the Amalekites and recover all they had lost. God provided guidance for David, as well, through the priest and the ephod, and arranged for an ill Egyptian man who was a slave of the Amalekites to direct David to their camp, enabling a surprise attack. Finally, God allowed David to share the spoils with the people of Judah, which increased their confidence in their soon-to-be king.

King David, Nicolas Cordier (1567–1612)

Saul's Last Battle at Mount Gilboa

1 SAMUEL 28; 31; 1 CHRONICLES 10

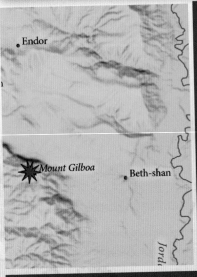

LOCATION

Mount Gilboa, an eight-mile-long range of hills in northern Israel, borders the highlands of the modern-day West Bank and the Beit She'an Valley. The Philistines had been unable to establish a presence in the central part of Israel, so they made their move from the south to the central plains. The region just below Mount Gilboa, known as the Valley of Jezreel, was a lush area with small ponds and grassy fields. This fertile area could support both livestock and farming.

KEY PLAYERS

- David: the second king of Israel's united kingdom and—according to the New Testament Gospels of Matthew and Luke—an ancestor of Jesus
- Saul: the son of Kish from the tribe of Benjamin; God's chosen leader to rule the scattered nation of Israel as its first king
- Philistines: an aggressive, warmongering sea people who occupied part of southwest Canaan between the Mediterranean Sea and the Jordan River; Israel's main enemy before the Assyrian invasion in the eighth century BC

WEAPONS AND WARRIORS

Both the Israelites and Philistines were heavily armed. They planned on fighting an intense war with a full-scale attack on each other. This battle was fought with arrows, then spears, then with slings and hand-to-hand sword fighting. The terrain would have been a challenge for both sides because of the uneven ground in the lower foothills of Gilboa.

Gilboa ridge, Israel

Battle Synopsis

The Philistines launched a major offensive against Israel. They combined all their forces to make a final push into the central plains of Israel. As the Philistines moved north, Saul encamped at the foothills of Mount Gilboa. It was there that the two armies clashed. Saul's men became afraid and fled; many died on the mountain. The Israelites did not put up much of a fight. As a result, the Philistines overtook Saul and his sons, killing Jonathan, Abinadab, and Malchi-shua. Philistine archers were able to reach Saul and critically wound him. Saul asked his armor-bearer to finish the job so that he would not fall into the hands of the Philistines. The armor-bearer refused, so Saul fell on his own sword and died.

Saul had known this battle was coming and was afraid. Samuel had died, and Saul did not trust that God was on his side anymore (and for good reason). Rather than seeking the Lord's guidance, Saul sought the help of a medium to see if she could make contact with Samuel's spirit. Apparently the medium was able to contact Samuel, who told Saul he was an enemy of the Lord and predicted he would die along with his sons. Also, Samuel revealed that Israel would fall into the Philistines' hands. It was God who allowed Saul to communicate with Samuel—only to hear words of judgment rather than hope. Saul refused to turn to the Lord in his darkest hour and instead turned to witchcraft—and he paid a heavy price for it.

Outcome

Short-Term

The Philistine army seized territory on both sides of the Jordan, essentially cutting Israel in half, making the fledgling nation ripe for total conquest by the Philistines.

Long-Term

The years of Saul's reign taught the Israelite tribes that trusting God was the only thing that brought success and strength. David demonstrated this truth over and over again during his reign.

God's Role

God spoke to Saul through a medium; but sadly, the words that came were words of judgment. God's hand was also present in allowing Saul's three sons to die. Their deaths were tragic, yet they played a role in God's unfolding plan. If Jonathan had lived, he would have likely given the throne to David (1 Samuel 18:1–4); Saul's other sons, however, would probably not have responded in this same way. Their involvement in this battle revealed God's mercy to the nation of Israel and to David.

Things to Think About

- What did you learn about trusting in God from the stories in this chapter?

- What are some of the lessons you can learn from Saul about what to do when you are jealous or afraid?

- God is able to use all things to carry out His will. What are some of the unique ways God protected David?

- When David had a chance to kill Saul, he did not. Why?

- What did you observe about the faith of David from the way he lived and fought?

- Can you think of anything in your life for which God deserves exclusive credit?

King Saul. Postage stamp (Israel, 1960)
© irisphoto1 / Shutterstock.com

THE ILLUSTRATED GUIDE TO BIBLE BATTLES

Chapter 4

BATTLES OF THE UNITED KINGDOM: DAVID

"And your house and your kingdom shall be made sure forever before me. Your throne shall be established forever."

(2 Samuel 7:16)

INTRODUCTION

Israel's greatest king, David, defeated the Philistines and began to reign over Judah in 1010 BC, and all Israel in 1003 BC. The united kingdom lasted until 930 BC, when it split. During David's reign, he conquered the entire coastal region from Gaza to Phoenicia. His authority extended from the Euphrates River in the north to as far as Egypt in the south. His reign was known as Israel's golden age because of the extent of his empire.

From the moment the Israelites entered the promised land, they were confronted with enemies. This is why the people begged for a king in the first place: They wanted protection from enemies who continually provoked and attacked them. When Israel's first king, Saul, died, Israel faced internal conflict on top of the external threat. Even though the kingdom had been promised to David, Saul's son Ish-bosheth tried to take the throne. It was several years before David was able to rule over a united kingdom.

Mediterranean Sea, Ashkelon, southern Israel

Even after David had established his throne, war did not cease. David encountered numerous threats and fought many battles during his reign. The first such battle took place when David dislodged the Jebusites from Jerusalem and made the city his capital. In the thirty years that followed, David fought the Philistines repeatedly. Israel's chief rivals proved a formidable foe because of their advanced weaponry and well-trained warriors. The Philistine city of Gath was populated with some tall men, or giants, who were strong and armed to the teeth. These prized warriors were notoriously difficult to defeat, and they made life in Israel very difficult. Yet through each battle, God showed that no earthly power could match His. He is the Lord of hosts—the Lord of angelic armies. No human being or weapon can thwart His plans and purposes.

David is a central figure in the Old Testament story, not because he was perfect (far from it), but because he was a man of conviction. He served God wholeheartedly. He believed God alone was worthy of worship. God's glory and power inspired his praise, in both good times and bad. David was also a man of faith. He believed God would be faithful to His promises; therefore, he was able to trust God for what he couldn't see. When God spoke, David listened and obeyed.

David also understood God's mercy firsthand. When David sinned, he humbled himself and sought God's forgiveness. David understood that it was important to seek the Lord in all things. Before going into battle, David would ask the Lord where to go and what to do. He knew God was the One who orchestrated all things and that without God leading him in battle, there would be no victory. The Lord provided the key to success in every battle, even when victory seemed impossible. David also believed that God was a God of justice. Knowing this, David desired to act fairly toward all people, even his enemies. Though he was by no means perfect, David desired deep in his heart to serve God, act justly, and love mercy. David was God's choice to rule Israel. He was the king through whom God promised to establish an eternal throne, and he was the one who would deal with the internal and external threats to the nation so that God's people could enjoy a time of peace, growth, and stability.

David's battles were evidence of God's faithfulness to the promises He had made to Israel and the world. Through these battles, God established His king, dealt with internal enemies, provided security for His people, and displayed His hand of justice and righteousness—not only for Israel, but also for the world. God took Israel from a state of fear to a place of security, from a place of constant war to a place of peace, from internal strife to a place of stability, and from a nation always on the brink of destruction to a world power. God kept His promise to Abraham and established Israel, giving assurance that He will continue to fulfill His promises in the future.

BATTLES OF THE UNITED KINGDOM: DAVID

War between David and Ish-bosheth

2 SAMUEL 4

ISH-BOSHETH'S KINGDOM
(later ruled by David)

Shechem

Aphek

Gezer
Gibeon
VALLEY OF
REPHAIM?
Geba
Bahurim?
Gilgal?
Jebus (Jerusalem)
Bethlehem
DAVID'S
KINGDOM
Tekoa
Hebron
En-gedi
Carmel

Jordan River
Dead Sea

LOCATION

The flash point of conflict was Mahanaim, the city where Ish-bosheth, the king of the northern tribes, lived. Mahanaim was a city near the Jabbok River, which flowed into the Jordan from the east, situated in the same general area as Jabesh-gilead. The precise location of Mahanaim is uncertain, though the Bible says the fighting took place in the bedroom of the palace where Ish-bosheth slept. The most widely agreed upon location sits about ten miles east of the Jordan River.

KEY PLAYERS

- David: the second king of Israel's united kingdom and—according to the New Testament Gospels of Matthew and Luke—an ancestor of Jesus
- Abner: Saul's first cousin and commander in chief of his army
- Ish-bosheth: Saul's youngest and only surviving son, who became king over the northern tribes of Israel after his father's death (Judah was loyal to David)

WEAPONS AND WARRIORS

This was a targeted attack meant to remove any hindrance to David being made king over the entire nation of Israel. Two soldiers made their way into Ish-bosheth's bedroom while he was sleeping and stabbed him. The weapon used was a simple dagger.

Iron dagger (500–300 BC)

BATTLE SYNOPSIS

Tension between the houses of Saul and David provided the backdrop to this battle. When Ish-bosheth, the king of the northern tribes in Israel, heard that his chief adviser, Abner, had died, he lost heart. All in Israel were troubled, too. Two captains from Ish-bosheth's army, Baanah and Rechab, set out during the heat of the day, making their way to Ish-bosheth's house. When they arrived, Ish-bosheth was lying on his bed. They entered the house, pretending to get some wheat. Once inside, they snuck into the king's chambers, stabbed him in the stomach, and beheaded him before escaping. Rechab and Baanah brought Ish-bosheth's severed head to David, thinking he would be pleased with their savagery. Instead, David was furious. He trusted God to hand over the kingdom in His own time; David never intended to murder anyone in Saul's family. David had Baanah and Rechab executed for murder and ordered Ish-bosheth's head buried out of respect for the slain leader.

Landscape of Jordan, between the capital of Amman and the city of Jerash

OUTCOME

SHORT-TERM

The house of Saul was dealt a crippling blow. All the tribes of Israel anointed David, and Saul's dynasty officially came to an end.

LONG-TERM

The house of David became even stronger, setting the stage for Jerusalem to become his capital. Even today Jerusalem is known as the city of David.

GOD'S ROLE

Ish-bosheth's murder was wrong in God's eyes, yet He was able to use the situation to ensure that David became the undisputed king of Israel. David made God's integrity known in how he honored his slain rival. His response showed the people God could be trusted, even when things did not seem to be going in the right direction.

Combat Soldiers of Ish-bosheth and David, Gustave Doré (1832–1883)

David's Capture of Jerusalem

2 SAMUEL 5:6-16; 1 CHRONICLES 11:4-9

DAVID'S KINGDOM

LOCATION

Jerusalem is situated on a plateau in the Judaean Mountains between the Mediterranean and the Dead Seas. It played a treasured part in ancient Israel's history. The first time Jerusalem appears in the Bible is in Genesis 14:18–20. Back then Jerusalem was called Salem and was ruled by a mysterious figure named Melchizedek. The city sat on the border between Judah and Benjamin; both tribes had attacked it during the conquest of Canaan but were unable to control it (Joshua 15:63; Judges 1:8, 21). David needed to conquer Jerusalem so that one like Melchizedek could come and bless the whole world.

KEY PLAYERS

- David: the second king of Israel's united kingdom and—according to the New Testament Gospels of Matthew and Luke—an ancestor of Jesus
- Jebusites: descendants of Noah's grandson Canaan who occupied Jerusalem before it was captured by Israel

WEAPONS AND WARRIORS

Jerusalem was a fortified city located on top of a hill—in other words, it was not the easiest place to conquer. David's army did not make a frontal attack and lay siege to the city. Instead, a guerilla force snuck in through the water supply. Once inside, they engaged in hand-to-hand combat, fighting with swords, spears, and fists.

A remnant of Herod's temple walls in Jerusalem, with an inscription in Hebrew that reads, "To the trumpeting place."

Battle Synopsis

In roughly 1000 BC, David sought to take down the Jebusite stronghold in Jerusalem. The Jebusites were confident their defenses would hold; they boasted that even the disabled or blind could defend the city from attack. This angered David, who came up with a plan to breach the city through its water supply. Because the water supply was not heavily guarded, it offered a perfect avenue into the city. Once inside, David's army attacked and conquered Jerusalem. The Jebusites were caught off guard, unprepared for a battle inside their city walls. Once conquered, David renamed Jerusalem the "city of David." He further fortified Jerusalem, which provided an ideal seat for his kingdom.

Judaean mountains, sunset

OUTCOME

SHORT-TERM

The Jebusites' arrogance proved to be their downfall, and David reclaimed the last unconquered city of the promised land. All twelve tribes of Israel recognized David as king.

LONG-TERM

Jerusalem became a great city, Israel's political and religious capital. Eventually David's son Solomon built the temple there.

GOD'S ROLE

God's hand was evident in the conquest of Jerusalem. According to 2 Samuel 5:10, "the LORD, the God of hosts"—that is, the God of the armies—was with David. "Lord of hosts" was a title God used to refer to His strength and power to conquer. There was no king, no army, no power, and no nation that could triumph over God. God's presence gave David supernatural power to overcome his enemies. Thus, God was the source of the military wisdom, power, and strength that allowed David and his men to overcome the Jebusites.

Model of Jerusalem

David's Battles against the Philistines
2 SAMUEL 5:17-25

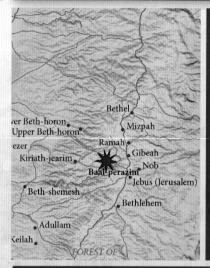

LOCATION

The Philistines waged two campaigns against Israel in the Valley of Rephaim in a city called Baal-perazim, to the west of Jerusalem. The tough terrain in the Valley of Rephaim made fighting difficult. The name *Baal-perazim* means "Lord of the breakthrough." This was the place where God helped David break through the Philistine garrison and further unify the nation.

KEY PLAYERS

- David: the second king of Israel's united kingdom and—according to the New Testament Gospels of Matthew and Luke—an ancestor of Jesus
- The Philistines: an aggressive, warmongering sea people who occupied part of southwest Canaan between the Mediterranean Sea and the Jordan River; Israel's main enemy before the Assyrian invasion in the eighth century BC

WEAPONS AND WARRIORS

David brought his fighting men down from the "stronghold" (2 Samuel 5:17), likely the area where he had hidden from Saul, to meet the Philistine army that was mustered for battle. This battle was a straightforward, army-to-army conflict. The soldiers would have used bows for long-range shots as the enemy approached. Next, they would have used spears for shorter-range fighting, and then swords and slings for the up-close combat.

Assyrian bow and arrow (911–605 BC)

Battle Synopsis

After David became king over the whole nation of Israel and conquered Jerusalem, the Philistines recognized him as a serious threat. So they began to move toward Jerusalem. When David heard of their movements, he left Jerusalem and made his way to his former stronghold in the wilderness of Judah and sought the Lord as to what to do. God told David to attack. The king and his men did so and were victorious. The Philistines regrouped for another attack, and again David sought the Lord's guidance. God told David to wait until he heard the sound of marching in the tops of the trees; then he was to attack. David obeyed and was victorious against the Philistines once more.

Near the Valley of Rephaim

Outcome

SHORT-TERM

David further established his rule in the region and emerged as a conquering king.

LONG-TERM

The civil war that had broken out between those loyal to Saul and those loyal to David had ended. Under David's uncontested rule, the nation enjoyed a period of unity.

GOD'S ROLE

God promised to deliver the Philistines into David's hands and gave him the ability to break through their defenses. David understood that even though it seemed impossible to overcome the Philistines' line of defense through human power alone, God was powerful enough to accomplish this incredible feat. This victory served as a small taste of what God would do in sending Jesus to the world to break through the bondage of sin that held humankind captive. God alone would break its power and restore us to life.

History of Jerusalem
GENESIS 14:18-20

Jerusalem was the spiritual and political capital of the Israelite kingdom. The city first appears in the Bible as "Salem" in Genesis 14:18–20. In this passage, the priest-king of Salem, Melchizedek, blessed Abraham. Melchizedek's name means "king of righteousness." The first blessing to God's people came from the king of righteousness who reigned in what later became Jerusalem—a beautiful foreshadowing of the blessing that was to come in Jesus, the eternal King of righteousness.

Later God commanded Abraham to sacrifice his son Isaac on Mount Moriah, a site associated with Jerusalem. Abraham referred to Mount Moriah as "the mount of the LORD" (Genesis 22:14). When the Israelites were told to seek out a place to make their center of worship (Deuteronomy 12:5), God chose Mount Moriah as the eventual place. Centuries later this became the location for Solomon's temple.

During the earliest stages of Israel's conquest of the promised land—and throughout the reign of Saul (1050–1010 BC), Israel's first king—Jerusalem was in Jebusite hands. The Jebusites were a tribal group whose land lay on the border between Benjamin and Judah. The Bible refers to the Jebusites as a people of a Canaanite tribe.

In the tenth century BC, King David seized Jerusalem from the Jebusites and established it as his residence. He brought the ark of the covenant to rest there. For David, Jerusalem's location offered several advantages. Its position halfway between Saul's capital of Gibeah and David's own birthplace of Bethlehem helped to unify the nation—at least for a while. Jerusalem was not associated with any tribal traditions, so its status as capital prompted little jealousy among the twelve tribes. Jerusalem was built on a high ridge bordered by steep valleys on three sides, making it a natural fortress that was easy to defend against attacks from Israel's enemies, especially the powerful Philistines. The city was more central than Hebron, David's capital during the seven years he reigned over Judah (2 Samuel 5:4–5), and it benefited from

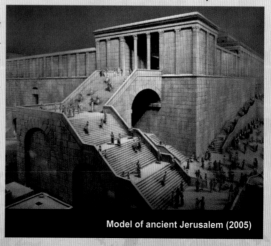

Model of ancient Jerusalem (2005)

the nearby spring of Gihon—a source of fresh water. Perhaps most importantly, Jerusalem lay near two highways, one going north–south between Shechem and Hebron, and another running east–west. This strategic location made Jerusalem the "center of the nations" (Ezekiel 5:5). After establishing Jerusalem as his capital, David bought the upper part of the hill from Araunah the Jebusite (2 Samuel 24:18–25; 1 Chronicles 21:18–22:1). This hill is Mount Moriah.

Jerusalem is also referred to as Zion in the Bible (Psalm 76:2). Originally the name appears to have been given to the southernmost hill of the city on which the Jebusite fortress was located. As the city expanded (from the days of Solomon onward), the name continued to apply to the entire city (see Isaiah 1:8; 2:3).

Under David's leadership, Jerusalem became the center of political and spiritual life for Israel. It was David who conceived of building a temple to serve as a permanent house of God. However, God did not allow David to build His dwelling place; instead, He promised David that an eternal kingdom would emerge from his line and that a King would rule for all eternity from this city (2 Samuel 7). God gave David's son Solomon the task of building the temple for the Lord. Jerusalem was the city where God chose to dwell, the place where He promised to judge the nations one day. Centuries later, when John received a vision of eternity, as recorded in Revelation 21:2, he described a new Jerusalem coming down from heaven—the eternal kingdom.

When the Babylonians conquered Jerusalem in 586 BC, they destroyed the temple. The people of Judah who survived the battle and were sent into exile pledged that they would never forget the city or its temple:

> *By the waters of Babylon,*
> *there we sat down and wept,*
> *when we remembered Zion.*
> *On the willows there*
> *we hung up our lyres.*
> *For there our captors*
> *required of us songs,*
> *and our tormentors, mirth, saying,*
> *"Sing us one of the songs of Zion!"*
> *How shall we sing the LORD's song*
> *in a foreign land?*
> *If I forget you, O Jerusalem,*
> *let my right hand forget its skill!*
> *Let my tongue stick to the roof of my mouth,*
> *if I do not remember you,*
> *if I do not set Jerusalem*
> *above my highest joy! (Psalm 137:1–6)*

King David's Great Conquests
2 SAMUEL 8; 1 CHRONICLES 18

LOCATION

As king, David secured the nation of Israel by taking his enemies' key cities. He captured Metheg-ammah, better known as Gath, from the Philistines. *Metheg-ammah* literally means "the bridle of the mother city." Located west of Jerusalem, it was the central city of the Philistines. In addition to his triumph over Gath, David was victorious over the Moabites, who lived east of the Dead Sea, and defeated the king of Zobah. Though the city of Zobah was located in Syria, northeast of Israel, David won this battle near the Euphrates River. Thus, David was able to establish the northern, southern, eastern, and western borders of the united kingdom.

KEY PLAYERS

- David: the second king of Israel's united kingdom and—according to the New Testament Gospels of Matthew and Luke—an ancestor of Jesus
- The Philistines: an aggressive, warmongering sea people who occupied part of southwest Canaan between the Mediterranean Sea and the Jordan River; Israel's main enemy before the Assyrian invasion in the eighth century BC
- Moabites: a tribe descended from Moab, the son of Lot
- Edomites: descendants of Isaac's son Esau who occupied territory south and southeast of the Dead Sea

WEAPONS AND WARRIORS

King David's army had two divisions, unlike his predecessor's army. The first consisted of Israelite warriors, including soldiers who had been faithful to David from the moment he fled Saul. The second division was a mercenary force comprised of Cherethites and Pelethites. These were Philistine soldiers and possibly soldiers from Crete as well. David had made alliances with these people while living as a fugitive. The swords and armor of his mercenary force were heavier and stronger than those of the Israelite division because the Philistines were master metalworkers.

BATTLE SYNOPSIS

Second Samuel 8 provides the account of a series of battles that David fought to secure his kingdom. God had promised to establish an eternal throne through David. These battles reveal how God made His plan come to pass through human events. God established David's throne by guarding Israel against the Philistines, Moabites, and Syrians. He struck down eighteen thousand Edomites in the Valley of Salt. David went on the offensive in all these battles and attacked the heart of each enemy's stronghold, securing the kingdom and ensuring the stability of the region.

Ruins of ancient Gath

OUTCOME

SHORT-TERM

Neighboring nations brought David honor and gifts. Under David's reign, Israel possessed more of the land that had been promised to Abraham (Genesis 15:18–21) than at any other time in its history.

LONG-TERM

David's plunder included bronze, which was later used to construct the bronze sea, the pillars, and other articles for Solomon's temple. God established the line of David and protected the lineage of the future Messiah, Jesus.

GOD'S ROLE

God was present with David through all these battles. God made it clear that He would establish an eternal throne through the line of David. Jesus was the King who would reign forever from David's throne. The Lord preserved David wherever he went in order to fulfill what He had promised. Every victory that David experienced was due to God's provision and protection. David attacked three enemies who were much stronger than Israel, yet with God's help, he was able to triumph over the strongholds of Israel's enemies

Military Heroes and Villains: David

David, whose name means "beloved," is one of the best-loved heroes in scripture. Born around 1040 BC, David was the eighth and youngest son of Jesse from Bethlehem. David was from the tribe of Judah and was a direct ancestor of Jesus (Matthew 1:1–17). The Bible describes David as handsome, with red hair and beautiful eyes (1 Samuel 16:12; 17:42). He was a shepherd and also had great musical skills, playing the flute and harp.

When the people of Israel begged God for a king to lead them, they had a certain type of king in mind—quite different from the one God had in mind. So God gave them Saul. A young David served Saul periodically as a musician and armorbearer (1 Samuel 16:21–23)—an ironic appointment, as David would eventually replace Saul on the throne. At one point, David found himself in the odd situation of fighting Saul's enemies while fleeing from Saul at the same time. Though Saul continually sought to kill David, David refused to lift his weapon against Saul—even saving Saul's life on occasion. The transition from Saul's reign to David's was slow, but God's Spirit eventually left Saul and rested on David, who was a man after God's own heart. David was the true type of king God desired for His people. To understand David is to understand much of God's plan for the world.

David Playing the Harp, Jan de Bray (1627–1697)

David was marked by several key traits:

1. ***David was a man of faith.*** He trusted that God was in control and rested his life on the Word of the Lord. When David needed direction, he sought the Lord before he acted.

2. ***David was a man of worship.*** He understood God was not only worthy to be trusted but worthy to be praised. He composed many of the songs recorded in the book of Psalms. When King David brought the ark of the covenant to Jerusalem, an occasion of great communal happiness, David danced wildly before the Lord.

3. ***David was a man of valor.*** He fought for the glory of God. Whenever God was maligned by His enemies, David was not shy about defending His holy name.

4. ***David was a man of justice.*** While waiting for God to give him the throne, David did not try to circumvent God's timing. He served Saul and waited. Once he was seated on the throne, David ruled with justice and righteousness.

5. ***David was a man of repentance.*** David was not a perfect man. He sinned—sometimes horribly. Yet when confronted with his sin, David repented and sought God's mercy and grace.

6. ***David was a man of promise.*** David was God's king because God used him to bring the Messiah, who would sit on David's throne forever (2 Samuel 7:13).

> *For God alone my soul waits in silence;*
> *from him comes my salvation.*
> *He alone is my rock and my salvation,*
> *my fortress; I shall not be greatly shaken.*
> *(Psalm 62:1–2, a psalm of David)*

BATTLES OF THE UNITED KINGDOM: DAVID

Battles against the Ammonites

2 SAMUEL 10-12; 1 CHRONICLES 19-20

LOCATION

Rabbah was the Ammonite capital, a heavily fortified, walled city located in modern-day Jordan. This Ammonite region was spread across the eastern hills. Rabbah is about twenty miles east of the Jordan, and about forty miles east of Jerusalem.

KEY PLAYERS

- David: the second king of Israel's united kingdom and—according to the New Testament Gospels of Matthew and Luke—an ancestor of Jesus.
- Hanun: the Ammonite king
- Ammonites: a Semitic people, closely related to the Israelites, tracing their ancestry to Lot's son Ben-ammi
- Syrians: the mercenaries hired by the Ammonites to fight against David's army
- Joab: David's commanding officer and chief counselor during most of his reign

WEAPONS AND WARRIORS

The Ammonites hired the Syrians of Beth-rehob and the Syrians of Zobah, totaling twenty thousand foot soldiers. They also hired a thousand men from the king of Maacah, and twelve thousand from Tob. When David heard of this, he sent Joab and his army of mighty men. Both sides were armed with traditional weapons: swords, spears, bows, slings, and a mounted cavalry.

BATTLE SYNOPSIS

This was a long, protracted battle. It began with the death of Hanun's father, king of the Ammonites. David had made an alliance with Hanun's father, so he sent his servants to Ammon to pay their respects. The new king of Ammon, Hanun, did not believe David's sympathy was genuine. He thought David was gathering intelligence on the city so he might attack it. Instead of welcoming David's representatives, Hanun humiliated them before sending them back to Jerusalem. David was furious. Hanun soon realized he had provoked David, so he hired a military force from Syria to help him fight. When David learned of this, he sent Joab with an army across the Jordan River toward the capital of Ammon, the city of Rabbah.

Zarqa River, identified with the biblical river Jabbok, which runs through Jordan

The mercenary force hired by Hanun made its way down to Medeba, south of Rabbah. When the Israelites approached Rabbah, the Ammonites came out of their city to meet them in battle. Joab's army saw the Ammonites approaching from the north and looked south—no doubt to scout out a path of retreat if

Ruins of an Ammonite tower in Rujm Al-Malfouf in Amman, Jordan

BATTLES OF THE UNITED KINGDOM: DAVID

needed. It was at that point they saw the mercenary force behind them. The two forces closed in around Israel, surrounding them. The Israelites reacted quickly, splitting their force into two divisions. The first division attacked the Syrian force, while the other engaged the Ammonites. The Syrians fled; when the Ammonites saw their allies had been routed, they followed suit. The Ammonites returned

David and Uriah
Rembrandt (1606–1669)

THE ILLUSTRATED GUIDE TO BIBLE BATTLES

home to Rabbah, and Joab returned home to Israel. However, this was not the end of the hostilities.

David again sent Joab to battle, this time to lay siege to Rabbah itself. David should have gone as well, but he did not. While Joab was attacking the city, David fell into his darkest hour as king, committing adultery with a woman named Bathsheba, whose husband was part of Joab's army. To make matters worse, David attempted to cover his sin. He had Bathsheba's husband, Uriah, sent to the wall of Rabbah, knowing he would almost certainly be killed, since the most intense part of any siege took place at the city wall. Sure enough, Bathsheba's husband was struck dead. After two years, the walls finally came down; the Israelites plundered the city and made the Ammonites their slaves.

Bathsheba, **Notre Dame Cathedral, Paris Portal of St. Anne**

OUTCOME

SHORT-TERM

The destruction of Rabbah was David's last great conquest. His kingdom extended to its farthest limits, but David's sexual sin had repercussions, including a civil war.

LONG-TERM

David eventually made Bathsheba his wife, and they gave birth to Solomon, who became heir to the throne and ancestor of the Messiah. This demonstrates that God forgives repentant sinners. In addition, Israel was safe from any Ammonite threat, and a labor force was put in place to work on various building projects.

GOD'S ROLE

God protected David's throne against threats from without (like the Ammonites) and within (such as David's own sin). God extended His grace to the woman with whom David sinned—Bathsheba was later mentioned in the New Testament as an ancestor of Jesus, the Messiah (Matthew 1:6). In addition, God extended mercy to David, despite his lies, depravity, and murder. God showed the nation that sin has consequences and that He must always be respected, but He also showed that He is gracious and forgiving to those who humbly turn to Him in wholehearted repentance.

BATTLES OF THE UNITED KINGDOM: DAVID

Absalom's Conspiracy against David
2 SAMUEL 13-19

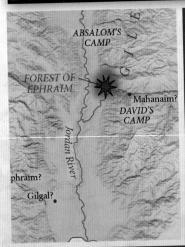

ABSALOM'S CAMP

FOREST OF EPHRAIM

Mahanaim?

DAVID'S CAMP

Jordan River

phraim?

Gilgal?

LOCATION

The heartrending battle between David and Absalom took place in the forest of Ephraim. The forest was located on the east side of the Jordan, not far from Mahanaim, in the territory of Gad, and was marked by very rough terrain. The region abounded in rocks, stones, scrub, and trees surrounded by thickets. This made it a perfect place to hide from enemies, because it was so difficult to navigate. It would have been difficult to wage a full-scale battle in the forest of Ephraim because of the terrain.

KEY PLAYERS

- David: the second king of Israel's united kingdom and—according to the New Testament Gospels of Matthew and Luke—an ancestor of Jesus
- Absalom: David's third son (born to his wife Maacah), who usurped his father's throne
- Amnon: the heir apparent to David's throne who brutally raped his half sister Tamar, who was Absalom's sister and daughter of David and Maacah
- Joab: David's commanding officer and chief counselor during most of his reign

WEAPONS AND WARRIORS

Absalom rallied support, especially from the northern tribes of Israel. He obtained a chariot and horses and fifty men to run before him (2 Samuel 15). Yet in the forest of Ephraim, where the battle took place, his weapons were not as powerful as the terrain itself, which was what killed most of the twenty thousand men who died. Typical military formations were useless in the forest. Most of the battle was fought hand to hand.

Forest landscape north of Israel

Battle Synopsis

At the heart of this battle was a broken family. Absalom's half brother Amnon violated Absalom's sister Tamar. Absalom was furious, but his father, David, did not bring Amnon to justice. Absalom took matters into his own hands and killed Amnon. A skilled politician, Absalom then worked successfully to turn the hearts of the Israelites against his father (2 Samuel 15:6). Eventually, David fled Jerusalem because Absalom had been effective at rallying support to himself. This eventually led to a decisive battle in the forest of Ephraim. The forest was filled with rocks, thorns, thistles, and trees, making it difficult to fight. At one point, Absalom was riding his mule through the forest when his long hair became caught in some thick branches of a tree. His mule ran off, leaving him hanging in the air and unable to free himself. David's military commander, Joab, heard that Absalom was caught—and killed him. When word spread that Absalom had died, the war between his supporters and those loyal to David ended. A bereaved David returned to Jerusalem.

Death of Absalom, Gustave Doré (1832–1883)

Outcome

SHORT-TERM

David was reinstated as king, and his kingdom was restored.

LONG-TERM

David's escort back across the Jordan consisted of all the troops of Judah and half the troops of Israel, leading to tension between the two groups that would eventually end in the division of the united kingdom into two separate nations.

God's Role

God protected David, thereby maintaining the lineage of the Messiah. Despite Absalom's early advances, God did not allow him to triumph over his father, David. God had told David that because of his sin with Bathsheba and the murder of her husband, the sword would not depart from David's family (2 Samuel 12:10–12). When David faced Absalom's rebellion, he knew it was a result of his own failure. Yet even in the midst of the fallout from David's sin, God was faithful to preserve David's throne so He could bring the Messiah through David.

David Mourns the Death of Absalom Gustave Doré (1832–1883)

Battle with the Philistines

2 SAMUEL 21:15-17

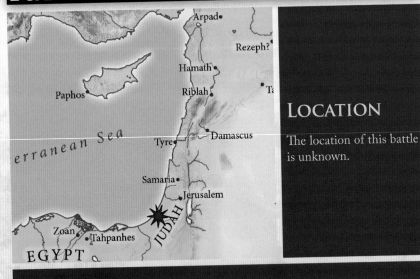

LOCATION

The location of this battle is unknown.

KEY PLAYERS

- David: the second king of Israel's united kingdom and—according to the New Testament Gospels of Matthew and Luke—an ancestor of Jesus.
- The Philistines: an aggressive, warmongering sea people who occupied part of southwest Canaan between the Mediterranean Sea and the Jordan River; Israel's main enemy before the Assyrian invasion in the eighth century BC

WEAPONS AND WARRIORS

The Philistines were known for their master metalworking. Because there were giants living among them, their weapons were bigger and more powerful than those of the Israelites. In this particular battle, one Philistine soldier had a spear that weighed 7.5 pounds. Between their strength and the power of these weapons, the Philistines could easily penetrate their enemies' armor, killing them with brutal efficiency.

Ancient iron spearhead

BATTLE SYNOPSIS

Israel's archenemies, the Philistines, mounted yet another offensive against God's people. At one point during the fight, David's strength gave out, and he found himself unable to continue. Perhaps this was because David was getting older and hand-to-hand combat was becoming more difficult for the weakening king. Ishbi-benob, one of the descendants of Rapha (a Philistine giant from Gath), noticed that David was vulnerable. Ishbi-benob took his heavy spear, which weighed 7.5 pounds, and made a move to kill Israel's king. David had no chance to defend himself, but Abishai, one of David's men, saw what was happening and counterattacked, saving David's life. After David's brush with death, his men swore never to let him fight in battle again. If he were to be slain, the light of Israel would go out.

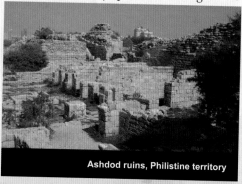

Ashdod ruins, Philistine territory

OUTCOME

SHORT-TERM

David's life was spared, and the Philistines were defeated again.

LONG-TERM

The godly line of David was preserved once more. Israel was spared from the Philistines in preparation for Solomon's rule.

GOD'S ROLE

The Philistines were strong warriors with superior weapons, and one Philistine in particular had marked David for death. God placed the right man in the right place to protect David from certain demise. It's likely the loss of their king would have been too much for the fragile nation of Israel to withstand. If Israel had fallen into the Philistines' hands, the messianic line would have been broken. Solomon would surely have been killed, and the promise of God to send a Messiah through the line of David would have been thwarted.

**Bronze javelin thrower,
Laconian style
(sixth century BC)**

Slaying the Giants
2 SAMUEL 21:18-22

LOCATION

It is difficult to establish a precise location for the first of the three battles mentioned in 2 Samuel 21:18–22. In the first two battles, David's army fought the descendants of the giants in Gob; this is the only time Gob is mentioned in the Bible. In 1 Chronicles 20:4, however, a parallel account to 2 Samuel 21:18–22, the city is identified as the Canaanite city of Gezer. Gezer was located in the Judaean Mountains, along the border of Shephelah. Gezer was a fortified city, a stronghold for the Philistines. A battle also took place in Gath, where many of the giant Philistines lived. Goliath, whom young David killed, lived in Gath.

KEY PLAYERS

- Israelite army: the Israelite soldiers, who were courageous fighters and not afraid of the Philistines' size
- The Philistine giants: larger-than-average Philistine warriors who made the Israelites fearful the first time they saw the promised land

WEAPONS AND WARRIORS

Some of the Philistine warriors descended from men of large stature. With their size and strength—along with their skill in forging metal—they were able to wield large and heavy weapons. Their weapons of choice were spears. Philistine warriors were able to throw heavy spears at fast speeds and pierce their enemies' armor.

Ancient iron spearhead

BATTLE SYNOPSIS

The rivalry between the Philistines and the Israelites continued well into David's reign. But this time Israel had to go to war without its king. David may have been growing too old to fight. If David were killed in battle, his loss would have been debilitating for the fledgling nation. The four battles mentioned in 2 Samuel 21 were important not so much for their military strategy but because of the Philistine giants who were killed. These "descendants of the giants" (2 Samuel 21:18) were most likely the giants suggested by the author of Deuteronomy 2:10–11, 20–21. The giants were powerful warriors who had terrorized Israel. God gave the Israelites the ability to overcome these warriors and neutralize the Philistine threat.

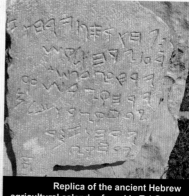

Replica of the ancient Hebrew agricultural calendar found in Tel Gezer, evidence of Israelite occupation

OUTCOME

SHORT-TERM

Once again, God protected David and the nation of Israel from the threat of the Philistines.

LONG-TERM

Eliminating the Philistine giants gave the people of Israel peace and protection from their arch-enemies once and for all. During the ensuing period of peace, Solomon was able to strengthen the nation and build God's temple.

GOD'S ROLE

The Philistine giants posed a massive threat to Israel. Because of their size and superior armament, they were difficult to defeat. As long as they were alive, Israel was not safe. God had promised that an eternal King would come from David's line, and the Philistines were the greatest threat to that line. God enabled Israel to defeat these massive soldiers. He proved His power was greater than that of any man or nation. By protecting Israel, He demonstrated His faithfulness to the promise He made to David to establish an everlasting throne.

David and Goliath
Osmar Schindler (1869–1927)

There lived in the city of Gath men the Bible refers to as "descendants of the giants" (2 Samuel 21:16, 18, 20, 22). The Philistine giants gave Israel's arch-enemies a tactical advantage in battle. The giants who fought against Israel were Gittites. They were unusually tall, strong, and powerful warriors.

The most common term used for giants in the Bible is *Rephaim* (Deuteronomy 2:10–11, 20–21; 3:11, 13). Other words to describe these large people are *Nephilim* and *Anakim* (or the Anakites). The sons of Anak were part of the Nephilim. The Nephilim and Anakim were mentioned when Joshua's spies returned from exploring Canaan. The spies reported, "The land, through which we have gone to spy it out, is a land that devours its inhabitants, and all the people that we saw in it are of great height. And there we saw the Nephilim (the sons of Anak, who come from the Nephilim), and we seemed to ourselves like grasshoppers, and so we seemed to them" (Numbers 13:32–33).

David's mighty men once killed a giant named Ishbi-benob (2 Samuel 21:15–17). Ishbi-benob wielded a large sword and spear. Other giants mentioned in scripture include Saph (Sippai) (2 Samuel 21:18; 1 Chronicles 20:4) and Lahmi (1 Chronicles 20:5), as well as an unidentified giant with six fingers on each hand and six toes on each foot (2 Samuel 21:20; 1 Chronicles 20:6). These giants may have descended from the few remaining Anakim who lived in Gath, Gaza, and Ashdod (Joshua 11:21–22). The Anakim ("sons of Anak") appear frequently in the accounts of the conquest (Numbers 13:22, 28, 33; Deuteronomy 1:28; 9:2; Joshua 14:12, 15; Judges 1:20).

Of course, the most renowned giant in the Bible is Goliath, a towering warrior who stood more than nine feet tall. His armor was made of bronze, and his protective coat of mail weighed 125 pounds. The fronts of his legs were covered with

Philistine Giant, Gebhard Fugel (1863–1939)

greaves of bronze bound by leather straps. The Bible compares the shaft of Goliath's spear to a weaver's beam, and it describes his spearhead as being made of iron and weighing fifteen pounds (1 Samuel 17:7).

These Philistine giants were intimidating because of their size, power, and strength. It was not until David's reign that Israel annihilated these fierce warriors, providing the land with a time of relative peace.

David and Goliath, Ilya Repin (1844–1930)

Things to Think About

- Many battles are described in 1 and 2 Samuel. In light of Psalm 2, why do you think there was so much war in and around the land?
- What can we learn from David's life about the nature of faith and trust in God?
- First John 4:4 says, "He who is in you is greater than he who is in the world." How can this statement be understood in light of the wars that David fought?
- Why did God protect David and the nation of Israel as He did?
- How was God's justice seen in the battles that tore apart David's family?

Statue of King David, Mount Zion, Jerusalem

Chapter 5

THE DIVIDED KINGDOM: ISRAEL'S EARLY DAYS

And when all Israel heard that Jeroboam had returned, they sent and called him to the assembly and made him king over all Israel. There was none that followed the house of David but the tribe of Judah only.

(1 Kings 12:20)

INTRODUCTION

Solomon's son Rehoboam was in line to become the next king of Israel after his father died. Jeroboam, who had fled after making an unsuccessful bid for power during Solomon's reign, returned from Egypt, where he had sought refuge with King Shishak I. Shishak lacked the strength to attack Israel's united monarchy, so it is theorized that he hatched a plan to destroy it from within and that Jeroboam was his pawn. Encouraged by Shishak, Jeroboam led a delegation to ask Rehoboam to ease the heavy burden of labor and taxation imposed by his father, Solomon.

Sunrise in the Peace Valley, northern Israel

Rehoboam foolishly refused their demand, so ten of the tribes rejected Rehoboam and David's dynasty (1 Kings 12:16), fulfilling the prediction from a prophet named Ahijah. God had spoken to Jeroboam through Ahijah, saying, "I am about to tear the kingdom from the hand of Solomon and will give you ten tribes (but he shall have one tribe, for the sake of my servant David and for the sake of Jerusalem, the city that I have chosen out of all the tribes of Israel)" (1 Kings 11:31–32).

After Jeroboam's defection, only Judah and Simeon (which had been absorbed by Judah), along with a small portion of Benjamin, remained loyal to Rehoboam. Although the bulk of Benjamin was aligned with the northern tribes, the area around Jerusalem remained under Rehoboam's control. Jeroboam was enthroned as king of the northern tribes. While Rehoboam planned to launch an attack on the secessionist tribes, God prevented him from doing so (1 Kings 12:21–24). The fracturing of Israel was part of God's plan.

From the north, Jeroboam consolidated his power base and instituted a distinct form of worship involving two golden calves. He discouraged his people from making annual pilgrimages to Jerusalem to celebrate the feasts that God had commanded (Leviticus 23). These actions on Jeroboam's part constituted outright rebellion against God and caused further separation from the southern tribes. King Shishak of Egypt attacked Jerusalem, invaded the temple, and took all the gold (1 Kings 14:25–26).

The northern kingdom became known as Israel (or sometimes "Ephraim"), while the southern kingdom was referred to as Judah. From a human perspective, the splintering of God's chosen nation seemed to be the result of tribal enmity and political unrest. However, the real root of the problem was spiritual. This division was tied up in the people of Israel's failure to keep God's commands, specifically those prohibiting idolatry. Sin against God naturally brings division (1 Corinthians 1:10–13; 11:18; James 4:1).

For northern Israel, the main threat to its supremacy was the Aramean kingdom, or Syria, and its capital, Damascus. The Philistines also emerged as a military adversary. Unlike their counterparts in Judah, the kings of northern Israel lacked the support of the priestly tribe of Levi. This contributed to frequent internal strife that further weakened the kingdom.

The fracturing of the kingdom caused great tension long after the ten northern tribes went their own way. Civil war, international pressure, espionage, betrayals, and spiritual rebellion typified this period. The result of conflicting ideologies led to hate, tension, war, and bloodshed in the two kingdoms, and this sorry state of affairs continued for many years. As one Old Testament writer put it, "So Israel has been in rebellion against the house of David to this day" (1 Kings 12:19). There were divine repercussions from Israel's rebellion as well. Yet God did not allow the sins of kings to thwart His plan to bring the Messiah to earth through the line of David.

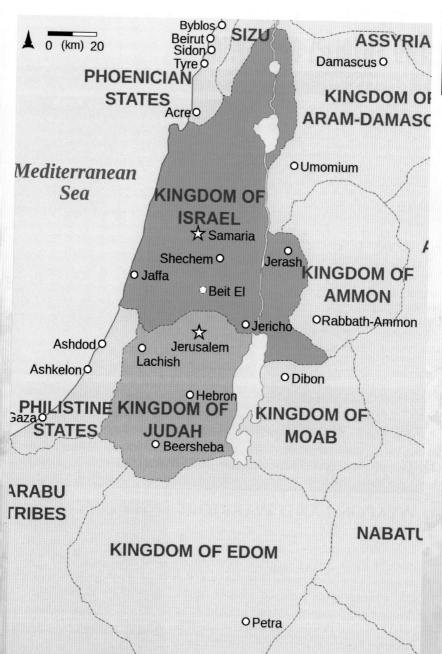

The wars of Israel and Judah stand as a sober warning to all who read them: *Do not take God lightly.* God will not be mocked. He is the Lord of the universe. He is to be worshipped, followed, and adored. His word must be obeyed.

THE DIVIDED KINGDOM: ISRAEL'S EARLY DAYS

Two Victories over Syria

1 KINGS 20

LOCATION

First Kings 20 describes two battles with Syria that took place on Israelite territory. The first took place in Samaria, the capital of the northern kingdom. The city was the capital from about 880 BC until 722 BC, when the Assyrians conquered the northern ten tribes (see 1 Kings 16:23–24). The second battle was fought in the city of Aphek, approximately three miles east of the Sea of Galilee. The name *Aphek* means "fortress." This city was located on the military road that connected Syria with Israel. Because of its location and fortification, Aphek made an excellent base for Syria to launch its offensive against Israel.

KEY PLAYERS

- Ben-hadad: king of Syria during the reign of King Ahab of Israel
- Ahab: king over the northern ten tribes of Israel; one of the most evil and powerful rulers Israel ever had

WEAPONS AND WARRIORS

Ben-hadad gathered together thirty-two kings, along with a number of horses and chariots, for battle (1 Kings 20:1). One of the most unlikely weapons of the battle turned out to be a wall that fell on twenty-seven thousand troops in Aphek. Another surprising weapon that brought defeat upon Syria was Ben-hadad's own character. His calloused heart that moved him to attack Israel in the first place also led him to get drunk with his thirty-two kings, rendering him ill-prepared for battle.

Old wall in Jerusalem, similar to what may have fallen on the troops in Aphek

Battle Synopsis

The Syrians viewed Israel's growing strength with great consternation. In the days of Ahab, who succeeded Omri (885–874 BC), Syria's king, Ben-hadad, decided to launch a preventative war before Israel could grow even more powerful. He advanced all the way to the capital of Israel, Samaria, and demanded Ahab's gold and silver, wives and children. When Ahab complied, Ben-hadad sensed weakness and upped his demands, requiring the surrender of the city. This time Ahab rejected Syria's humiliating terms of peace. A prophet told Ahab that God would lead Israel to victory over the Syrians, who had settled down for a long siege.

God kept His promise. Ahab outsmarted Ben-hadad, sending out his forces while Ben-hadad and his allies were getting drunk in their tents. The Israelites easily overran the Syrians. But Syria wasn't finished. Ben-hadad's forces returned the following spring, only to be slaughtered by the Israelites. One hundred thousand troops were struck down in a single day; twenty-seven thousand died when a wall collapsed on them. Seeing that all was lost, Ben-hadad negotiated a treaty with Ahab. Then he was released with honor and given safe passage home.

Ancient fortress in the Negeb (Negev), Israel

Outcome

Short-Term

The Lord had given Ben-hadad into Ahab's hand; Ahab was responsible to the Lord for his custody.

Long-Term

Ahab's negotiations with Ben-hadad affected him as well as the people of the northern kingdom. Israel ended up being humiliated by the Syrians.

God's Role

Ahab formed Israel into a powerful nation, but Syria was a much larger and stronger force. God allowed the Israelites to defeat the Syrians twice, showing them that He is a miracle worker and King over all the earth. God also brought down a massive wall in Aphek, killing twenty-seven thousand troops. Evidently, He intended for Ben-hadad's forces to be utterly destroyed by Israel's army.

The Israelites Slaughter the Syrians
Gustave Doré (1832–1883)

THE DIVIDED KINGDOM: ISRAEL'S EARLY DAYS

Military Heroes and Villains: Ahab

Ahab ruled over the northern ten tribes of Israel from 874 to 853 BC. He is one of the most colorful characters in the Bible. Ahab inherited the throne from his father, Omri, and ruled during the time of Elijah the prophet. Throughout his reign, he was a champion of evil. Ahab even married Jezebel, a princess from Sidon, a city where paganism and its associated evil were widespread. God forbade marriage to pagan foreigners in order to prevent His people from polluting their worship (Deuteronomy 7:3–4), but that didn't stop Ahab.

Not content with the form of worship instituted by Jeroboam, Ahab and his wife Jezebel promoted worship of Baal and Asherah. The rituals associated with these cults included detestable practices such as prostitution and child sacrifice. Ahab, influenced by Jezebel, built a temple to the pagan god Baal in Samaria (1 Kings 16:32). Jezebel was so evil that she rallied a large group of false prophets, together with the devotees of Baal (1 Kings 18:19–20), to participate in open rebellion toward God. She murdered prophets of the true God, tore down altars of the Lord, and forced Elijah to flee for his life.

Ahab did not discourage his wife from acting in such a despicable manner. He was so wicked himself that the Old Testament devotes roughly four chapters to his exploits; no other ruler from the northern kingdom of Israel has as much written about him. This portion of the Bible expounds on his sin and depravity, presenting Ahab as Israel's worst king.

Ahab also fortified many of Israel's cities (1 Kings 16:34; 22:39). He undertook a massive upgrade to his palace in Samaria. Excavation shows that his palace was ornate and adorned with ivory. Ahab negotiated trade agreements with Phoenician merchant cities in the north, and his twenty-two-year reign included three wars with neighboring Syria. God graciously aided Ahab and twice gave him victory. God also gave him an opportunity to repent—clear evidence of God's power and grace.

Though Ahab did eventually humble himself before the Lord, his change of heart came too late; his kingdom would never recover. Elijah predicted the fates of Ahab, his wife, and his dynasty (1 Kings 21:20–22). Because Ahab did evil in God's eyes, God pronounced disaster on him. God promised to bring Ahab to a dismal end. His family line would be cut off from Israel completely. God also said that dogs would eat Jezebel within the walls of Jezreel. During the third war with Syria, Ahab was killed, fulfilling part of Elijah's prophecy.

Modern-day Samarian landscape

THE DIVIDED KINGDOM: ISRAEL'S EARLY DAYS

Israel and Judah's Fight against Syria

1 Kings 22; 2 Chronicles 18:1-19:3

LOCATION

This important battle took place at Ramoth-gilead, a location originally established as a city of refuge for the tribe of Gad (see Joshua 20:1–8). A city of refuge was a place designated by God where someone could flee if he had accidently killed someone. Located east of the Jordan River, Ramoth-gilead fell to Syria after the division of Israel.

KEY PLAYERS

- Jehoshaphat: the fourth king of Judah, who took over from his father, Asa, and was known for combating idol worship in the land
- Ahab: king over the northern ten tribes of Israel; one of the most evil and powerful rulers Israel ever had

WEAPONS AND WARRIORS

Warriors fought this battle in close proximity using arrows, slings, spears, and swords. During the course of conflict, a barrage of arrows would be launched at a target, not unlike modern artillery. Such a volley could strike down anyone, which is exactly what happened to King Ahab.

Battle Synopsis

Ahab was perhaps the most wicked king of Israel. He disregarded the Lord and worshipped idols. Wanting to reclaim Ramoth-gilead from the Syrians, he sought help from Jehoshaphat, the king of Judah. Jehoshaphat was willing to fight alongside Ahab, but he feared God and announced he would only enter the battle if he was sure the Lord's favor was with them. When Ahab consulted with his false prophets, they assured him that the Lord was in favor of war. However, Micaiah, a true prophet of the Lord, foretold that Ahab would die in battle. Ahab refused to listen to Micaiah and went into battle disguised as a normal soldier. God protected Jehoshaphat; Ahab, however, was killed with an arrow. The battle ended, and Israel's soldiers returned home.

Outcome

Short-term

Ahab's rebellious pattern was followed by his son Ahaziah.

Long-term

Eventually, the Israelites were defeated by the Assyrians and scattered among the nations, as forewarned in Leviticus 26:33.

God's Role

This was more than the story of two kings, one good and one bad. This was also the story of a God who was orchestrating events even when there was an evil king who would not listen to Him. God allowed false prophets to lead Ahab astray, enticing him into a war in which he would die. God was faithful to His word; Ahab was killed in battle by what appeared to be a random shot. Meanwhile, God protected Jehoshaphat during the battle, showing His faithfulness to the people of Judah and to their king.

Israel and Judah's Fight against Moab
2 KINGS 3

LOCATION

A plateau in the southeast area of the Dead Sea served as the battlefield for a war involving Israel, Judah, and Moab. The Moabites occupied the plateau. The surrounding terrain was dotted with steep but fertile limestone hills. In the spring, they were covered with grass, and the tabletops of the plateau produced much grain. This territory consisted of three distinct portions: the enclosed corner just south of the Valley of Arnon, referred to as the "fields of Moab" (Ruth 1:6); the rolling country north of the Arnon, opposite Jericho and leading up to the hills of Gilead, referred to as the "land of Moab" (Judges 11:18); and finally, the district below sea level in the tropical depths of the Jordan Valley.

KEY PLAYERS

- Elisha: Elijah's successor and a prophet of God
- Jehoram (or Joram): the ruler of the northern kingdom of Israel; son of Ahab and Jezebel
- Mesha: king of Moab and a sheep breeder who sought independence from the northern kingdom of Israel and worshipped the Moabite god Chemosh
- Jehoshaphat: the fourth king of Judah, who took over from his father, Asa, and was known for combating idol worship in the land

WEAPONS AND WARRIORS

A rather unusual "weapon" played a role in this battle: ditches filled with water. This water sustained the armies of Judah, Israel, and Edom. To the Moabites, however, the water looked like blood. Thus they were deceived into thinking that the enemy armies had turned on each other and the field had turned to blood.

BATTLE SYNOPSIS

When the Moabites rebelled against Israel sometime between 852 and 841 BC, Jehoram (or Joram) decided to retaliate. He enlisted the help of Jehoshaphat, king of Judah. Together they traversed Edom and joined forces with the Edomite king. However, after a week, they had accomplished nothing except wandering in the desert. Their troops were becoming dehydrated, and the situation was dire. The three kings decided to consult Elisha to find out if God was in favor of their undertaking. The Lord told Elisha that He would give the Moabites into the hands of the three kings, and that the next morning there would be pools of water around them from which the soldiers could drink. When the Moabites saw the water, however, they mistook it for blood and thought the armies of the three kings had slaughtered each other. They rushed to plunder the camp but instead found their enemy poised to fight. The Moabites were defeated and their land destroyed.

Southern Israel near ancient Moab

OUTCOME

SHORT-TERM

The Moabites were defeated. Later Elisha assisted Jehoram in a war against Syria.

LONG-TERM

Because Moab's king, Mesha, was not killed in battle, he maintained his leadership over the Moabites.

GOD'S ROLE

Convinced of their own strength, Jehoram and Jehoshaphat marched into battle without first seeking God's favor. It wasn't until extreme thirst and dehydration threatened their undertaking that they called on the Lord. Elisha was summoned; initially he did not want to help. However, since Jehoshaphat honored God, Elisha eventually spoke, revealing that God intended to give the Moabites into the hands of the kings. To make clear that victory would be due to His intervention alone, God worked a miracle in the middle of a parched desert, creating pools of water.

THE DIVIDED KINGDOM: ISRAEL'S EARLY DAYS

Israelite Fortifications and Military

The main threats to Israel's sovereignty came from Syria (the Aramean kingdom) and, to a lesser degree, Philistia. In time, however, Assyria began building a massive empire, extending its control over Babylon and the Medes to the east, the kingdom of Urartu to the north, eastern Asia Minor, Phoenicia (Tyre), and Syria (Damascus) to the west, and well into northern Israelite territory.

In response to this threat, Israel began to fortify its northern borders, including what could be called the Naphtali line. This line of defense blocked enemy descent

The Golan Heights, Israel

from the Syrian plateau, known today as the Golan Heights. It also impeded military ascent into Galilee from the east. If and when Israel went to war with enemies from the north, its military operated from this region in Naphtali.

In an attempt to secure this northern border, Israel fortified several cities. Prominent fortifications were erected under King Omri (885–874 BC), and this effort continued during the reign of his son Ahab (874–853 BC). It was Ahab who made the kingdom a regional power. As the Assyrian threat intensified, the house of Omri introduced a new kind of wall: a solid, thick barricade featuring inset and offset sections to withstand powerful siege works. Without question, these walls were among the most sophisticated and complex in the ancient world. City gates in northern Israel became smaller, changing from the common six-chambered gates to four-chambered gates. To further prevent invasion, they were reinforced by an outer one-chambered gate.

The biblical narratives detailing the Philistine campaigns (1 Kings 15:27; 16:15–17) provide clues to the composition of Israelite forces prior to the Assyrian invasion in 722 BC. Carrying on the Solomonic tradition under Omri, the Israelite military force formed two strategic divisions. The first was called the general national levy, or the people in arms. This division was a reserve force that would be called up in the event of war. The second division consisted of charioteers. This was most likely a full-time force that trained in combat maneuvers and provided security for the nation. The chariot division also served as royal guards to protect the king, his palace, and all his associates.

The last great king of northern Israel was Jeroboam II (782–753 BC), who extended Israel's borders to their farthest reaches, "from Lebo-hamath as far as the Sea of the Arabah" (2 Kings 14:25; Amos 6:14). Jeroboam was succeeded by Zechariah. From that point on, Israel degenerated into political instability, which eventually led to the Assyrian invasion.

Israel's Deliverance from Syria

2 KINGS 6:8-7:20

Megiddo•
•Jezreel
Ke
Dothan•
Abel-meholah?•
Samaria ✦ I S R A E L
P.
•Gilgal?
Bethel•
Mizpah• Michmash
Ramah• Geba •Jericho
•Jerusalem
• Gath J U D A H   Dead Sea
Jordan River

LOCATION

Israel's capital city, Samaria, was the site of these extraordinary events involving Israel and Syria. The name *Samaria* means "watch-tower." The capital was located in a mountainous region just a few miles northwest of Shechem. This region was bordered by Galilee to the north, Judah to the south, the Mediterranean Sea to the west, and the Jordan River to the east.

KEY PLAYERS

- Elisha: Elijah's successor and a prophet of God
- Ben-hadad II: king of Syria during this time; either a son or grandson of Ben-hadad I, who reigned during the time of King Ahab of Israel

WEAPONS AND WARRIORS

A siege is a specialized military operation where an invading force surrounds a town or building and cuts off all traffic in and out of the city in order to force the surrender of those inside. This was the primary "weapon" used here. Ben-hadad's army laid siege to Samaria, trying to starve its people into submission.

God allowed the Syrian army to hear the sound of horses and a mighty marching army; panicked, they fled for their lives—leaving the whole camp just as it was (2 Kings 7:5–7).

Battle Synopsis

Syria (ancient Aram) was at war with its neighbor to the south, Israel. Furious that the king of Israel seemed to anticipate his plans, Ben-hadad accused his servants of being informants. Upon learning that Elisha was responsible for revealing his plans, Ben-hadad set out to capture the prophet to prevent him from helping Israel win the war. However, God protected Elisha, surrounding him with a massive army of angels in charge of horses and chariots of fire. In addition, God struck the Syrian soldiers with blindness so they could not see this angelic army. This allowed Elisha to lead the Syrian soldiers into Israel's capital city of Samaria. Elisha instructed the king of Israel to treat the enemy soldiers with kindness and generosity. Consequently, the Syrians stopped raiding Israel's territory. But some time later Ben-hadad launched a full-scale attack on Samaria; his siege led to a terrible famine in Samaria so extreme that women resorted to eating their own children. Outraged, the king of Israel demanded Elisha's head. The Lord ultimately gave Israel victory over Ben-hadad, bringing much-needed relief from the famine (2 Kings 7).

Mountains near Samaria

OUTCOME

SHORT-TERM

Within twenty-four hours, the economic situation in Samaria was completely reversed; food was abundant and prices dropped.

LONG-TERM

God allowed the people of Israel to suffer through the siege, but He also reminded them of His grace.

GOD'S ROLE

God conveyed messages through Elisha to the king of Israel. Significantly, He did not forsake His prophet but worked in miraculous ways to protect Elisha. When Ben-hadad surrounded the town where Elisha was staying, God's angel armies surrounded Elisha. God opened the eyes of Elisha's servant, allowing him to see the vast but invisible army. When Elisha asked that the Syrians be struck down with blindness, God granted his request. Later God reversed a famine caused by the Syrian siege of Samaria, and He provided abundantly for the people of the city.

Things to Think About

- What did you learn from reading about the leaders of Israel and their sinful choices? Despite their sin, how did God keep His promises to His people?

- What are some of the character traits God displayed in these battles?

- Make a list of some of the consequences of sin that were displayed in these stories.

- What do these battles teach about the mercy of God? (*Mercy* is defined as not getting a deserved punishment.)

- What do these battles teach about the grace of God? (*Grace* is defined as receiving an undeserved blessing.)

- In what ways do these battles reveal God's holiness?

- Why is it important to follow God with your entire life?

Chapter 6

THE DIVIDED KINGDOM: ISRAEL'S DECLINE

"And if you faithfully obey the voice of the LORD your God, being careful to do all his commandments that I command you today, the LORD your God will set you high above all the nations of the earth."

(Deuteronomy 28:1)

INTRODUCTION

God brought Israel into a specific piece of land, which He had promised the nation through Abraham (Genesis 12:1–3). He did so not for privilege but for purpose. The nation of Israel was to be a sign for all nations, a distinctive people set apart for God (Deuteronomy 14:2). The Israelites were to put the glory of God on display for the surrounding nations, who would be drawn toward God as a result.

God promised that if the people of Israel obeyed Him while they lived in the land He had given them, He would bless them beyond all measure. They would enjoy the fruits of the land and find peace and prosperity in all they did. God made it crystal clear what He wanted from His people: obedience.

God also made it clear that if His people ignored Him, they would face the consequences. Though the land was to be an everlasting possession, God warned the Israelites that they would only live in the land if they obeyed Him. God did not give His people the land for their own pleasure but for His. Disobedience would

Sand hills of Samaria, Israel

bring curse after curse on the nation—including disease, confusion, and famine (Deuteronomy 28:15–26).

But the most devastating consequence of not listening to God would be dispersion from the land: "And I will scatter you among the nations, and I will unsheathe the sword after you, and your land shall be a desolation, and your cities shall be a waste" (Leviticus 26:33; see also Deuteronomy 4:27; 28:64; Nehemiah 1:8).

Sadly, the people of the northern kingdom of Israel continued to rebel against God. Every king did evil in the sight of the Lord and walked in rebellion. They relied on other nations to protect them instead of trusting in God's promises. They disregarded the God of their redemption, conformed to the pagan nations around them, openly practiced idolatry, and ignored God's warnings (2 Kings 17:7–23).

Thus the Assyrians were God's instrument of judgment on Israel's unbridled corruption and depravity. After King Jeroboam II, the northern kingdom moved steadily and blindly toward the historical storm that would eventually spell its downfall. A series of insurrections erupted, like those that had toppled earlier dynasties such as Jeroboam I's, Baasha's, and Omri's. Then Assyria's Tiglath-pileser III (745–727 BC) intensified the threat against the northern kingdom. Israel's kings Menahem, Pekah, and Hoshea had to reckon with their Assyrian overlords—either by paying tribute or by being ravaged.

During Pekah's reign over the northern kingdom, Tiglath-pileser had pared away large portions of Israel, leaving only the core around Samaria intact (2 Kings 15:29). Hoshea (732–722 BC) took the throne after Pekah and had no choice but to yield to Tiglath-pileser's demands for tribute. Thus he began his reign as

Ruins at Mount Gerizim, West Bank, Israel

an Assyrian vassal. Israel secretly began to conspire with Egypt against Assyria. When Shalmaneser V, Tiglath-pileser's successor, became privy to this information, the Assyrians stormed into Samaria. Though the fortress capital held out for a few years, Shalmaneser's successor, Sargon II, finished the assault with a vengeance in 722 BC.

The results were disastrous; Israel was finally subdued. The proud northern kingdom of Israel came to an end. This divine judgment was followed by the deportation of the surviving remnant; Israel was scattered, just as the ancient prophets had foretold.

> *"And the* LORD *will scatter you among the peoples, and you will be left few in number among the nations where the* LORD *will drive you."*
>
> *(Deuteronomy 4:27)*

Assyrian battle scene (728 BC)

THE DIVIDED KINGDOM: ISRAEL'S DECLINE

King Joram and King Ahaziah against Syria

2 KINGS 8:25–9:29; 2 CHRONICLES 22:1-9

LOCATION

Ramoth-gilead, or the "heights of Gilead," was the setting for a war between Israel and Judah on one side and Syria on the other. When Solomon divided the united kingdom of Israel into different districts, Ramoth-gilead was made a district capital. Eventually, it became the seat of a governor (1 Kings 4:7, 13). During the Syrian wars, Ben-hadad captured Ramoth-gilead from the Israelites and made it a frontier post. The Israelite king Ahab was killed in an attempt to recapture the city (1 Kings 22:29–40).

KEY PLAYERS

- Ahaziah: king of Judah; Athaliah's son
- Joram: Ahab's son, who succeeded his brother Ahaziah as king of Israel
- Hazael: became king of Syria after he murdered Ben-hadad II by suffocating him; fought the kings of Judah and Israel with some success
- Athaliah: Ahab's daughter and Ahaziah's mother; the only woman to reign as queen of Judah; a wicked queen whose marriage to Jehoram sealed a treaty between the northern and southern kingdoms

WEAPONS AND WARRIORS

Of the various weapons used by the Israelites, slings were among the most exact. The sling was a more archaic weapon than the bow and arrow, but even after the latter was introduced, many fighters preferred the sling because of its long range. Slingers could launch a stone at such a velocity that it could easily kill someone. Slung stones were also less visible in flight.

BATTLE SYNOPSIS

Judah's evil king Ahaziah maintained close ties with the house of Ahab. This relationship developed into a war alliance between Judah and Israel against their enemy, Syria. Ahaziah was the "son-in-law to the house of Ahab" (2 Kings 8:27). Together Ahaziah and Israel's king Joram attacked Syria's king Hazael at Ramoth-gilead. Joram was wounded and withdrew from fighting. He traveled to Jezreel to recover. Later Ahaziah visited Joram. Unfortunately for Ahaziah, the visit led to his death. Ahaziah and Joram went to meet a man named Jehu. Little did they know that God had told Jehu to kill every male in Ahab's family, which included Joram and perhaps Ahaziah. According to 2 Kings 9:27, Ahaziah witnessed Joram's death and then escaped by road to Beth-haggan. Jehu mortally wounded Ahaziah near Ibleam, between Jezreel and Samaria. Ahaziah fled by chariot northwest to Megiddo, where he died.

Tel Jezreel looking east toward Gilboa

OUTCOME

SHORT-TERM

Israel was later ravaged during a series of campaigns, and parts of its territory were incorporated in the Syrian kingdom. The people living in the rest of northern Israel, as well as Judah, were forced to capitulate to King Hazael.

LONG-TERM

Jehu's assassinations of Joram and Ahaziah marked the beginning of years of decline for both the northern and southern kingdoms.

GOD'S ROLE

God was angry with Ahaziah because he had emulated Ahab's evil conduct. God allowed Ahaziah to fight the Syrians unscathed, but Joram was wounded in battle. This turned out to be part of God's plan to ensure the downfall of both men. God had raised Jehu up for the purpose of bringing judgment against the dynasty of Omri and Ahab, which ruled the northern kingdom of Israel (2 Kings 9:1–26). Jehu was used by God to kill Ahaziah and Joram, neither of whom saw any need in life to humble themselves before the Lord.

Depiction of King Jehu of Israel

Israel's Losses to Syria
2 KINGS 10:32-33; 13:1-7

LOCATION

Gradually, the Israelites lost all the territory they had possessed east of the Jordan River—land once held by the tribes of Gad, Reuben, and the half-tribe of Manasseh. Their losses reached as far south as the city of Aroer near the Valley of the Arnon, along the Arnon River, up through the land of the Reubenites and Gadites—and as far north as the land of the Manassites (Gilead and Bashan). Centuries earlier, when Joshua and the Israelites had set off to conquer the promised land, this was the first stretch of property they took for themselves and settled.

KEY PLAYERS

- Jehu: tenth king of Israel, notable for exterminating the house of Ahab at God's command and having Jezebel thrown out of a window
- Jehoahaz: Jehu's son, known for his wickedness
- Hazael: became king of Syria after he murdered Ben-hadad by suffocating him; fought the kings of Judah and Israel with some success

WEAPONS AND WARRIORS

Typical Syrian weaponry included bows, slings, and swords. Syrian fighters also used javelins or lances to spear their opponents, along with axes to hack at them in close combat. At times in their history, Syrians used lightweight chariots, striking fear into the hearts of their enemies.

Typical Syrian armor included full-length coats of mail, composed of overlapping bronze or iron scales that were sown onto tunics of wool, linen, or leather. Much like the skin of an alligator, these bronze or iron scales would overlap each other, giving the wearer a great deal of protection. Though heavy, a bit cumbersome, and often hot, they also allowed a degree of mobility that solid armor could not give.

Detail of a fragment of scale armor

Battle Synopsis

King Jehu obeyed the Lord and eliminated the house of Ahab according to God's plan. However, he did not follow all of God's commands, especially with respect to idolatry. "Jehu did not turn aside from the sins of Jeroboam the son of Nebat, which he made Israel to sin—that is, the golden calves that were in Bethel and in Dan" (2 Kings 10:29). As a result, judgment fell on Jehu and his people through God's agent of wrath, Hazael, king of Syria. In general, the Assyrian Empire kept the Syrians weak and subdued, unable to expand their territory. However, internal strife forced the Assyrians to withdraw their troops. The Syrians did not squander this opportunity to profit from Assyria's distraction. God allowed Hazael, king of Syria, to conquer large portions of Israelite territory on the eastern side of the Jordan River—land Israel had possessed since the time of the nation's entry into the promised land nearly six hundred years before. Hazael,

and later his son Ben-hadad III, continued to attack Israel throughout King Jehoahaz's reign. Jehoahaz followed in the evil footsteps of his father, Jehu. Eventually, Jehoahaz realized his sin and turned to the Lord for help. God heard his prayer, though it did not lead to a lasting change in Jehoahaz's life. Still, God provided a deliverer for His people. The Israelites were able to return to their land, but they continued to worship pagan idols.

Ancient mosaic, Assyria

Outcome

Short-term

Although some land was regained, the Syrians had decimated Jehoahaz's kingdom, reducing its army to fifty horsemen, ten chariots, and ten thousand infantry (2 Kings 13:7).

Long-term

The nation would never fully recover from these attacks; Israel would eventually fall to Assyria.

God's Role

It was the Lord who caused the Syrians to conquer Israelite land east of the Jordan; this was a direct consequence of the Israelites' unfaithfulness to their covenant with God. The Syrians did not stop their attacks when Jehoahaz became king. Nor did Jehoahaz change his ways and return to the Lord. However, even when he partially repented, God showed immeasurable kindness and mercy by providing a deliverer and restoring lost territory to the Israelites.

Syrian king Hazael

Israel's Kings

KINGS OF THE NORTHERN KINGDOM

ISRAEL		
King	**Reign (BC)**	**Character**
Jeroboam I	930–910	Bad
Nadab	910–909	Bad
Baasha	909–886	Bad
Elah	886–885	Bad
Zimri	885	Bad
Omri	885–874	Bad
Ahab	874–853	Bad
Ahaziah	853–852	Bad
Joram/Jehoram	852–841	Bad
Jehu	841–814	Bad
Jehoahaz	814–798	Bad
Joash/Jehoash	798–782	Bad
Jeroboam II	782–753	Bad
Zechariah	753–752	Bad
Shallum	752	Bad
Menahem	752–742	Bad
Pekahiah	742–740	Bad
Pekah	740–732	Bad
Hoshea	732–722	Bad

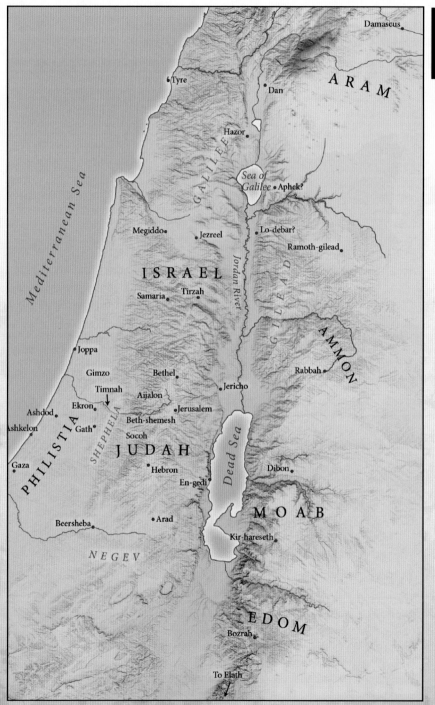

THE DIVIDED KINGDOM: ISRAEL'S DECLINE

Israel and Syria against Judah
2 KINGS 16:5-6; 2 CHRONICLES 28:1-21

LOCATION

Rebuilt by Judah's King Uzziah (also known as Azariah) as a port city, Elath was located in Edom near Ezion-geber and the Gulf of Aqaba. Years later, when the northern kingdom of Israel joined forces with Syria to attack Judah, Elath fell to the king of Syria. According to 2 Kings 16, Edomites then moved in, and Judah never controlled Elath again.

Much of the fighting in this episode seems to have been concentrated around Jerusalem, which the Syrian-Israelite coalition failed to capture. However, they seized many prisoners; some were taken to Damascus in Syria, and others were taken by Israel to the northern kingdom's capital of Samaria.

KEY PLAYERS

- Ahaz: king of Judah who succeeded Jotham and was known for his wicked behavior, worshipping idols and even practicing child sacrifice
- Pekah: an army general who later became king of Israel and continued the worship of false idols that had been started by Jeroboam I
- Rezin: king of Syria during the reigns of Pekah in Israel and Ahaz in Judah
- Oded: a prophet who warned the Israelites that they would receive God's wrath if they enslaved their fellow Israelites

WEAPONS AND WARRIORS

The major military difference between Judah and Israel was Judah's dominance of infantry as its main offensive arm. The chariot continued to be Judah's primary strength. The tribe of Judah was known for its pikesmen. Pikes (or pole weapons) were weapons fitted to the ends of long poles, extending the users' effective range. The tribe of Benjamin provided skilled archers.

Iron arrowhead, Lebanon (700 BC–AD 400)

Battle Synopsis

Immediately after introducing Judah's king Ahaz, 2 Chronicles 28 reveals the depth of Ahaz's wickedness: "He even made metal images for the Baals, and he made offerings in the Valley of the Son of Hinnom and burned his sons as an offering, according to the abominations of the nations whom the LORD drove out before the people of Israel" (verses 2–3). Displeased, God "humbled Judah because of Ahaz king of Israel, for he had made Judah act sinfully and had been very unfaithful to the LORD" (verse 19). God allowed Judah's enemies to carve up parts of its territory. Ahaz faced attacks from Rezin, the king of Syria, as well as from Edom and the northern kingdom of Israel. Pekah, the king of Israel, killed one hundred twenty thousand soldiers of Judah, in addition to members of the royal court. Even worse, he took two hundred thousand women and children captive and reaped the benefit of the plunder. However, when Pekah attempted to bring the women and children back to Samaria, a prophet of the Lord, Oded, warned Pekah to release them. The Lord was already angry at Israel for a long list of sins, and the king would only multiply that anger if he were to force his own relatives, the people of Judah, into slavery. Some of Israel's leaders took care of the captives' needs and returned them to Judah.

OUTCOME

SHORT-TERM

The loss of Judah's one hundred twenty thousand soldiers and members of the royal court set the ball rolling for the decline of the dynasty in Judah.

LONG-TERM

Judah lost Elath forever.

GOD'S ROLE

Judah was under attack from its enemies because of Ahaz's utter disregard for God. God taught him a lesson in humility by allowing Syria and Israel to inflict intense suffering upon Judah. Thousands were killed or captured, and many houses were plundered. God allowed Israel, a sinful nation, to conquer Judah. However, when Pekah tried to enslave thousands of captives from Judah, God drew the line. Israel did not have the right to inflict such humiliation on Judah, especially since Pekah himself was hardly without sin.

Hinnom Valley near Jerusalem

Battles Leading Up to Israel's Demise

2 KINGS 15:13-20

LOCATION

Menahem traveled to Samaria from Tirzah, a city in the central highlands northeast of Shechem and about eight miles from Samaria. Tirzah had been Israel's original capital city after the northern kingdom split from Judah. Menahem conspired to kill his predecessor, Shallum, in the city of Samaria, Israel's capital. Afterward, Menahem returned to Tirzah; from there he attacked the town of Tiphsah, an Israelite town whose location remains a mystery. Later in Menahem's reign, the Assyrian army invaded Israel, though the location of the invasion is not specified.

KEY PLAYERS

- Menahem: the son of Gadi who became king over Israel after deposing Shallum
- Pul (Tiglath-pileser III): a prominent king of Assyria

WEAPONS AND WARRIORS

Tiglath-pileser III, also known as Pul, introduced major changes to the structure of the Assyrian military. One of these changes was the institution of a full-time army that trained and studied military tactics, even while not at war. Tiglath-pileser III enlisted the help of vassal states such as Israel to support his military.

Assyrian warriors and warhorses

Battle Synopsis

King Shallum of Israel had reigned for a mere four weeks when Menahem struck him dead and appointed himself as king over the land. Menahem's violent and evil roots surfaced early on as he dragged the whole nation of Israel into sin with him. Menahem seemed to imitate King Jeroboam, who had given free rein to the Israelites' evil desires and savage behavior.

One of Menahem's first victories was against the Israelite town of Tiphsah. When the people of Tiphsah refused to acknowledge Menahem's rise to power, his deep, unbridled rage spewed forth as he attacked his own people. In an act of unthinkable cruelty, Menahem's forces ripped open pregnant women. Clearly, Menahem was influenced by the brutality of the nations surrounding Israel, given that this particular form of violence had been inflicted on the Israelites themselves by Syria (2 Kings 8:12), Ammon (Amos 1:13), and Assyria (Hosea 13:16).

Sometime later, when Tiglath-pileser III (Pul) attacked Israel, Menahem purchased the Assyrian king's support, giving Pul a thousand talents of silver raised from taxing the rich in his own kingdom. Menahem ruled with Assyria's strength behind him, and only because of this did Pul recognize Menahem as the rightful king over Israel.

Outcome

Short-Term

Menahem passed the kingdom to his son Pekahiah, who also ruled with an evil heart.

Long-Term

Israel became a vassal to Assyria, but a few years later, King Hoshea refused to pay the required tribute; this further propelled Israel in its decline.

God's Role

Menahem did not honor God in any way; instead, he chose to emulate Jeroboam, who was known for disobedience toward God. This was a dark period in Israel's history—a time when God allowed people to walk in their rebellion and experience the consequences of sin. Those who chose to rebel against Him experienced the pain and misery of their own sin. Downtrodden and tyrannized, the people of Israel continued to sin with their fists raised high against God.

Ancient Assyrian warriors

The Assyrian Empire flourished as one of the fiercest powers of its time. Beginning in 745 BC, Tiglath-pileser III inaugurated the last and greatest phase of this empire. When he seized control of the Assyrian throne, he made such sweeping reforms that Assyria quickly became a force to be reckoned with. By 743 BC, Tiglath-pileser III had subjugated a vast expanse of nations. Included in this group was Israel under King Menahem. Both the biblical account (2 Kings 15:19) and Assyrian records agree that Menahem paid heavy tribute to Tiglath-pileser in order to keep the peace.

The first thing Tiglath-pileser did during his reign was to reorganize his territory to prevent rebellion from within surrounding provinces. He subdivided larger provinces that harbored aspirations of independence from Assyria, and he appointed Assyrian officials who were directly accountable to him and responsible for controlling what took place in the kingdom. Within a few years, all regions reported directly to the king, who continuously monitored the loyalty and efficiency of his officials. Each governor, for example, was responsible for taxing the local population, storing military supplies, and calling up regional forces to support the new Assyrian army.

Tiglath-pileser III

When Tiglath-pileser III took the throne, Assyria was in the middle of an ugly civil war. During his reign, Tiglath-pileser developed a more highly skilled, better trained, and more advanced military compared with its predecessor. A new intelligence system relied on reports transmitted from staging posts; this provided the Assyrians with much better reconnaissance, which increased their effectiveness in battle.

In 735 BC, Syria and Israel united against Judah. Ahaz, the king of Judah, sent messengers to Tiglath-pileser carrying tribute in hopes that Tiglath-pileser would come to his aid. Tiglath-pileser conceded, and in 734 BC he marched his army into Syria to find Rezin, the Syrian king, waiting for him. The Assyrians completely decimated Rezin's army and laid siege to Damascus. Tiglath-pileser's army was so substantial that he was able to leave part of his infantry in Syria and take the rest to attack Israel. Fleeing for his life, Israel's king Pekah took refuge in Samaria. Tiglath-pileser then conquered the Ammonites and Moabites, and he placed the king of Gaza under tribute. Finally, in 732 BC, the Damascene siege was completed, and Tiglath-pileser invaded Babylon yet again. In October 729 BC, Tiglath-pileser assumed total control of Babylon. By 730 BC, Assyria had made itself known as the undisputed superpower of the Middle East.

Assyrian warships

Assyrian Invasion of Israel under Pekah

2 KINGS 15:27-31

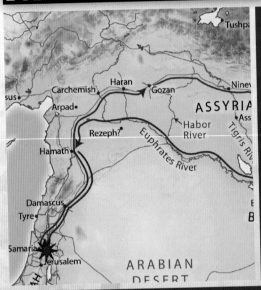

LOCATION

The Assyrians captured Ijon, Abel-beth-maacah, Janoah, Kedesh, Hazor, Gilead, and Galilee, and all the land of Naphtali. These cities and areas were all located in the northern part of Israel. As the Assyrians made their way south, conquering land as they went, Naphtali would have been one of the first stretches of Israelite territory they encountered.

KEY PLAYERS

- Pekah: an army general who later became king of Israel and continued the worship of false idols that had been started by Jeroboam I
- Tiglath-pileser III (Pul): a prominent king of Assyria
- Hoshea: the last king of the northern kingdom of Israel, who came to the throne after killing his predecessor, Pekah

WEAPONS AND WARRIORS

Assyria was a plain and fertile area with few natural defenses, making a strong defensive posture near impossible. To compensate, the Assyrians formed a powerful army that attacked with force, speed, and skill; they fought with iron swords, lances, and the most advanced armor of the day. When laying siege to a city, the Assyrians used battering rams to devastating effect, breaking open masonry walls of fortifications or splintering the city gates.

Assyrian battering ram

BATTLE SYNOPSIS

King Pekah was no better than Menahem, for he, too, followed in the footsteps of Jeroboam I—the infamous king of Israel who rebelled against God. Not for the first time, the king of Assyria, Tiglath-pileser, attacked Israel and carried away captives, in addition to seizing the whole land of Naphtali. Because of Pekah's disobedience, God abandoned him, leaving him powerless to stop Tiglath-pileser. In fact, Pekah was such a weak leader that he was eventually assassinated. Hoshea conspired against Pekah, killed him, and ruled as king in his place.

Looking up to Mount Arbel, Galilee, Israel

OUTCOME

SHORT-TERM

This was the beginning of the displacement of Israel. The territory of Naphtali was never regained by Israel, setting the stage for Assyria's complete conquest of the nation.

LONG-TERM

Israel's time of judgment had finally come. After centuries of rebellion against God, Israel was about to find itself totally conquered, its people carried off into captivity in Assyria.

GOD'S ROLE

Israel's sin had been piling up for centuries, and God's prophets had continually warned of impending judgment. An intransigent people continued to turn their backs on the One who had rescued them from their enemies time after time. Faithful to His word, God stirred the Assyrians to attack Israel; they captured many Israelites and took them as prisoners to Assyria. Angered at Pekah's rebellion, God refused to offer assistance during his reign. Pekah was eventually assassinated, no doubt because of his divergence from the ways of God.

Assyrian warriors

THE DIVIDED KINGDOM: ISRAEL'S DECLINE

Assyrian Conquests

TREATIES OF THE ANCIENT NEAR EASTERN WORLD

Treaties were part of the culture of international relations in the ancient Near East. These treaties (or covenants) were binding agreements between two or more parties in which certain expectations were outlined, so that nations could function in relation to each other. In the ancient Near East, there were three kinds of covenants used between parties.

1. The *suzerainty* (or vassal) *treaty*: an agreement between two unequal parties, one of higher status and one of lower status. In the treaty, the party of higher status typically asserted its dominance over the party of lower status.
2. The *parity treaty*: an agreement between two parties of equal status in which both parties worked as equals toward a common end.
3. The *land grant treaty*: an agreement between two parties concerning the shared use of territory.

Throughout Old Testament history, the suzerainty (or vassal) treaty was the one most often used. The word *suzerainty* literally means "the dominion of a lord." This type of treaty called to mind the image of a king who had taken control of someone else's territory and made it part of his kingdom. In a suzerainty treaty, an alliance was made between a great monarch and a subjugated king. Normally, the weaker party was a ruler who had either surrendered or lost his capital in battle. The weaker king was required to pay allegiance or tribute to the superior monarch, or dominant entity, called the *suzerain*.

He was also subject to heavy taxation. The weaker party had to keep their borders secure, provide military assets, and promise not to make alliances with other countries or kings. In short, they became servants to the suzerain.

Often a conquering king would use the suzerainty treaty as a means of extending his kingdom, while preserving the infrastructure of the defeated kingdom. Rule of the weaker nation was transferred to the victorious king. This approach served to prevent needless rebuilding efforts after a war.

Assyrian warrior

THE DIVIDED KINGDOM: ISRAEL'S DECLINE

Assyria's Three-Year Siege of Israel under Hoshea
2 KINGS 17:1-23

Mount Carmel
Megiddo
Jezreel
Dothan
Abel-meholah?
Samaria
ISRA
Jordan River
Gilgal?
Bethel
Mizpah
Michmash
Ramah
Geba
Jericho
Jerusalem
Gath
JUDAH
Dea
Sea

LOCATION

Samaria was the capital of Israel and the home of kings who reigned from the time of Omri (885–874 BC) until Hoshea, who was king during the nation's collapse in 722 BC. Omri had purchased the land from its owner, Shemer (1 Kings 16:23–24). This turned out to be a strategic move on Omri's part because Samaria was near two major roads running north and west. Samaria provided protection from enemies since it was located on rocky, mountainous terrain about seven miles northwest of Shechem. Samaria became a worship center for Baal and other foreign gods, which were brought to Israel by disobedient kings and their families.

KEY PLAYERS

- Shalmaneser: king of Assyria who subdued Israel and attempted to put an end to the rebellion led by its king, Hoshea.
- Hoshea: the last king of the northern kingdom of Israel, who ascended to the throne after killing his predecessor, Pekah

WEAPONS AND WARRIORS

Israel's soldiers were no match for the mighty and brutal Assyrian army. The Assyrians were known for being lovers of violence and the hunt. They thrived on massacring enemy soldiers, conquering land, and then scattering the more powerful classes all over the Assyrian Empire. They humiliated their opponents into submission, which allowed the Assyrians to rule without fear of an organized revolt.

Assyrian soldiers skinning captives alive

Battle Synopsis

After leading a conspiracy against Pekah, Hoshea began his own dynasty, taking the throne for a brief time. He was an evil man but hardly the worst king in Israel's history. Like Menahem before him (2 Kings 15:17–22), Hoshea accepted the status of vassal to the king of Assyria. As long as Hoshea paid his money and did as he was told by his overlord, he would be allowed to remain on Israel's throne. However, Hoshea saw a strategic opportunity to revolt when a new king rose to power in Assyria: Shalmaneser. How wrong Hoshea was. Hoping to find an ally in the delta of Egypt, Hoshea conspired against Assyria. Shalmaneser discovered the plan and, having found Hoshea to be a treacherous vassal, besieged the capital city of Samaria for three years—a long, unwavering campaign to decimate the northern kingdom of Israel. Eventually, the Assyrians conquered Samaria, took more Israelites captive, and brought them back to Assyria. Ancient Assyrian annals claim that 27,290 captives were taken from Israel during this time. Thus the Assyrians completed their conquest of Israel. Some Israelites were assimilated into other cultures, while others hung on to their Israelite identity as exiles in other lands.

Outcome

Short-Term

The Assyrian invasion of Israel brought to an end the ten northern tribes as an independent kingdom.

Long-Term

Israel's exile led to the eventual "birth" of the Samaritans, the descendants of those who were left behind and intermarried with others who were settled in Israel after the collapse of the nation.

God's Role

Typical of the kings of Israel, Hoshea did not look to God for help in his time of need; he turned instead to Egypt and placed his trust in their chariots and horses (Psalm 20:7). Therefore, the prophet Hosea prophesied about him: "Samaria's king shall perish like a twig on the face of the waters" (Hosea 10:7). For centuries, the people of Israel conformed to the godless nations around them, worshipping idols and forsaking God. They indulged in all sorts of pagan practices, including worshipping fertility goddesses and participating in child sacrifice. Because of this, God allowed them to be carried off into captivity (2 Kings 17:9–18). Though the people of the southern kingdom of Judah clung to their territory, they, too, were rejecting God's commandments. They chose to ignore the object lesson right in front of them by imitating Israel's sins (2 Kings 17:18–19).

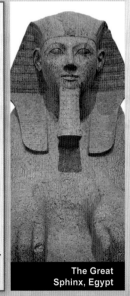

The Great Sphinx, Egypt

Military Heroes and Villains: Hoshea

Hoshea, whose name means "salvation," was the last ruler of the northern kingdom of Israel. He reigned from 732 to 722 BC. His rise to power took place when he conspired against and murdered the previous king, Pekah (2 Kings 15:30). Assyria's king Tiglath-pileser III claimed that it was he who had made Hoshea king, and he forced Hoshea to become a vassal to his kingdom.

Hoshea revolted against Tiglath-pileser's successor, Shalmaneser, thus violating the terms of his agreement with Assyria. Hoshea refused to pay the annual tribute due to Assyria's king and sought help from Egypt, believing the alliance would provide the protection needed to break free from Assyria. However, the hoped-for relationship with Egypt never developed. Hoshea's rebellion revealed his outright hatred for the Assyrians, who promptly invaded an already weakened Israel. Shalmaneser took Hoshea prisoner and besieged Samaria for three years. When the city finally fell, many of Israel's citizens were scattered throughout the Assyrian Empire.

The prophet Hosea spoke of Hoshea's rule: "Ephraim [Israel] is like a dove, silly and without sense, calling to Egypt, going to Assyria" (Hosea 7:11). Hoshea's disobedience brought about his own demise. What happened to him after the collapse of Israel is not known. No more is said about his existence in the Bible; he disappeared "like a twig on the face of the waters" (Hosea 10:7).

Assyrian warriors

Things to Think About

Depiction of ancient Assyrian warriors

- What were the blessings promised to the people of Israel if they obeyed God (see Deuteronomy 28:1–14)?

- What were the judgments threatened upon the people of Israel if they disobeyed God (see Deuteronomy 28:15–68)?

- What can you learn about what God wanted from the Israelites in Deuteronomy 28?

- How did God use Assyria as His tool?

- What can you learn about God's response to rebellion from the story of the northern kingdom of Israel?

- How does this chapter remind you of your need for Jesus?

THE DIVIDED KINGDOM: ISRAEL'S DECLINE

Chapter 7

THE DIVIDED KINGDOM: JUDAH'S FORTIFICATIONS

"Yet the LORD was not willing to destroy the house of David, because of the covenant that he had made with David, and since he had promised to give a lamp to him and to his sons forever."

(2 Chronicles 21:7)

INTRODUCTION

After the northern kingdom of Israel collapsed, concerns began to surface for Judah. Would the southern kingdom survive? Would its people also experience judgment for turning their backs on God? Or would they renew their commitment to God and experience His grace? God takes His glory seriously, and though He is extraordinarily long-suffering with rebellious nations and individuals, His patience will eventually reach its end. Despite the powerful object lesson provided by the demise and exile of the people of Israel, the people of Judah would eventually follow their lead, suffering a similar fate as their neighbors to the north.

The failure of leadership is one of the most discouraging aspects of Judah's history. The number of kings who were dedicated to serving God is very small. However, kings alone can't be blamed for the tragedies that befell both Israel and Judah. According to the great prophets of Judah, especially Jeremiah, most of the leaders were corrupt. "Both prophet and priest are ungodly; even in my house I have

Walls of Jerusalem, near the Tower of David

found their evil, declares the LORD. . . . But in the prophets of Jerusalem I have seen a horrible thing: they commit adultery and walk in lies; they strengthen the hands of evildoers, so that no one turns from his evil; all of them have become like Sodom to me, and its inhabitants like Gomorrah" (Jeremiah 23:11, 14).

The story of Judah is a complicated one. There were times when the kings of the south lived for the glory and honor of God. There were dark times as well, when Judah's people swelled with pride, neglected the poor, and worshipped idols. In response, God used nations around Judah to chastise His people, a painful reminder of the consequences for violating their covenant with Him. God allowed for war to humble His people and prompt them to repentance.

With great kindness, God sent prophets to warn of impending judgment; these prophets spoke vehemently against foreign military alliances, especially those with Egypt. God had already demonstrated His power over Egypt in the past, when He overwhelmed Pharaoh and his army at the Red Sea. But the temptation to trust Egypt for help continued to tug at Judah's leaders. Meanwhile, Babylonian rulers tried to woo Judah with talk of treaties that were really traps in disguise.

Sunset on the Judaean Desert

The wars fought by the southern kingdom of Judah during this time, though terrible, were like a curtain being pulled back to reveal the heart of God. It was during this time that some of God's most remarkable promises for the future—the messianic prophecies of the Old Testament—were revealed. During the reign of Ahaz, perhaps the most evil king in the nation's history, God broke into time and space and spoke through prophets. He proclaimed a promise of hope: God would someday act to bring salvation—not just to Judah, but to the whole world. This was an echo of a promise made centuries earlier to the patriarch Abraham: "I will bless those who bless you, and him who dishonors you I will curse, and in you all the families of the earth shall be blessed" (Genesis 12:3). It was during Ahaz's reign that God announced that the sign of salvation would be a virgin who would conceive and give birth to a son called Immanuel (Isaiah 7:14), which means "God with us." In the midst of a very dark time in Judah's history, when war was imminent and people faced the reality of destruction, God spoke a word of hope; He had not forgotten His people.

This promise had its immediate fulfillment in events during the reign of Ahaz. However, Judah eventually fell into the hands of the Babylonians, and its people were held captive for seventy years. But God still kept His promise. A virgin conceived and gave birth to a son, who saved—and continues to save—people from every tribe and nation. The promise found its ultimate fulfillment in the life of Jesus, the Son of God.

The long, bloody history of Israel's and Judah's battles is more than stories of two nations warring against other nations for the sole purpose of gaining power. These battles reveal something about God's heart, affirming His holy and just character. They are a reminder that God is in control of all things. It is God alone who "removes kings and sets up kings; he gives wisdom to the wise and knowledge to those who have understanding" (Daniel 2:21). From the beginning of time, God revealed the end of time (Isaiah 46:10), and He maneuvers kings and peoples and nations to cause His plan to come to pass.

Because Judah's army had to defend their mountains, a contingent of foot soldiers was nonnegotiable. Elsewhere in Judah, valleys and plains demanded the use of chariots—the war vehicle of choice during this time in history. Spears, shields, and bows were common weapons of tribal warfare, which the men of Judah continued to use: "And Asa had an army of 300,000 from Judah, armed with large shields and spears, and 280,000 men from Benjamin that carried shields and drew bows. All these were mighty men of valor" (2 Chronicles 14:8).

However, Judah's main focus was on strengthening its defensive fortifications. These efforts included building city walls and rerouting water supplies, both of which helped to protect the city of Jerusalem during the reign of Hezekiah.

The Egyptian Invasion of Judah

LOCATION

The battle materialized in the fortified cities of Judah, including Jerusalem, the capital of Judah. Other fortified cities affected by the fighting included Bethlehem, Etam, Tekoa, Beth-zur, Soco, Adullam, Gath, Mareshah, Ziph, Adoraim, Lachish, Azekah, Zorah, Aijalon, and Hebron (2 Chronicles 11:5–10).

KEY PLAYERS

- Judah: the southern kingdom, consisting of the tribes of Judah and Simeon, whose capital was Jerusalem
- Shishak I: the king of Egypt who provided refuge to Jeroboam during the latter years of Solomon's reign
- Rehoboam: ruler of the united kingdom of Israel for a short reign, which involved the rebellion of the ten northern nations that formed the northern kingdom of Israel; first king of Judah, the southern kingdom

WEAPONS AND WARRIORS

Shishak I, the king of Egypt (and the first Egyptian king to be mentioned by name in the Bible), organized a military force from the entire region of North Africa. His invading force included twelve hundred chariots and sixty thousand horsemen, along with Libyan and Ethiopian, or Cushite, infantries. A large army like this was designed for one purpose: to wage a strong attack against fortified cities and win.

Shishak I

BATTLE SYNOPSIS

Rehoboam, Solomon's son and king of Judah, disregarded God's commands. As a result, the Lord became angry with him. God allowed Shishak to attack Judah during the fifth year of Rehoboam's reign. After biding his time waiting for the struggle between Judah and Israel to wear out both kingdoms, Shishak launched a major offensive in about 924 BC. His goal was to debilitate his neighbor to the north.

However, before Shishak entered Jerusalem, Shemaiah, a prophet of the Lord, conveyed a message from God to Rehoboam and the princes: God was deeply displeased with them. They immediately humbled themselves; consequently, God lightened their punishment and prevented Shishak from conquering Judah completely. Shishak was able to plunder the gold and riches from the temple and the palace—including all the treasures the people of Israel had brought with them during the exodus from Egypt. Other valuable spoils included the golden shields Solomon had made for the royal bodyguard. Attempting to hide the embarrassing loss and protect his image, King Rehoboam arranged for shields to be made out of bronze to replace the golden ones. The Egyptians retreated as swiftly as they came, leaving behind a weakened nation.

OUTCOME

SHORT-TERM

Despite Rehoboam's refusal to honor God, he ruled for seventeen years in Jerusalem. After his death, his son Ahijah took his place.

LONG-TERM

Instability plagued the line of Judah's kings, until the people of the nation were finally scattered and carried away to captivity in Babylon.

GOD'S ROLE

Rehoboam fluctuated between obeying God and doing his own thing, protecting his own image and interests along the way. Though he attempted to keep up his outward appearances, his intents were evil—so much so that the author of 2 Chronicles concluded that "he did not set his heart to seek the LORD" (12:14). Through the king of Egypt who came against Jerusalem, God punished Rehoboam for his hypocrisy and disobedient spirit. Showing great patience, God did not destroy His people. God gave the people the opportunity to repent by revealing to Rehoboam why He was punishing the nation.

Deliverance from the Ethiopians
2 CHRONICLES 14

LOCATION

Even though the exact location of this battle is not known, it is possible to identify the general setting as south of Mareshah, in the space between Mareshah and Gerar. *Zephathah* means "watchtower," and *Mareshah* means "crest of a hill." Mareshah was a town in the western foothills of Judah, about twenty-four miles southwest of Jerusalem, in what is now considered the Judaean Lowlands. The Valley of Zephathah was a valley outside Mareshah that stretched from Mareshah to Gerar. This region was at one time a Philistine stronghold but later fell under Judah's control.

KEY PLAYERS

- Zerah: a local Cushite (Ethiopian) chief who enjoyed the support of Egypt's pharaoh and may have had some kind of official standing in the Egyptian court
- Asa: Rehoboam's grandson and Solomon's great-grandson; the third king of Judah, and the fifth king from the house of David, who was zealous in rooting out idolatry and following God
- Judah: the southern kingdom, consisting of the tribes of Judah and Simeon, whose capital was Jerusalem

WEAPONS AND WARRIORS

The Egyptians supported Zerah's efforts to weaken Judah. With this support, the Ethiopians were able to amass three hundred chariots—each having roughly the same impact as a modern tank— along with an army of one million men. Judah's inferior army of five hundred eighty thousand men (their biggest army since the northern kingdom had split) was no match for the Egyptians. However, Judah had built up its fortified cites—building strong walls and stockpiling food and weapons—to withstand a long siege.

Egyptian war chariot, papyrus

BATTLE SYNOPSIS

Asa, king of Judah, honored God during his reign as king. He sought to obey all of God's commands. The great-grandson of Solomon, Asa ascended to the throne after the death of his father, Abijah. When Zerah the Ethiopian invaded Judah, King Asa pleaded with God for help before marching into battle. Judah's army then moved against the Ethiopians and massacred them. Zerah retreated, but the warriors of Judah pursued them to the Philistine border, inflicting heavy casualties from which Ethiopia could not recover. On the return trip, the men of Judah gathered spoils from their defeated enemy.

Tel Burna, an archaeological site near Mareshah, Israel

OUTCOME

SHORT-TERM

After defeating the Ethiopians, Asa led the people to renew their covenant with the Lord, and Judah enjoyed peace for about twenty years.

LONG-TERM

After Asa's reign, his successor, Jehoshaphat, inherited a nation whose people were following the Lord.

GOD'S ROLE

Asa's first action before going to war was to pray to God and ask for deliverance. Prior to this particular crisis, Asa had launched a reform movement to wipe out foreign gods and high places of worship. He spent considerable time strengthening the nation's defense; yet when Ethiopia attacked, he knew it would not be enough without the Lord's help: "Help us, O Lord our God, for we rely on you, and in your name we have come against this multitude" (2 Chronicles 14:11). God heard Asa's prayer and allowed Judah to annihilate the Ethiopian army—nothing short of a miracle. Scripture makes it very clear who won the battle: "So the Lord defeated the Ethiopians before Asa and before Judah, and the Ethiopians fled" (2 Chronicles 14:12).

16

Judah's Worship in the Face of Battle

2 CHRONICLES 20

LOCATION

The enemies of Judah approached through the ascent of Ziz, which is traditionally associated with a valley by which an ancient road ran from Engedi to Jerusalem. The fighting force made it as far as the wilderness of Jeruel, a desert located on the way from Engedi to Jerusalem. This desert area was later renamed the Valley of Beracah, meaning "valley of blessing."

KEY PLAYERS

- Jehoshaphat: the fourth king of Judah, who took over from his father, Asa, and was known for combating idol worship in the land
- Ammonites: a Semitic people, closely related to the Israelites, tracing their ancestry to Lot's son Ben-ammi
- Moabites: a tribe descended from Moab, the son of Lot
- People of Mount Seir: Edomites who lived in a mountainous area between the Gulf of Aqaba and the Dead Sea
- Jahaziel: a Levite upon whom the Spirit of the Lord came and who prophesied victory for Jehoshaphat

WEAPONS AND WARRIORS

The armies opposing Judah threatened with chariots and a mass of lightly armed, nomadic fighters. Judah, on the other hand, boasted a most unusual weapon: the sound of song and praise to the Lord.

Battle Synopsis

During Jehoshaphat's reign, the Ammonites, Moabites, and Meunites attacked Judah. Aware of his weakness, Jehoshaphat assembled all the men of Judah at the temple—along with their wives and children—and cried out to the Lord. Jehoshaphat reminded God that the land they were fighting to preserve had been promised to the people of Israel through Abraham. Jehoshaphat prayed, "We do not know what to do, but our eyes are on you" (2 Chronicles 20:12). In response, God's Spirit came upon a Levite named Jahaziel, who assured Jehoshaphat that God would indeed deliver their enemies into their hands. The next day, Jehoshaphat and his men prepared for battle, trusting God to do what they could not. Jehoshaphat exhorted his people, saying, "Believe in the LORD your God, and you will be established" (2 Chronicles 20:20); then he appointed men to walk in front of Judah's army and sing praises to Yahweh—an odd military tactic! Miraculously, the men of Judah did not have to lift a sword; God confused Judah's enemies, who fought among themselves and killed each other. The people of Judah then spent the next three days collecting plunder from among the dead.

Outcome

Short-Term

Fear gripped Judah's neighbors, who heard how God had fought against the enemies of His people. Jehoshaphat's kingdom experienced a period of rest.

Long-Term

Sometime later, Jehoshaphat made an alliance with Ahaziah, king of Israel, whose ways were wicked; this weakened the nation of Judah.

God's Role

Jehoshaphat knew he was powerless against his enemies and could do nothing to stop them from decimating Judah. Pleased with Jehoshaphat's humility, God sent His Spirit upon Jahaziel with the message that the people of Judah need not fear their enemies; the battle was not theirs to fight, but the Lord's. Jehoshaphat believed God's promise, and his faith was rewarded. It was God Himself who set ambushes against the people of Ammon, Moab, and Mount Seir who invaded Judah. It was God who wiped out every single one of His enemies, leaving a sea of plunder for Jehoshaphat and his men. Jehoshaphat humbly realized this victory was an act of God; he and his people spent a whole day in the Valley of Beracah worshipping God for the miraculous victory.

King Jehoram's Battle against the Edomites
2 Kings 8:20-22; 2 Chronicles 21:4-10

Location

King Jehoram (also known as Joram) battled the Edomites at Zair, most likely a town near the southern end of the Dead Sea, in Edom's territory. Some scholars equate Zair with Zoar (Genesis 13:10). Edom and Israel were often in conflict. King David conquered the Edomites at one point, but later they revolted against Judah. The terrain of Zair included a vast mountain range bordered by a desert and the Dead Sea.

Key Players

- Jehoram (or Joram): became king of Judah after his father, Jehoshaphat; did evil in the sight of God
- Edomites: the descendants of Esau, the firstborn son of Isaac and twin brother of Jacob. Even though the Edomites regularly attacked Israel, God forbade the Israelites from totally destroying them because the Edomites and Israelites were close relatives.

Weapons and Warriors

Basic structure of an ancient chariot

Judah fought using a mobilized infantry of chariots. King Jehoram mustered all his chariots, to fight against the Edomite army that surrounded Jehoram's troops in Zair.

Battle Synopsis

Mountains of Edom, modern day

Jehoram did not follow the Lord. Instead, he worshipped false idols, just like the rulers of the northern kingdom of Israel did. Because of his rebellion against God, Judah began to weaken. The Edomites sensed an opportunity to free themselves from Judah's rule. For years, the Edomites had paid homage to Judah through taxation. As a result, the Edomites loathed their Israelite relatives in Judah. Their revolt was an attempt to break the shackle that tied Edom to Judah. During the conflict, the Edomite army surrounded Judah's army, but Jehoram broke through the Edomite line at night. The battle was ultimately inconclusive. The Edomites continued their revolt against Judah, winning some measure of independence. The days of Judah's undisputed control over Edom were at an end (2 Kings 8:22).

Outcome

Short-Term

Weakened, Judah lost control over some of the territories they had ruled. This sent a signal to other nations that Judah had become fragile.

Long-Term

Judah's disobedience and weakened state helped pave the way for the future Babylonian invasion.

God's Role

Jehoram was an evil king who deserved to be punished. Yet because of the covenant with David, God did not destroy Jehoram. David's line remained intact, as God had promised to "give a lamp to him and to his sons forever" (2 Chronicles 21:7). God stayed faithful to His promises even when His children strayed from Him.

Judah's Battle against the Syrians and Edomites

2 KINGS 12:17-18; 14:1-22; 2 CHRONICLES 24:17-25:28

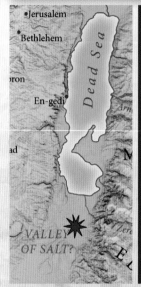

LOCATION

Located 2,460 feet above sea level on a rocky hill, Jerusalem is surrounded by valleys on all sides. It sits thirty-three miles east of the Mediterranean Sea and fourteen miles west of the Dead Sea. The Syrians (Arameans) attacked Jerusalem during Joash's reign. Jerusalem had become Judah's capital when David settled there and brought the ark of the covenant to the city, which thereafter became known as the city of David. When David's son Solomon built the temple to house the ark, Jerusalem became the center of Jewish worship as well as the nation's capital. Amaziah succeeded Joash and fought a second battle against ten thousand Edomites, or men from Seir. This battle took place in the Valley of Salt, likely located directly south of the Dead Sea, in the Negev.

KEY PLAYERS

- Syrians: Arameans who lived in what is today known as Syria
- Edomites: the descendants of Esau, the firstborn son of Isaac and twin brother of Jacob. Even though the Edomites regularly attacked Israel, God forbade the Israelites from totally destroying them because the Edomites and Israelites were close relatives.
- Joash: the king of Judah after Ahaziah
- Amaziah: the king of Judah after his father, Joash

WEAPONS AND WARRIORS

Amaziah boasted an army of three hundred thousand men who could skillfully handle spears and shields. In 2 Chronicles 25, the author gives insight into the strength of this army. Mandatory national service in Judah began at the age of twenty. These young soldiers remained on the home front. They were expected to take over jobs abandoned by the older men who were on the front lines and to ensure those at home were not left without protection. Amaziah also hired one hundred thousand mercenary soldiers from Israel, though he did not make use of them.

Battle Synopsis

The two battles mentioned in these passages of scripture highlight God's judgment and provision. While Joash was king over Judah, God became angry over the nation's continued disobedience. As punishment, God allowed the Syrians to defeat Judah and kill many of its leaders and plunder the people. This was in fulfillment of God's promise in the book of Leviticus, foretelling that the Israelites would be punished and defeated by a force much smaller than their own (Leviticus 26:17, 37).

A short time later in Judah's history, Amaziah, Joash's son, advanced into battle against the Edomites, killing twenty thousand men. Amaziah assembled three hundred thousand of his own men and then paid one hundred talents of silver for one hundred additional Ephraimite soldiers from Israel to secure a victory. However, a man of God warned Amaziah not to make use of the Ephraimites, for God's favor was not on them. Amaziah would only defeat his enemies if he trusted in the Lord alone and not in his mercenary army. Amaziah listened to the messenger and went into battle without the Ephraimites, emerging victorious.

Outcome

Short-Term

Amaziah worshipped idols he had brought back from the people of Seir.

Long-Term

Amaziah laid the foundation for his son and heir, who would later bring prosperity to his kingdom.

God's Role

Joash began his role as king of Judah doing what was right in the eyes of the Lord. However, at the end of his rule, Joash, puffed up and arrogant, rebelled against God—and following his lead, so did the people of Judah. God punished Judah and allowed the Syrians to completely defeat the nation and attack the royal line, killing nearly all the princes. When Amaziah became king after Joash, he honored God—for a while. As a result, God enabled him to defeat the Edomites. Sadly, Amaziah turned from God and began to worship idols.

Reconstruction of Solomon's Temple

Uzziah and the Philistines
2 CHRONICLES 26

LOCATION

Philistine territory stretched from the narrow plain along the Mediterranean Sea, south of the Yarkon River, down toward the Brook (wadi) of Egypt, to the coast eastward toward Judah. This was a fertile, flat territory.

Gath, Jabneh, and Ashdod were Philistine towns.

KEY PLAYERS

- Uzziah (also known as Azariah): Amaziah's son who became king of Judah
- The Philistines: an aggressive, warmongering sea people who occupied part of southwest Canaan between the Mediterranean Sea and the Jordan River; Israel's main enemy before the Assyrian invasion in the eighth century BC
- Meunites: a people who lived in the area of Mount Seir in Edom, south of the Dead Sea
- Ammonites: a Semitic people closely related to the Israelites, tracing their ancestry to Lot's son Ben-ammi

WEAPONS AND WARRIORS

Uzziah's army boasted war machines that shot arrows and great stones at the enemy. In addition, he provided his army with "shields, spears, helmets, coats of mail, bows, and stones for slinging" (2 Chronicles 26:14).

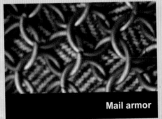

Mail armor

BATTLE SYNOPSIS

17

Uzziah was a king of Judah who honored God in the way he reigned. Blessed for his faith, he earned a reputation among the surrounding nations as a strong king buttressed by a large army. Uzziah fought against the Philistines and destroyed many of their cities, replacing them with new ones and reducing the Philistines to a state of servitude. God helped Uzziah to defeat the Arabians and the Meunites as well. In addition, Uzziah exacted tribute from the Ammonites. God blessed Uzziah and enabled him to fortify Jerusalem with strong towers and to build towers and dig cisterns in the wilderness. Uzziah was also very fond of agriculture and promoted its development in that area.

OUTCOME

SHORT-TERM

Much of the Philistines' territory, along with the Negeb, came firmly under Judah's control.

LONG-TERM

Jabneh, one of the cities the Philistines lost, later became Jamnia, where the Sanhedrin—the Jewish ruling council—was reestablished after Jerusalem's destruction in AD 70.

GOD'S ROLE

In the past, God had used the Philistines to chastise Judah for disobedience; but in an ironic twist, God used Judah to punish the Philistines for their own wickedness. God heaped blessings on Uzziah during his reign, allowing him to grow strong and create a nation known for its wealth and power. Though God had graciously fought for Uzziah, the king forgot where his strength came from. Uzziah pridefully entered the sanctuary of the temple to burn incense. Uzziah knew full well that only the priests of Aaron's lineage were allowed to do this. God punished Uzziah for his foolish act; Uzziah developed leprosy.

Judah and the Ammonites
2 KINGS 15:32-38; 2 CHRONICLES 27:1-6

Shiloh

Bethel

h-horon

Jericho • Gilgal?

Gibeon •

• Jerusalem

Bethlehem

• Hebron

En-gedi

• Arad

Rabbah •

Jazer •

AMMON

Heshbon •

▲ Mount Nebo

Medeba •

Dead Sea

Dibon •

Arnon River

M O A B

LOCATION

The Ammonites lived on the east side of the Dead Sea from the Jabbok River in the north to the territory of Moab in the south—that is, modern-day Jordan. Although a nomadic people, the Ammonites retained a capital city, Rabbah.

KEY PLAYERS

- Jotham: king of Judah who was generally good and did right in God's eyes
- Ammonites: a Semitic people, closely related to the Israelites, tracing their ancestry to Lot's son Ben-ammi

WEAPONS AND WARRIORS

Jotham built impregnable walls to withstand siege and repel his enemies. This proved key to his success as a king and military leader.

Battle Synopsis

Jotham was the son of Uzziah. Like his father, he honored God with his reign. Jotham created a strong kingdom by building new forts and cities. When he waged war against the Ammonites, he was victorious. After winning one battle against the Ammonites, Jotham exacted tribute for three years in the form of silver, wheat, and barley. Despite the fact that Jotham lived in keeping with God's law, the rest of the people of Judah did not emulate him. They continued to worship false gods and participate in pagan ceremonies. Though Jotham was a strong ruler, his nation was spiritually weak.

Wheat

Barley

Silver

OUTCOME

SHORT-TERM

Jotham continued the work of his father. Throughout his reign (750–735 BC), he contributed to the enlargement of Jerusalemite defenses.

LONG-TERM

Hezekiah later continued Jotham's work in fortifying Jerusalem.

GOD'S ROLE

Jotham found favor with God and was blessed with a stable rule and a rich kingdom. However, even though he was such a strong ruler, his people were prone to idol worship, frequenting the high places that had not been removed. Because of this, according to 2 Kings 15–16, God raised up Rezin, king of Syria, and Pekah, the son of Remaliah, to attack Judah and cause disturbance during Jotham's reign. God's heart was to motivate His people to return to Him and trust Him for provision and security.

Military Heroes and Villains: Ahaz

Ahaz was the twelfth king of Judah, ruling from 735 to 715 BC. With the exception of his grandson Manasseh, he was the wickedest man to sit on the throne of Judah.

Many of the people of the pagan nations around Judah sacrificed their sons and daughters to heathen deities, but God made it clear that His people were not to follow suit (Leviticus 18:21). Nonetheless, Ahaz sacrificed his own children by fire in the Hinnom Valley (also known as Gehenna) to the false gods Baal and Molech (2 Chronicles 28:1–4; see also Jeremiah 32:35). The prophets Isaiah, Micah, and Hosea had warned Ahaz to turn back to the Lord, but Ahaz was too steeped in his own sin to listen.

At the beginning of his reign, Ahaz was thrust into an international conflict. Assyria was threatening Aram (modern-day Syria) and the northern kingdom of Israel. Although the Israelites and Arameans had been enemies for years, they formed an alliance in an effort to protect themselves from Assyrian expansion.

Many believe that Gehenna was a location used for burning trash, waste, and burying criminals

18

The two kingdoms requested Ahaz to join their anti-Assyrian coalition to provide a strong enough force to fight off Assyria. Ahaz refused, so Israel and Aram conspired to invade Judah. Ahaz knew his army was no match for these two stronger forces, and he was justifiably nervous.

It was then that the prophet Isaiah approached Ahaz with a word from the Lord (Isaiah 7). God's message to Ahaz and his people was that He had not abandoned them; His promise of protection was still in place, but Ahaz needed to trust God through all the conflicts he faced. The Lord told Ahaz to ask for a sign to confirm this promised protection.

The Flight of Moloch
William Blake (1757–1827)

Ahaz refused. He had his heart set on another plan for protection. He wanted to form an alliance with the king of Assyria and hoped this would keep the Assyrians from attacking Judah. Any sign from God would be an embarrassment to Ahaz. God gave the promised sign of His protection in spite of Ahaz's sin: "Therefore the Lord himself will give you a sign. Behold, the virgin shall conceive and bear a son, and shall call his name Immanuel" (Isaiah 7:14).

God revealed that His sign of protection and deliverance would come in the birth of a male child named Immanuel, which means "God with us." In the midst of Ahaz's rebellion against Yahweh, when Judah was at a place of despair and hopelessness, God provided a message of hope.

Gehenna (Hinnom) Valley near the Old City in Jerusalem

THE DIVIDED KINGDOM: JUDAH'S FORTIFICATIONS

Judah Weakened by Battles

2 KINGS 16; 2 CHRONICLES 28

LOCATION

Rezin, the king of Syria, successfully attacked Elath, which was located in Edom near Ezion Geber and the Gulf of Aqaba. It had been rebuilt by Uzziah (Azariah), king of Judah (767–750 BC), as a port city for Judah on the Red Sea. After its conquest, it was inhabited by Edomites and was never returned to Israel again. The captured men of Judah were taken north to Damascus, the capital of Syria.

When the Israelites conquered Judah, they brought captives to Samaria. When they decided to return the captives to Judah, they brought them approximately thirty-two miles southeast to Jericho, a city on the border between the two kingdoms.

KEY PLAYERS

- Ahaz: king of Judah who succeeded Jotham and was known for his wicked behavior, worshipping idols and even practicing child sacrifice
- Pekah: an army general who later became king of Israel and continued the worship of false idols that had been started by Jeroboam I
- Rezin: king of Syria during the reigns of Pekah in Israel and Ahaz in Judah
- Tiglath-pileser III (Pul): a prominent king of Assyria

WEAPONS AND WARRIORS

The battle between Israel and Judah was fought using hand-to-hand combat. The strategy of this style of fighting was simple: to force the enemy to surrender by overwhelming their foot soldiers in close conflict. If an attacking force could then convince the enemy that continued war was more costly than surrendering, they could achieve their objective.

Battle Synopsis

Pekah, an evil king of Israel, and Rezin, king of Syria, besieged Jerusalem, attempting to defeat Ahaz of Judah. According to 2 Chronicles, Judah lost one hundred twenty thousand troops in a single day, including many key officials and the king's son. However, Jerusalem was not captured. Ahaz feared the alliance between Israel and Syria; on top of that, the Philistines and the Edomites were taking advantage of the situation by invading towns and villages in southern Judah. In an effort to save his kingdom, Ahaz forged an alliance with the king of Assyria, Tiglath-pileser, who defended Judah after Ahaz presented him with the treasuries from the temple. This alliance only brought future trouble for the nation.

Ahaz met Tiglath-pileser in Damascus. While there, he noticed the altar in the Syrian temple. He commissioned Uriah the priest to make an identical one for Judah. Uriah did so, and upon Ahaz's return to Judah, the king offered sacrifices to false gods—moving the true altar of the temple aside. Ahaz paid the price for his rebellion against God. David's dynasty came very close to disappearing in that dark period.

Outcome

Short-Term

By asking Assyria to come to his aid, Ahaz unknowingly facilitated the ascendant empire's influence over the entire region, directly affecting Israel.

Long-Term

Assyria conquered and deported much of the northern kingdom of Israel in 733 BC; the remaining deportations followed.

God's Role

God was displeased with Ahaz, a disobedient king who did not even pretend to worship the one true God. He embraced the detestable practices of his day, including horrific ones like killing his own son in order to appease pagan gods. With the help of Assyria, Ahaz was able to defeat his enemies. Ahaz's kingdom was no longer his to control.

Tiglath-pileser III, stone panel (728 BC)

THE DIVIDED KINGDOM: JUDAH'S FORTIFICATIONS

Judah versus the Edomites and Philistines

2 CHRONICLES 28:16-21

LOCATION

The territory of the Edomites extended from the Dead Sea south to the Gulf of Aqaba.

Shephelah, a hilly tract of land between the coastal plain and the hills of Judah and Samaria, was the land closest to Philistia. The terrain was rocky and full of limestone. Beth-shemesh, Aijalon, Gederoth, Soco, Timnah, and Gimzo were all located in or near the Shephelah region.

The Negeb (or Negev), located at the southern end of Judah, was also targeted in this conflict. The Negeb consisted of rolling hills from the Dead Sea to the Mediterranean, stretching about seventy miles south to the desert.

KEY PLAYERS

- Edomites: the descendants of Esau, the firstborn son of Isaac and twin brother of Jacob. Even though the Edomites regularly attacked Israel, God forbade the Israelites from totally destroying them because the Edomites and Israelites were close relatives.

- The Philistines: an aggressive, warmongering sea people who occupied part of southwest Canaan between the Mediterranean Sea and the Jordan River; Israel's main enemy before the Assyrian invasion in the eighth century BC

WEAPONS AND WARRIORS

Judah was facing the worst situation a nation could face—multiple attacks from various forces. No city in Judah could withstand such a heavy bombardment without divine intervention. While under siege, a city would lock its gates and hide its people inside. The opposing force would surround the city, preventing its inhabitants from escaping. Then the opposing force would cut off the city's water supply. Next, the enemy would attack with catapults and arrows until the city exhausted its food, water, and defenses. Finally, the invading force would scale the city walls and cut down the inhabitants.

BATTLE SYNOPSIS

Israel and Syria had repeatedly attacked Judah; soon the Edomites and Philistines invaded, too, defeating Judah and carrying away many of its people. Instead of turning to God for help, Ahaz looked to the king of Assyria. Ahaz complained that the Philistines were occupying his territory and the Edomites had taken captives back to their country. God humbled both Ahaz and Judah. Tiglath-pileser, king of Assyria, helped Ahaz in the short run by attacking Syria and Israel (2 Kings 16:5–9) but brought Ahaz trouble in the long run. It was during this time that God gave the sign of the Messiah to Ahaz through the prophet Isaiah (see Isaiah 7:14).

Assyrian horse and archer

OUTCOME

SHORT-TERM

This time of distress led to the eventual decline and downfall of Ahaz.

LONG-TERM

Judah continued to weaken. The Philistines captured southern villages in Judah, and captives were taken as prisoners. Isaiah's prophecy to Ahaz found its ultimate fulfillment in the birth of Jesus.

GOD'S ROLE

God is a just and holy God. He cannot tolerate sin. He is also a jealous God who cannot stand to have praise given to any false god. Those who disobey Him receive punishment unless they confess their sin. Ahaz did not see his need for God and blatantly ignored Him. Therefore, God allowed for Judah to be under constant enemy attack. Even though Ahaz faced an insurmountable force, God had promised to deliver him and his people if he returned to God. Unfortunately, Ahaz refused God's hand of grace and faced defeat as a result. Had Ahaz pleaded for mercy, God would have granted him a reprieve, but Ahaz was too proud.

Hills next to the Dead Sea, Israel

THE DIVIDED KINGDOM: JUDAH'S FORTIFICATIONS

Assyrian Warfare

The Assyrians were fierce warriors who had conquered territory stretching from the Persian Gulf to the Mediterranean Sea. Not content with what they already possessed, the Assyrians sought to expand their rule beyond Mesopotamia into the region of Israel, thus posing a threat to both the northern and southern kingdoms. Their army grew to be the largest of its time, and their warfare proved the cruelest. It was the Assyrians' intent that the rest of the world view them as an invincible military power with a single goal: total annihilation of their enemies.

Infamous for their use of psychological terror, the Assyrians created a deep sense of dread in their enemies. Captives were burned alive or used as human shields on the battlefield. The Assyrians induced terror in those they conquered by skinning their victims alive. They also cut off hands, feet, noses, ears, and eyes; and they pulled out tongues. Those who survived were forced into servitude or made to resettle in distant lands, which destroyed any sense of nationalism. This kept the people subjugated by Assyria in a constant state of fear.

Because their territory was an expansive area without natural protection from oceans, mountains, or rocky plains, the Assyrians were vulnerable to attack from all directions. They compensated for this weakness by forming a strong offensive army that could attack with heartless and brutal aggression.

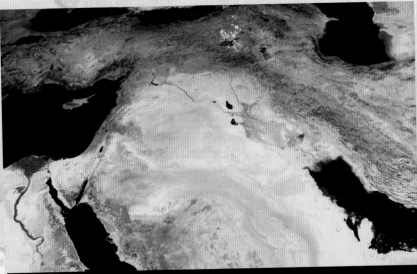

The Assyrian Empire stretched from the Persian Gulf to the Mediterranean Sea

Large cavalry squadrons would line up for battle, filling a space almost one and a half miles across and approximately one hundred yards deep. By the seventh century BC, Assyria had established a guild of engineers whose job was to perfect an assault on fortified cities and walls. Battering rams emerged as a key weapon in siege warfare. Assyrian rams consisted of large, heavy logs carried by several people who propelled them with force against a wall or gate.

The Assyrians also used ladders to scale high city walls in order to slaughter the guards. While this would take place, other soldiers would dig tunnels underneath the walls, causing them to crumble, which paved the way for an all-out assault. The Assyrians besieged town after town, massacring people and piling human heads outside the city walls. Any rulers left alive were deported and made to obey their new masters out of fear and humiliation.

The glory of the Assyrian Empire lasted about three hundred years. Under Ashurbanipal, the Assyrian Empire's last great ruler (669–627 BC), Assyria's brutality and control reached its highest point. When Ashurbanipal died, however, Assyria's power and influence rapidly declined. In 612 BC, the Medes and the Babylonians took over Nineveh, Assyria's capital city. Just a few years later, in 605 BC, the Assyrian Empire ended when the Babylonians and Medes defeated both Assyria and Egypt at Carchemish (see Jeremiah 46:2).

Ashurbanipal, the Assyrian king
Michael A. Rhea / Shutterstock.com

THE DIVIDED KINGDOM: JUDAH'S FORTIFICATIONS

Hezekiah's Rebellion against Assyria
2 KINGS 18:1-12

LOCATION

Gaza, a trade city, was located along a highway three miles inland from the Mediterranean Sea. It was bursting with lush gardens and olive trees. At the time of this campaign, the people of Gaza were paying tribute to the Assyrians, so a victory over Assyria's vassal made a statement to Assyria as well. It was also an opportunity for Hezekiah, king of Judah, to recapture Judah's cities in the Shephelah region, which stretched from Jerusalem to Gaza.

KEY PLAYERS

- Hezekiah: king of Judah who succeeded his father, Ahaz, and was known for having a heart that followed God
- The Philistines: an aggressive, warmongering sea people who occupied part of southwest Canaan between the Mediterranean Sea and the Jordan River; Israel's main enemy before the Assyrian invasion in the eighth century BC
- Assyrians: people who engaged in gruesome physical and psychological warfare and formed a mighty empire that dominated the ancient Near East from the ninth to the seventh century BC

WEAPONS AND WARRIORS

Hezekiah's priority was the fortification of Judah's cities. The Bible reveals in 2 Chronicles 32:2–4 that Hezekiah managed to block the water supply outside Jerusalem, preventing the Assyrian army from accessing the water they needed to refresh themselves and their animals. Hezekiah also repaired Jerusalem's defensive walls and rebuilt its towers, giving the people of Judah the strength they needed to withstand a siege and retain the upper hand in combat.

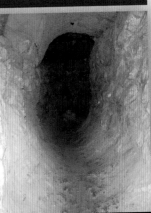

Hezekiah's aqueduct, city of David

BATTLE SYNOPSIS

The Assyrians were operating at full force during Hezekiah's reign, were decimating the northern kingdom of Israel. Yet miraculously, Judah was able to withstand their assault. The reason? Hezekiah's dependence on God alone. Hezekiah was the complete opposite of his father, Ahaz. He tore down all the high places of worship, broke the Asherah poles, and even destroyed the bronze serpent Moses had made, which had since become an idol to the people of Judah. Hezekiah wanted all the people of Judah to follow the Lord as he did. God honored Hezekiah's actions; as a result, Hezekiah's refusal to continue being subservient to the king of Assyria went without reprisal. He also drove the Philistines out of his territory. This campaign was so great that it is often compared to David's triumph over the Philistines (2 Samuel 5:25).

Grove of ancient olive trees, Israel

OUTCOME

SHORT-TERM

Hezekiah's assertiveness paved the way for a short de facto understanding between Judah and Assyria; Judah abstained from interfering with Assyria, and Assyria refrained from attacking Judah.

LONG-TERM

The Assyrians were overextended and eventually struggled to hold together their vast empire. Judah soon found itself caught between two warring giants: Assyria and Babylonia.

GOD'S ROLE

Hezekiah dedicated his life to serving the Lord. God blessed Hezekiah with victory on the battlefield and a strong and united country. However, dark clouds were looming. It was during Hezekiah's reign that the Assyrians carried the people of the northern kingdom of Israel into exile. This should have awoken the people of Judah to the consequences of disobedience. If they turned away from the Lord again, they, too, could face judgment. According to 2 Chronicles 30, Hezekiah invited those from the northern kingdom who were not taken captive in the Assyrian invasion to come to Jerusalem to celebrate the Passover. For the first time since King Solomon, people from the northern tribes worshipped alongside those from the southern tribes.

Judah's Kings

JUDAH		
King of Judah	**Reign (BC)**	**Character**
Rehoboam	930–914	Bad
Abijah/Abijam	914–911	Bad
Asa	911–870	Good
Jehoshaphat	870–848	Good
Jehoram/Joram	848–842	Bad
Ahaziah	842–841	Bad
Athaliah (queen)	841–835	Bad
Joash/Jehoash	835–796	Good
Amaziah	796–767	Good
Uzziah/Azariah	767–740	Good
Jotham	750–735	Good
Ahaz	735–715	Bad
Hezekiah	715–686	Good
Manasseh	686–642	Bad
Amon	642–640	Bad
Josiah	640–609	Good
Jehoahaz	609	Bad
Jehoiakim	609–598	Bad
Jehoiachin/Jeconiah	598–597	Bad
Zedekiah	597–586	Bad

Michelangelo's *David*.
Judah's kings were
from the house of David.

THE DIVIDED KINGDOM: JUDAH'S FORTIFICATIONS

Military Heroes and Villains: Hezekiah

H ezekiah, whose name means "God has strengthened," ascended to the throne after the death of his father, Ahaz. As a new king, Hezekiah introduced comprehensive religious reforms and made major changes to the southern kingdom of Judah. The writer of 2 Kings held Hezekiah in high regard: "He trusted in the LORD, the God of Israel, so that there was none like him among all the kings of Judah after him, nor among those who were before him" (18:5).

Hezekiah's first royal action gave a strong indicator of his priorities. In the very first month of his reign, "he opened the doors of the house of the LORD and repaired them" (2 Chronicles 29:3), the same doors his father, Ahaz, had tried to shut forever. Hezekiah then renewed full-scale worship of God after a long period of idol worship that had taken root in the city. Hezekiah abolished the high places of worship, smashed pillars, and cut down the sacred Asherah pole. The Israelites had begun to offer sacrifices to the bronze serpent Moses had made, so Hezekiah destroyed it (2 Kings 18:4). Most importantly, Hezekiah renewed the tradition of the Passover pilgrimage. This was a major achievement. Israelites who had not been taken into Assyrian exile were invited to worship God by celebrating Passover in Jerusalem, the place God had prepared (2 Chronicles 6:6). This hadn't happened since the division of the kingdom under Rehoboam. Hezekiah's proclamation to Judah was clear: Yahweh would be a national priority once more.

Moses and the Brazen Serpent, Adriaen van Nieulandt the Younger (1587–1658)

Defensive wall of ancient Jerusalem

Hezekiah also developed a major defensive plan to protect Jerusalem from the Assyrians. He stopped the flow of the springs outside the city so that the Assyrians would not have access to any water if they came to Jerusalem to attack. Because of the typical length of sieges, it was important for the opposing force to have a source of water for their soldiers and animals. Cutting off their water supply put Jerusalem in a much stronger defensive position. At the same time, Hezekiah constructed a nearly six-hundred-yard-long aqueduct to provide Jerusalem water in the event of an attack by the Assyrians. The aqueduct—a technical wonder in its day—routed water into the city for his people. It was dug underneath the city by two teams coming from different directions. They met up at the exact same location. The aqueduct connected the Gihon spring, Jerusalem's fresh water supply, to the Siloam pool.

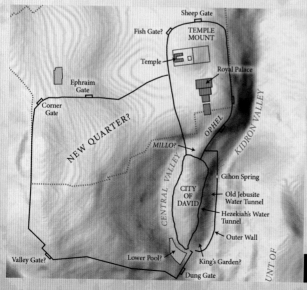

Hezekiah left an indelible mark in the history of Judah. His faith, coupled with his successful governing of Judah, brought him great recognition (2 Chronicles 32:33). His firm commitment to God left a legacy of devotion, making him an appropriate predecessor to Jesus.

Jerusalem at the time of Hezekiah

THE DIVIDED KINGDOM: JUDAH'S FORTIFICATIONS

Things to Think About

- It is clear that God blesses His children. What are some of the blessings that you can see from the ways He protected Judah?

- What were some of the traits of the good kings that you can observe?

- How did the good kings of Judah show their allegiance to God?

- What were some of the traits of the bad kings of Judah?

- How did God humble the people of Judah when they forgot Him?

- What are some of the lessons you can learn from the kings of Judah?

- Make a list of what you learned about what God values from the wars of Judah.

- Reflect on the meaning of Isaiah 7:14 in view of what you learned in this chapter. How does the context of the life of Ahaz shed light on the promise of verse 14?

Walls of the Old City of Jerusalem, Israel

Chapter 8

THE DIVIDED KINGDOM: JUDAH'S DECLINE

For because of the anger of the LORD it came to the point in Jerusalem and Judah that he cast them out from his presence.

(2 Kings 24:20)

INTRODUCTION

The events leading up to Judah's eventual destruction were more than just a series of random happenings. During this period of bloody wars and stubborn rebellion, good kings and wicked kings, not to mention death and utter destruction, God was orchestrating His plan of redemption. This plan hadn't changed since Abraham's time: through one unique nation God would make His entrance into the world, in order that His blessings might flow to all nations (Genesis 12:1–3; Psalm 148:14). Even the machinations of powerful kings could not disrupt God's plan or impugn His character.

God allowed—and often directed—certain wars because He is just and fair; to avoid punishing evil would go against His character (Deuteronomy 9:4). God used warfare as a tool of judgment against His enemies, as well as against His own people when they rebelled. Ultimately, this ensured His plan would advance

Assyrian soldiers with bows, arrows, and spears

unhindered. His prime concern was the salvation of humankind. When Assyria and Babylon took up arms against Judah, it was not because God was weak or unaware of what was happening. God allowed Judah's enemies to increase in strength as a means for Him to carry out His purposes. God controlled how much, how far, and how long these nations could attack and overpower Judah.

The prophet Jeremiah penned words that brought hope to hopeless people: "For I know the plans I have for you, declares the LORD, plans for welfare and not for evil, to give you a future and a hope" (Jeremiah 29:11). Jeremiah was writing to the Jewish exiles of the second deportation of 597 BC. Eleven years later, in 586 BC, Jerusalem was utterly destroyed. The temple was in ruins, and city residents were being hauled off to Babylon as captives in a third and final deportation. God had called Jeremiah to proclaim stern warnings to the people of Judah to mend their ways, but now it looked like it might be too late. Though at first glance this popular verse from Jeremiah sounds like a general statement about God's plans, it was actually referencing a specific, pivotal time in the life of Israel, one that forever altered the course of history for God's people.

Both the northern and southern kingdoms would end up destroyed, and it would appear as if all were lost, as if God had walked away for good—or, perhaps, that He was not as powerful as the people of Judah thought. How could God be the true King of Israel when there was no more Israel? Was there any hope for the nation as it faced extinction?

Assyrian archers

It was at this moment that God spoke through Jeremiah. He reminded the nation that He knew what He was doing. In fact, God was well aware of what was taking place, and He had good things already planned for His people. His plan did not include the annihilation of the people of Israel. He was going to extend His ultimate act of loving-kindness to them and give them a true hope and future. It was a good plan, one of blessing and not of cursing, but one that necessitated traveling the road of heartache and pain first. God's plan would ultimately come to fruition in His Son, the Lord Jesus Christ, who would bring promised salvation to the world.

It was through the wars of this period that God revealed His good, merciful, gracious, and long-suffering character to the world. God wanted His people to walk by faith, to trust that He was in control, and to understand that no earthly king was greater than God. "Yet God my King is from of old, working salvation in the midst of the earth" (Psalm 74:12).

Ancient bas-relief of Assyrian soldiers from Iran

THE DIVIDED KINGDOM: JUDAH'S DECLINE

Judah's Deliverance from the Assyrians

2 Kings 18–19; 2 Chronicles 32; Isaiah 36–37

LOCATION

Lachish was a large Canaanite town later rebuilt as one of Judah's fortresses. Located in the lowlands of Judah about thirty miles southwest of Jerusalem, Lachish guarded the mountain pass to Jerusalem from the coast. Lachish was secured with a double line of massive mud-brick walls on stone foundations. The city gate was one of the largest and most strongly fortified gates known from this time period.

Hezekiah's aqueduct was built on the road to the Washer's Field opposite the upper pool in Jerusalem. This reservoir fed into Hezekiah's tunnel that he constructed to route water into Jerusalem and cut off the water supply to the attacking army during a siege.

KEY PLAYERS

- Hezekiah: king of Judah who succeeded his father, Ahaz, and was known for having a heart that followed God
- Sennacherib: king of Assyria who ascended the throne after the death of his father, Sargon II, and made Nineveh his capital
- Assyrians: people who engaged in gruesome physical and psychological warfare and formed a mighty empire that dominated the ancient Near East from the ninth to the seventh century BC. They conquered an area that includes what is now Iraq, Syria, Jordan, Lebanon, and much of Israel.

WEAPONS AND WARRIORS

King Hezekiah primed Jerusalem for an impending siege when he "closed the upper outlet of the waters of Gihon and directed them down to the west side of the city of David" (2 Chronicles 32:30).

The Assyrian army likely used battering rams and built a siege ramp against another city in Judah, Lachish, and employed terror to weaken the spirit of their enemies. Ancient reliefs show men impaled in plain sight of the city's wall. Excavators of Lachish found hundreds of missiles and arrowheads.

BATTLE SYNOPSIS

Hezekiah had conquered or subdued much of the Philistine territory and formed an alliance with Egypt. During Hezekiah's fourteenth year as king of Judah, Sennacherib, king of Assyria, attacked Judah (see Isaiah 36:1). His father, Sargon II, had overseen the demise of the northern kingdom of Israel.

Hezekiah wisely decided to focus on improving Jerusalem's defenses by restoring walls and fortifying towers. He also stopped up the springs outside the city to eliminate the Assyrians' water supply, which would have been necessary to sustain their large army. Hezekiah shipped his gold and silver to Sennacherib in an attempt to appease him, hoping the enemy might leave Judah alone. Sennacherib laughed at Hezekiah's overture. Upon arriving outside Jerusalem, by the aqueduct of the upper pool, Sennacherib's commander gave Hezekiah an ultimatum: "Resist and you will die. Concede and you will live—*maybe*."

Sennacherib's message disturbed Hezekiah. In desperation, he summoned the prophet Isaiah, who reassured Hezekiah that God would orchestrate Sennacherib's downfall. Sennacherib insisted this was a lie. God reminded Hezekiah again not to fear. That night an angel of the Lord descended upon the enemy camp and killed 185,000 soldiers. The next day the crippled Assyrian army retreated.

OUTCOME

SHORT-TERM

The Assyrians lived on, but Sennacherib never returned to Jerusalem. Jerusalem's fate continued to hang in the balance as the Babylonians began revolting against Assyria.

LONG-TERM

Hezekiah's aqueduct can still be seen in Jerusalem today; it empties into the pool of Siloam.

GOD'S ROLE

Although the people of Judah deserved to be punished, and did suffer greatly for their sins, God delivered the nation because of Hezekiah's faith and trust in Him (Isaiah 37:14–21, 36). Though Hezekiah did what he could to protect Jerusalem from an army much stronger than his own, his trust was ultimately in God. He pleaded for God to defend Judah so the Assyrians would see His glory and power, and acknowledge Yahweh as the one true God. Conversely, Sennacherib mocked God, blaspheming His name. This posture was more than God could tolerate, so He sent His angel to strike the Assyrians' camp with death. The people of Judah did not have to lift a finger to defend Jerusalem. After the victory, Hezekiah became a strong ruler and was respected among the nations (2 Chronicles 32:23). While there was a time when he became prideful, he quickly remembered where his power came from and gave glory to God.

Assyria's Defeat of Manasseh

2 CHRONICLES 33:1-20

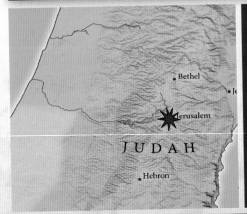

LOCATION

The location of this battle was likely Jerusalem, a city positioned in the center of Israel between the Mediterranean and Dead Seas. Jerusalem, the capital of Judah, was built on the top of a hill. Given the natural defenses of the city and the strength of its walls, Jerusalem would have been a difficult city to conquer.

KEY PLAYERS

- Manasseh: king of Judah who succeeded his father, Hezekiah, and whose reign was characterized by a relapse into idolatry
- Assyrians: people who engaged in gruesome physical and psychological warfare and formed a mighty empire that dominated the ancient Near East from the ninth to the seventh century BC. They conquered an area that includes what is now Iraq, Syria, Jordan, and Lebanon, and much of Israel.

WEAPONS AND WARRIORS

Assyrian soldiers and prisoners (ca. 700–692 BC), possibly from one of Sennacherib's campaigns

The Assyrians were warriors known for their brutality. They would often pierce the noses and lips of their captives, attach rings to their faces, and lead them back to Assyria with thick bronze chains that dug into their skin. In other words, the Assyrians used their superior might to treat their enemies like animals.

Battle Synopsis

Hezekiah's evil son Manasseh opened the door to pagan practices in Judah, thus undoing the religious reforms instituted by his father. Manasseh rebuilt the altars to Baal, erected Asherah poles, and established additional high places of worship. He followed all the heathen practices of his day, including sacrificing his own sons to gods like Molech. He consulted fortune-tellers and mediums, ultimately leading all of Judah astray. When God tried to speak to Manasseh and His people, they completely ignored Him. God gave His people ample opportunity to repent, but late in Manasseh's fifty-five-year reign, God punished the people of Judah by bringing the Assyrian army against them again. This time Assyria was successful. The Assyrians captured Manasseh, placed a hook in his nose, and took him nearly one thousand miles away to Babylon. Humiliated and defeated, Manasseh cried out to God and humbled himself. God showed him mercy and rescued him from the Assyrians.

Outcome

Short-Term

Manasseh completely disregarded God's law. The Book of the Law of Moses was either lost or misplaced during his reign, and the people of Judah forgot it even existed—an indication of just how corrupt the nation had become.

Long-Term

Manasseh's repentance did not alter Judah's destiny; soon the people of Judah would fall to the Babylonians. The writer of Kings blamed Judah's fate on Manasseh's sins (2 Kings 24:3–4).

God's Role

Manasseh disregarded everything having to do with God. He did not even pretend to worship the one true God but instead poured his energy and money into worshipping false gods. Eventually, Manasseh met the message of the prophets head-on, the theme of which was judgment: "I will wipe Jerusalem as one wipes a dish, wiping it and turning it upside down" (2 Kings 21:13). The Assyrian commander who took Manasseh captive was an agent God used to punish and humble the wayward king. Manasseh had become wicked and proud, so God allowed him to be taken away in chains—all for the purpose of bringing him to repentance. Just as disciplining a strong-willed child is a parent's demonstration of love, so was God's discipline of Manasseh. Afterward, in an amazing and undeserved act of mercy, God relented His punishment and allowed Manasseh to be restored to his place of leadership.

Military Heroes and Villains: Josiah

Judah's final hero, Josiah, reigned from 640 to 609 BC. His godly legacy was similar to Hezekiah's. Josiah became king at the age of eight, following the assassination of his father, king Amon. He ruled for thirty-one years; his reign is seen as the final attempt to set the nation back on track.

Military and political pressures kept the Assyrians nearby. However, their empire was beginning to weaken. The Assyrians were preoccupied with concerns aside from Judah and the former territory of Israel. The prophet Nahum's prediction of Assyria's demise looked like it would actually come to pass.

In the eighteenth year of his reign, Josiah used tax money to perform extensive repairs on the temple. During this rebuilding process in 622 BC, a scroll was discovered: the Book of the Law (2 Kings 22:8)—lost from the time of Manasseh. When Josiah read the scroll, he was overwhelmed with concern over the consequences for Judah's failure to heed the Law; this fear became the catalyst for Josiah's reform

King Josiah, Julius Schnorr von Carolsfeld (1794–1872)

Torah scroll

efforts. Josiah recognized that God's people had placed themselves under God's curse. His first action was to seek counsel from the prophetess Huldah; she validated the content of the scroll and predicted that consequences for disobedience would indeed come. However, because Josiah's heart was tender toward the Lord, Huldah promised that God would be gracious to him. Judah's downfall would not take place in his lifetime.

Josiah set his heart on purging the land of idolatry and led a dramatic ceremony to renew Israel's covenant with God. He then called the nation to worship God exclusively and outlawed the worship of any other gods. The temple was purged of all the instruments used to worship Baal. All local sanctuaries that had been erected to worship false gods were destroyed, and the statues and images of pagan gods were smashed. Josiah executed pagan priests and exhumed and burned the bones of dead pagan priests to desecrate their altars—a sign of complete rejection. Finally, Josiah reinstituted the Passover celebration, signaling that Judah was once more a land and people devoted to the Lord.

Sadly, Josiah's reign was cut short when he went into battle against Egypt and was killed in action, stunning his own people who greeted the chariot that brought his body home.

THE DIVIDED KINGDOM: JUDAH'S DECLINE

King Josiah's Battle with the King of Egypt
2 KINGS 23:28-30; 2 CHRONICLES 35:20-27

Tyre
Megiddo
Jerusalem
Mediterranean
Migdol

LOCATION

The plain of Megiddo, also known as Armageddon and Har Megiddo (Mount Megiddo), was located near the ancient city of Megiddo. The Via Maris, or "Way of the Sea," was an ancient trade route dating from the early Bronze Age that meandered through the Megiddo valley. This highway linked Egypt with Syria, north of Israel, and created a path for trade as well as conflict. The Valley of Jezreel stretched across the breadth of this entire region between Mount Carmel, Mount Gilboa, and the hills of lower Galilee. Several important battles of the Bible were fought on this plain, the largest valley in Israel.

KEY PLAYERS

- Josiah: the king of Judah who succeeded his father, Amon, when Amon was assassinated. Josiah instituted major reforms in the southern kingdom.
- Neco: an Egyptian king; the son and successor of Psammetichus I

WEAPONS AND WARRIORS

The ancient Egyptians took to archery as a central part of their military armament. Archery was widespread both for hunting and use in battle; images from the tombs of Thebes depict archery lessons being given. The Egyptians used their bows with precision and great effectiveness.

Carved stone, found near the west bank of the Nile in Egypt, showing Egyptians in battle

BATTLE SYNOPSIS

Egyptians and Assyrians formed an allied army and were fighting the Babylonians. Neco, the king of Egypt at this time, traveled to meet with the king of Assyria. Josiah decided to strike the Egyptians. Perhaps he feared Egypt and hoped to frustrate Egypt's objectives in order to foster a more balanced international scene. Neco sent a message to Josiah advising him not to attack, as Egypt was not at war with Judah. Neco told Josiah that God was on *Egypt's* side and it would be foolish for Judah to fight against God. Paying no attention to Egypt's offer of neutrality, Josiah continued with his battle plans against Neco. Josiah hoped to catch Egypt ill-prepared. Neco may have sensed Josiah's plan, so he massed archers to slow the assault. Early in the battle, Josiah was fatally shot with an arrow, and all of Judah mourned his death. Both the battle and Josiah's plan were lost.

Jezreel Valley, northern Israel

OUTCOME

SHORT-TERM

After Egypt's victory, the main core of the Egyptian army advanced northward to help the Assyrians attack the Babylonians.

LONG-TERM

Within four years, Nebuchadnezzar of Babylon destroyed the powerful Egyptian army. This helped set the stage for the invasion and eventual destruction of Judah by Babylon.

GOD'S ROLE

God blessed Josiah's faith with a successful reign—the last good thing to happen to Judah before the kingdom collapsed in 586 BC. Unfortunately, Josiah's rule was cut short by his untimely death. The Lord had been commanding Josiah and the people—speaking through the prophetess Huldah and now through a pagan Egyptian king—to trust Him alone and correspondingly refrain from international political affairs. Josiah "did not listen to the words of Neco from the mouth of God" (2 Chronicles 35:22). Josiah's disobedience resulted in his death in battle. The Egyptian ruler was eventually defeated, but God positioned Nebuchadnezzar of Babylon to first demolish the Egyptians and Assyrians, and then attack others, including Judah. Though God's ways are often confusing, they are sovereign and purposeful.

Babylonian Warfare

With the demise of the Assyrian Empire (626–605 BC), the Babylonians emerged as the dominant superpower of the region. They ended the Assyrian state and destroyed the Assyrian capital, Nineveh, in part by diverting the Tigris River into the city. During this time, Egyptians marched through Judah to assist the remnant of the Assyrian army in Carchemish, a Hittite city on the west bank of the Euphrates River, in their fight against Babylon, but they were defeated. With its victory, Babylon enlarged its territory all the way to the borders of Egypt. In 605 BC, and again in 597, the Babylonians conquered Jerusalem. When its vassal king revolted a decade later, the city was captured again. This time the Babylonians destroyed the city, took the people of Judah captive, and dispersed them throughout their empire.

Babylonian soldiers, the Apadana Palace, Iran

The army of Babylon used mounted bowmen and tools made from iron, including helmets and chain mail for armor. The Babylonians were master traders, able to barter their livestock and crops for metal. Their fertile land made for productive farming and animal husbandry, leaving them rich with food and animals to trade.

Though not as brutal as the Assyrian military, the Babylonians deported vanquished peoples, including women and children, in order to maintain control over conquered territories. Archaeological evidence depicts captives marching in neck stocks or walking with their elbows tied behind their backs. Prisoners were then mixed in with Babylonian society, thus eroding any sense of nationalism. Customs, traditions, and even language—things that give a nation its unique identity—were eventually lost, further preventing the nation from rebelling.

Lion on the reconstructed Ishtar Gate, a gate to the inner city of ancient Babylon, Villorejo / Shutterstock.com

Habakkuk 1:5–11 reveals just how fierce these Babylonians were as warriors:

> "Look among the nations, and see;
>> wonder and be astounded.
> For I am doing a work in your days
>> that you would not believe if told.
> For behold, I am raising up the Chaldeans,
>> that bitter and hasty nation,
> who march through the breadth of the earth,
>> to seize dwellings not their own.
> They are dreaded and fearsome;
>> their justice and dignity go forth from themselves.
> Their horses are swifter than leopards,
>> more fierce than the evening wolves;
>> their horsemen press proudly on.
> Their horsemen come from afar;
>> they fly like an eagle swift to devour.
> They all come for violence,
>> all their faces forward.
>> They gather captives like sand.
> At kings they scoff,
>> and at rulers they laugh.
> They laugh at every fortress,
>> for they pile up earth and take it.
> Then they sweep by like the wind and go on,
>> guilty men, whose own might is their god!"

Relief from the Ishtar Gate, Babylon

THE DIVIDED KINGDOM: JUDAH'S DECLINE

Jehoiakim's and Jehoiachin's Defeat

2 KINGS 23:36–24:17

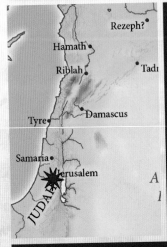

LOCATION

Jerusalem was the capital of Judah, located in the center of Israel, between the Mediterranean and Dead Seas. Also known as the city of David, it was home to the temple, the place God designated for His people to worship Him. Protecting Jerusalem was not only essential to retaining the seat of Judah's government but also to preserving the religious identity of everyone in Judah. If the temple were captured, there would be no place for God's people to perform their sacrifices—the prescribed way for them to draw near to God.

KEY PLAYERS

- Jehoiakim: Josiah's second son and the first king installed in Judah by an external power—namely, the Egyptian king Neco
- Jehoiachin: the son of Jehoiakim; another evil king
- Nebuchadnezzar: a brutal, powerful, and ambitious king of the Babylonian Empire who is credited for constructing the Hanging Gardens of Babylon and for conquering and destroying Judah

WEAPONS AND WARRIORS

Old City, Jerusalem

Prior to the Babylonians' destruction of Jerusalem, God allowed the Moabites, Syrians, and Ammonites to attack Judah. These forces were able to wear down Judah's defenses and weaken its military. When Nebuchadnezzar made his move on Jerusalem, he found its defenses depleted, which paved the way for his victory.

Battle Synopsis

Weakened by the sudden death of its beloved leader Josiah, the kingdom of Judah became a vassal state of the Babylonian king Nebuchadnezzar. Nebuchadnezzar conquered Judah and forced Jehoiakim to serve him for three years—the first, but not the last, encounter between the two rulers. Jehoiakim grew frustrated and rebelled against the Babylonians, which led to his ultimate downfall. This rebellion displeased God, who sent the Babylonians, Moabites, Syrians, and Ammonites to attack Judah. Jehoiachin, who reigned in his father's place for three months, was no better a king. Again, Nebuchadnezzar attacked and conquered Judah (597 BC). He took the young king, his family, and Judah's finest leaders and craftsmen to Babylon, but he left the poor behind. He also took the remaining valuables from the temple and the palace. Nebuchadnezzar inserted Jehoiachin's uncle Mattaniah (whom Nebuchadnezzar renamed Zedekiah) in Jehoiachin's place and made him a puppet king.

Israelites taken into captivity, Holman Bible (1890)

Outcome

Short-Term

Jerusalem was impoverished and weakened. Nebuchadnezzar's sieges were further steps toward the ultimate destruction and depopulation of Jerusalem.

Long-Term

The breakup and displacement of the people of Judah removed the threat of a rebellion against Babylon.

God's Role

Both Jehoiakim and Jehoiachin were evil rulers who disdained God's Word, but God used them (along with Nebuchadnezzar) as key players in the future destruction of Jerusalem. God did not allow either ruler to sit on Judah's throne for very long; instead, He orchestrated their captivity by Nebuchadnezzar. Jehoiakim and Jehoiachin did not understand that God was to be worshipped as King; He had true authority, power, and dominion over everything. God used other nations to remind the people of Judah and their leaders that continued disobedience would bring consequences. Even though Judah was eventually conquered, God was not.

The Fall of Jerusalem

2 KINGS 25; 2 CHRONICLES 36:11-21; JEREMIAH 52; DANIEL 1:1-7

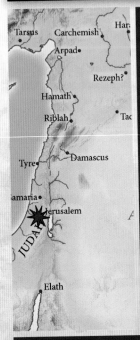

LOCATION

Jerusalem's decimation took place when Zedekiah rebelled against Nebuchadnezzar. The city had been plundered on March 16, 597 BC, but this time, in the summer of 586 BC, it was burned to the ground. The temple and the palace were completely destroyed, and the people were murdered or carted off to Babylon.

Although the direct distance between Jerusalem and Babylon was 520 miles, traveling between the two cities usually involved a nine-hundred-mile journey. Babylon, which was less than sixty miles from present-day Baghdad, was situated along the Euphrates River, enclosed by an eleven-mile-long outer wall. An inner wall, wide enough for two chariots to ride side by side, encompassed many suburbs. Babylon also boasted a great royal palace, complete with hanging gardens, which are now considered one of the Seven Wonders of the Ancient World.

KEY PLAYERS

- Nebuchadnezzar: a brutal, powerful, and ambitious king of the Babylonian Empire who is credited for constructing the Hanging Gardens of Babylon and for conquering and destroying Judah
- Zedekiah: the last king of Judah, who was put on the throne as a "puppet" by Nebuchadnezzar. Zedekiah (named Mattaniah before Nebuchadnezzar renamed him) succeeded his nephew King Jehoiachin.

WEAPONS AND WARRIORS

One common practice of invading armies in the ancient Near East was to plunder the cities they conquered, primarily to increase their own wealth. However, there was another perceived benefit. Most people in these ancient empires were polytheistic and believed if they took the idols or instruments of worship from the people they conquered and added them to their pantheon of gods, then blessings would follow. Ultimately, pillaging a city thoroughly demoralized the people of a conquered nation—and kept them under the thumb of their new overlords.

Battle Synopsis

After capturing Jerusalem for the first time, during Jehoiakim's reign in 605 BC, Nebuchadnezzar demanded that the youths of noble families—those who were handsome and without any defect—be brought to him. Nebuchadnezzar wanted them to be educated in Babylonian thought. Among those selected was a young man named Daniel. While Daniel was being trained in Nebuchadnezzar's court, Zedekiah was chosen to be the new client king of Judah. Zedekiah ruled for about eleven years but completely ignored God. Zedekiah eventually rebelled against Nebuchadnezzar; in return, the Babylonians laid siege to Jerusalem for two years. Judah's foolhardy leaders banked on the angel of the Lord showing up to save them, as He had in the days of Hezekiah, but no divine intervention took place. Famine spiraled out of control; when it was at its worst, the king and his army tried to leave the city. During their desperate bid to escape, the Babylonians intercepted them, put them in chains, and brought them to Babylon. Zedekiah paid a steep price for his rebellion. Nebuchadnezzar had Zedekiah's sons murdered in front of him before having him blinded and imprisoned.

Later the captain of the bodyguard, Nebuzaradan, went back to Jerusalem and razed the city, stealing all the valuables and capturing the people. The Babylonians plundered the temple and stole all the bronze pillars, beautiful gold basins, jars, and bowls used in temple worship. Only a few of the poorest people were left in Judah to work the fields. Nebuzaradan also brought the head priests, officials, and other important nobles of Judah to Nebuchadnezzar, who put them all to death. The Babylonian king appointed Gedaliah as governor over Judah. He was friendly to the people of Judah, but he was assassinated. The people of Judah feared the

Babylonians, and many fled to Egypt. Later Evil-merodach succeeded Nebuchadnezzar as king of Babylon; he freed Jehoiachin, who had been living in captivity for thirty-seven years, and gave him an allowance and royal treatment.

Thus the curtains closed on this period of Israelite history, the long-expected divine judgment for Manasseh's crimes having come to pass. Scripture records a somber epitaph for the nation: "So Judah was taken into exile out of its land" (2 Kings 25:21).

OUTCOME

SHORT-TERM

The fall of Jerusalem was a turning point in Israel's religious life. The Jews never returned to idol worship after their captivity.

LONG-TERM

The destruction of Jerusalem marked the beginning of Gentile dominion over Israel.

GOD'S ROLE

The people of Judah continually rebelled against God, and Judah fell completely under Nebuchadnezzar's control. While it seemed God was abandoning His people, He was actually bringing His plan to pass. Daniel, Shadrach, Meshach, and Abednego were being educated in the ways of the Babylonians; God was preparing them to be witnesses to the power of the one true God, right in the heart of the Babylonian Empire.

Zedekiah is chained and brought before Nebuchadnezzar, c. 1670

God used Jerusalem's ruin to bring about good for the nation (Jeremiah 29:10–14).

The prophets had correctly predicted destruction as punishment for Judah's continued disobedience. The people of Judah finally realized that the verdict of God's wrath had been poured out on them because of their continued sin—and they accepted it. The dark storm clouds would pass; God's people held on to Isaiah's promise of a better day in the future: "Speak tenderly to Jerusalem, and cry to her that her warfare is ended, that her iniquity is pardoned, that she has received from the LORD's hand double for all her sins" (Isaiah 40:2).

Painting by Gebhard Fugal depicting the exiled Jews at the waters of Babylon (c. 1920)

"By the waters of Babylon, there we sat down and wept, when we remembered Zion." (Psalm 137:1)

THE DIVIDED KINGDOM: JUDAH'S DECLINE

Military Heroes and Villains: Nebuchadnezzar

There is perhaps no other king in Babylonian history as great as Nebuchadnezzar, who ruled from 605 to 562 BC. He was the son of Nabopolassar, who was the neo-Babylonian Empire's first ruler from 626 to 605 BC. Nabopolassar played an important role in weakening the Assyrian Empire.

Following Nabopolassar's death, his son Nebuchadnezzar took the throne. Nebuchadnezzar's practice was to seize the best and the brightest young men from the nations he conquered and bring them to his palace. This enabled him to harness their talents and deplete conquered territories of anyone skilled enough to lead an uprising. Once the exiles were brought into his kingdom, they were subjected to an extensive indoctrination program that assimilated them into Babylonian life, customs, and thinking. The process included exposure to their foods, music, and philosophies.

One young man who experienced the pressure of embracing Babylonian ideology was Daniel. Daniel was among the nobility of Judah who were carried off to captivity during Nebuchadnezzar's reign. According to Daniel 1, the young man refused to eat Babylonian food; God had required His people to keep specific dietary laws in the Book of the Law, or the Torah. Daniel would not obey a man over Yahweh. God enabled Daniel to stay true to His laws, despite intense harassment.

Life was not altogether terrible for the captives under Nebuchadnezzar. The Jews were allowed to live together in communities, and they were permitted to farm and work to earn an income. Some became quite wealthy. The Lord intended for the Jews to settle in Babylon; they would not be leaving anytime soon. At times, however, Nebuchadnezzar was temperamental and

Shadrach, Meshach, and Abednego in the Furnace
Gustave Doré (1832–1883)

Nebuchadnezzar, William Blake (1757–1827)

turned on people, often ordering their deaths without warning. This left those under his rule living in constant fear. On one occasion, the king tried to force Daniel's friends Shadrach, Meshach, and Abednego to worship an idol at Dura; upon their refusal to do so, they were thrown into a fiery furnace that was made seven times hotter than usual. Peering into the furnace, Nebuchadnezzar was aghast; he saw not three but four men walking around in the fire, unharmed—Shadrach, Meshach, Abednego, and a mysterious divine presence. The Lord protected Daniel's friends; not one hair on their heads was burned. This led Nebuchadnezzar to join the men in praising God (see Daniel 3).

The king's double-minded nature finally caught up with him, however; he was convinced his success was due to his own inherent greatness. So God humbled Nebuchadnezzar; to punish his pride and vanity, God afflicted him with a strange mental illness, causing Nebuchadnezzar to behave like a wild animal, eat grass, and live outdoors until God finally restored his sanity (Daniel 4:28–37). It took sinking to his lowest point for Nebuchadnezzar to worship God and listen to Daniel's counsel.

Things to Think About

- List the ways that you have observed God's blessing upon His children.

- List some ways that God has disciplined His children.

- What have you learned about the character of God from these battle stories?

- Jeremiah 29:11 is a popular verse. When you read it in light of Jerusalem's destruction and the dispersion of people from Judah to Babylon, how does the meaning of this passage change or deepen for you?

- How did God use the Babylonian captivity for good—both in Israel and in the world?

The Burning of Jerusalem by Nebuchadnezzar's Army, Juan de la Corte (1597–1660)

Chapter 9

THE DIVIDED KINGDOM: ISRAEL AND JUDAH'S CIVIL WARS

Thus says the LORD GOD: Behold, I will take the people of Israel from the nations among which they have gone, and will gather them from all around, and bring them to their own land. And I will make them one nation in the land, on the mountains of Israel. And one king shall be king over them all, and they shall be no longer two nations, and no longer divided into two kingdoms.

(Ezekiel 37:21–22)

INTRODUCTION

The constant civil wars between Israel and Judah reveal just how far God's people had wandered from His plan for them. The Israelites were supposed to be united in their devotion to God and to each other. They were meant to be a royal priesthood, a light to other nations. But the people and their leaders couldn't even manage to hold the nation together. After Israel split in two—into Judah to the south and Israel to the north—the fractured kingdom went to war with itself from time to time. Both kingdoms also slipped further into idolatry. God repeatedly sent prophets to both nations, calling them back to love, worship, and serve Him alone—back to the relationship He had always intended for them. Hosea 14, for example, opens with the prophet's plea for repentance: "Return, O Israel, to the LORD your God, for you have stumbled because of your iniquity" (see also Joel 2:15–27; Micah 7:18–20). Sadly, a long list of rebellious kings refused to heed this call.

Sunrise in northern Israel

The wars between Israel and Judah were not simply the result of irreconcilable differences among neighbors. God sometimes used one kingdom against the other as a tool of judgment because of their rebellion as well as to provoke His people to return to Him.

When a king acted as if he was the true ruler instead of God, what he was really doing was rejecting the true King, Yahweh, and His rightful position of authority. Earthly kings who turned from the Lord, who ruled for their own glory rather than God's, wound up boastful, arrogant, and discontent. Full of their own pride, they attacked, fought, and took land that God had not given them.

The kings of both Israel and Judah were called to do one thing: be responsible for the people that God had entrusted to them. God did not call them to advance

Micah Preaching to the Israelites, Gustave Doré (1832–1883)

their own kingdoms or agendas. He did not call them to establish their own names throughout the earth. He did not call them to take advantage of others for their own wealth and glory. He called them to take care of His people and manage the land He entrusted to them.

However, those whom God made to be united—in the purposes of God, working together to make His name known among the nations—found themselves on opposite sides, seeking to destroy each other. Their refusal to return to God cost them many lives, and it eventually cost them their kingdoms.

HIEREMIAS

The Prophet Jeremiah, Michelangelo (1475–1564)

THE DIVIDED KINGDOM: ISRAEL AND JUDAH'S CIVIL WARS

Battle of Mount Zemaraim

2 CHRONICLES 13

LOCATION

Abijah stood on Mount Zemaraim and addressed Jeroboam and all of Israel. The exact location of Mount Zemaraim is unknown, but it was in the hill country of Ephraim and likely on the northern border of Benjamin's territory. Bethel, a city of the tribe of Benjamin where Jeroboam I had set up one of his two golden calves, was nearby. Zemaraim was a perfect location from which Abijah could address the people of the northern kingdom. From this mountain he declared that the true line of kings came from Judah, and he indirectly urged the people of Israel to submit to Judah so the two kingdoms could become a whole nation again.

KEY PLAYERS

- Jeroboam I: Israel's first king after the ten northern tribes revolted against Rehoboam, putting an end to the united monarchy. Jeroboam was known for being at constant war with the house of Judah.
- Abijah (also known as Abijam): Rehoboam's son who succeeded his father on the throne of Judah and was denounced in 1 Kings 15:3 for being an evil king

WEAPONS AND WARRIORS

Abijah boasted an army of four hundred thousand fighting men who were chosen because of their skill and valor. They were a highly trained military force. Jeroboam drew up a battle line against Judah's army with eight hundred thousand mighty warriors of his own, managing to surround Abijah.

Jeroboam Offering Sacrifice for the Idol, Jean-Honoré Fragonard (1732–1806)

BATTLE SYNOPSIS

King Abijah ascended to the edge of Israel's territory and stood on top of Mount Zemaraim. From there he shouted to the people of Israel, who were on the other side of the mountain. He reminded the Israelites that their kingdom had been founded on rebellion against the house of David, the legitimate house to rule over the tribes of Israel—including the ten northern tribes under Jeroboam. Implicitly, Abijah tried to compel the ten northern tribes to place themselves back under control of the house of Judah.

Abijah's army numbered four hundred thousand, half of Jeroboam's army of eight hundred thousand; it looked as if Judah would be easily defeated. While Abijah was yelling, Jeroboam's troops ambushed his forces from behind and from in front. When Abijah's army realized they were about to be decimated, their only hope was to cry out to God for help. The priests of Judah sounded their trumpets, and the battle was won. God heard the cries of the people of Judah and intervened.

Jeroboam's army fled, but his men could not escape Abijah and his troops. Jeroboam lost five hundred thousand men in this bloody battle, more than half his strength. He also lost Bethel. Evidently, the golden calf Jeroboam installed at Bethel was too feeble to protect its own sanctuary.

OUTCOME

SHORT-TERM	LONG-TERM
Jeroboam never fully recovered from this defeat, but Abijah grew in power.	Even though Judah was victorious, Abijah failed to unify Israel and Judah. The two kingdoms continued to fight border wars until Israel's destruction by the Assyrian Empire in 722 BC.

GOD'S ROLE

Scripture tells us that Abijah "walked in all the sins that his father did before him, and his heart was not wholly true to the LORD his God, as the heart of David his father. Nevertheless, for David's sake the LORD his God gave him a lamp in Jerusalem, setting up his son after him, and establishing Jerusalem" (1 Kings 15:3–4). God intervened on behalf of Judah because this victory was vital to His purpose of bringing the Messiah to earth through the line of Judah in order to provide an opportunity for all humankind to be saved. The line of Judah had to be preserved. Judah's men defeated Israel because they relied on God for strength. There was, quite simply, no other reason for their victory. Though it's not clear from scripture how God struck the army of Israel, His intervention was immediate, and His victory was complete.

War between Asa and Baasha
1 KINGS 15:9-24; 2 CHRONICLES 16

LOCATION

Ramah was an Israelite city only five miles north of Jerusalem near Gibeah; its fortification posed a severe threat to Judah's capital city. Damascus, the ancient capital of Syria, was located northeast of Mount Hermon and sixty miles inland from Sidon. Two important trade routes, the Via Maris and the King's Highway, both passed through Damascus, making it an important stop for trading—and fighting.

Ijon, Dan, Abel-beth-maacah, Chinneroth, and the land of Naphtali comprised a fertile stretch of Israelite territory in the north that was home to Israelites and many Gentiles. Geba of Benjamin was likely one of the northernmost cities of Judah at the time of this battle. Mizpah, which means "watchtower" or "lookout," was also situated to the north of Jerusalem.

KEY PLAYERS

- Asa: Rehoboam's grandson and Solomon's great-grandson; the third king of Judah, and the fifth king from the house of David, who was zealous in rooting out idolatry and following God
- Baasha: Ahijah's son and the third king of Israel, who usurped the throne from Jeroboam's son Nadab by killing him and exterminating the house of Jeroboam
- Ben-hadad: king of Syria

WEAPONS AND WARRIORS

Smaller nations often formed strategic military alliances with each other to offer mutual protection and to defend themselves against larger, more powerful nations. Often a third country would try to cause one of the two nations to break the covenant. In this civil war, Judah worked to break the alliance between Israel and Syria.

BATTLE SYNOPSIS

Asa, king of Judah, and Baasha, king of Israel, were long-standing enemies. Their two kingdoms had been feuding since the splintering of the united kingdom of Israel. Because many of his people had defected to the southern kingdom of Judah (2 Chronicles 15:9), Baasha blocked a main route into Judah by erecting a fortress at Ramah, which was only about five miles north of Jerusalem. Along with stopping additional defections, this action gave Baasha control of the trade routes. Feeling threatened, Asa devised a plan to compel Baasha to remove his troops from Ramah. Trusting in a political alliance rather than in God, Asa hired Ben-hadad—a sworn enemy and the king of Syria. At this time Syria was the strongest power in the region and was looking to increase its dominance. Asa bribed Ben-hadad with priceless temple and palace treasures so he would break his current treaty with Baasha. Ben-hadad agreed and welcomed the opportunity to expand his kingdom. From a political standpoint, Asa's plan worked; Baasha withdrew and redeployed to the north, while Syrian mercenaries fought for Asa. Asa proceeded to tear down the fortification at Ramah.

OUTCOME

SHORT-TERM

Asa carried away supplies from Ramah and used them to fortify Geba and Mizpah in order to protect Judah against attacks from Israel.

LONG-TERM

Syria conquered the northern cities of Israel, which gave the nation a military foothold in the promised land. Some of Asa's descendants would inherit his tendency to forge political alliances without God's blessing and consequently bring great pain upon Judah.

GOD'S ROLE

Asa offered treasures from the house of the Lord to a pagan king. Worse, he broke a covenant with God by making a treaty with Ben-hadad. Because Asa relied on the king of Syria and not the Lord, he failed to see what God saw. Asa wrongly believed Israel to be his main enemy because of Baasha building the fortress at Ramah. In reality, the more worrisome adversary was Syria, and God had wanted to give Asa victory over the greater enemy. Asa brought more conflict on himself and the kingdom of Judah because he foolishly trusted a pagan king and disobeyed God.

Several Torah scrolls enclosed in gold and silver

THE DIVIDED KINGDOM: ISRAEL AND JUDAH'S CIVIL WARS

Jehu Kills Joram and Ahaziah

2 KINGS 9-10

LOCATION

Jezreel, meaning "God sows," was the name of both a valley and a city in territory of the northern kingdom of Israel. Ahab and Joram's royal palace was located in this city. Nearby was a vineyard that Ahab had become obsessed with possessing; his evil actions in obtaining that vineyard led to this battle (1 Kings 21). The Valley of Jezreel was a beautiful, broad plain that stretched from Mount Carmel and the Sea of Galilee to the Jordan River. Nazareth lay on its northern side. It was also known as the Great Plain and the Plain of Esdraelon.

KEY PLAYERS

- Jehu: the tenth king of Israel, notable for exterminating the house of Ahab at God's command and having Jezebel thrown out of a window
- Joram: Ahab's son who succeeded him as king of Israel
- Ahab: king over the northern ten tribes of Israel; one of the most evil and powerful rulers Israel ever had
- Ahaziah: king of Judah and Athaliah's son

WEAPONS AND WARRIORS

Sometimes kingdoms are destroyed not because of outside forces but from attack within, which is something known as a *coup d'état*. The kingdom of Israel experienced an internal coup, leading to the deaths of two kings from arrows.

Battle Synopsis

Jehu, a commander in Joram's army, was in a council with other commanders in Ramoth-gilead when a prophet arrived and anointed him king of Israel. The prophet told Jehu he would be the one to bring down Ahab's house for their terrible sins. Jehu conspired against Joram, traveling in secret to Jezreel. As he approached King Joram, watchmen joined the coup. Joram and King Ahaziah of Judah, who happened to be visiting at the time, went out together to meet Jehu. Upon realizing that Jehu was there to exact justice on his family (particularly on his mother, Jezebel), Joram fled. Jehu shot him through his back into his heart and had his body thrown into a vineyard that had belonged to a man named Naboth. Jehu and his men also shot King Ahaziah, who did not die until he reached Megiddo. Ahaziah was taken back to Jerusalem and buried there.

Vineyard in Israel

Outcome

Short-Term

Jehu proceeded to execute Ahab's seventy sons, as well as the remaining members of Ahab's family. While Jehu was on the throne, Syria began to carve up large parts of Israel's territory.

Long-Term

Future judgment would come upon the house of Jehu for his halfhearted commitment to God. This contributed to the eventual demise of the northern kingdom of Israel (Hosea 1:4).

God's Role

Years earlier, Joram's mother, Jezebel, arranged for a vineyard owner named Naboth to be falsely accused and stoned to death so her husband, Ahab, could take Naboth's property for himself. In response, the prophet Elijah told Ahab he would die in the very place where Naboth had died. Ahab repented, so God spared him; but God revealed the punishment for this crime would fall on Ahab's son Joram. God raised up Jehu as His means for exacting judgment on Ahab. Joram was shot through the heart near the very vineyard his father had unlawfully taken. His body was then thrown on Naboth's property to fulfill God's word.

Stained glass of the prophet Elijah

Amaziah versus Joash
2 CHRONICLES 25:5-24

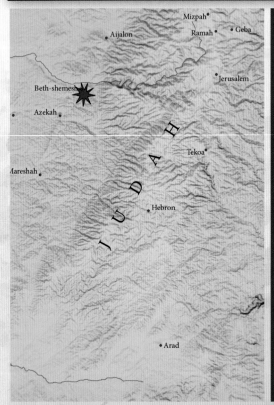

LOCATION

Beth-shemesh, which belonged to Judah, was a Levitical town in the Shephelah Valley, a lush plain. The town sat about fifteen miles west of Jerusalem and overlooked the Valley of Sorek. A road leading south to Lachish, the major artery through the Shephelah Valley, connected Beth-shemesh to other major cities during this time; this established Beth-shemesh as the most important city in the area.

KEY PLAYERS

- Amaziah: king of Judah who succeeded his father, Joash
- Joash (also known as Jehoash): king of Israel and grandson of Jehu

WEAPONS AND WARRIORS

Amaziah had assembled three hundred thousand men in an army that had killed twenty thousand enemy soldiers in a victory over Edom (2 Chronicles 25:5, 11–12). Under Joash's father, Jehoahaz, Israel's army had diminished to fifty horsemen, ten chariots, and ten thousand foot soldiers (2 Kings 13:7). Israel's militaristic situation had obviously improved in light of the boastful fable Joash communicated to Amaziah (2 Chronicles 25:18–19).

BATTLE SYNOPSIS

Amaziah of Judah relished in some military victories against Edom. Feeling perhaps overconfident, he decided to wage war against Israel, too. King Joash counseled Amaziah to give up the struggle. Joash was confident that his army would win the battle, so he wisely suggested Amaziah enjoy his recent triumph over Edom and stay home. Amaziah did not heed Joash's warning; he pressed on with his attack. Amaziah should have listened to his northern neighbor. Joash captured Amaziah at Beth-shemesh, brought the king to Jerusalem, and tore down a long section of the city's walls, from the Ephraim Gate to the northwest Corner Gate. Joash seized the temple articles that were under Obed-edom's care, as well as the palace treasures, and took the loot and prisoners back to Samaria.

OUTCOME

SHORT-TERM

Amaziah became Israel's prisoner for a time and was greatly humbled by God.

LONG-TERM

With Jerusalem's defensive wall broken, Judah found itself in a much weaker position when confronted with future attacks.

GOD'S ROLE

God did not allow Amaziah's sin to go unchecked; Joash became God's instrument of punishment on Amaziah.

Military Heroes and Villains: King Asa

Asa came from a family line consisting of a mixed batch of kings. He was the son of evil king Abijah (or Abijam) and grandson of Rehoboam (who was also wicked), but Asa was also the great-grandson of Solomon, who was famous for his wisdom and devotion to God (at least initially). Asa reigned for forty-one years. Then he was succeeded by his son Jehoshaphat.

As the third king of Judah, following the fracturing of Israel's united kingdom, and the fifth king from the house of David, Asa began his kingly reign with godly, fervent passion. Asa deposed his grandmother Maacah from the office of queen mother and demolished the idol she had erected for worship. Asa's goal was to uphold worship of the one true God, Yahweh.

Making the most of a long period of peace, Asa built fortified cities in Judah. His greatest challenge came against the Ethiopians. Asa stopped a raid by the Egyptian-backed chieftain Zerah (2 Chronicles 14:9–15)—all because of his faith in God. God's message to Asa is timeless: "Hear me, Asa, and all Judah and Benjamin: The LORD is with you while you are with him. If you seek him, he will be found by you, but if you forsake him, he will forsake you" (2 Chronicles 15:2).

However, Asa's goodness was not without its gaps. Near the end of Asa's reign, King Baasha of Israel threatened the kingdom of Judah (2 Chronicles 16:1). Baasha built the fortress of Ramah merely five miles north of Jerusalem, increasing the weight of military pressure on Judah. Asa bribed Ben-hadad I, king of Syria, with treasures from God's temple in exchange for the Syrian king reneging his peace treaty with Baasha. Ben-hadad attacked Israel, and Baasha was forced to withdraw from Ramah. Because he feared Israel, Asa sought help from Syria's king when he should have asked God to intervene in his time of need.

Asa's name means "physician" or "healer," which is ironic. He became seriously ill with a severe foot disease but relied only on physicians rather than trusting God to heal him. After his death, Asa was buried in the tomb he had carved out for himself in the city of David.

Things to Think About

- What are some of the key reasons for God's judgment against Amaziah?
- In the course of Amaziah's success, how should he have acted toward God and toward the northern kingdom?
- What do the civil wars between Israel and Judah teach you about the nature of God?
- What were some of the root causes of fighting between Israel and Judah?
- What can you learn about your own walk with God from the civil wars in Israel?
- How does this chapter make you appreciate the person of Jesus Christ and the way He serves as King?

Judaean hills near Beth-shemesh (modern-day Beith Shemesh, Israel)

THE DIVIDED KINGDOM: ISRAEL AND JUDAH'S CIVIL WARS

Chapter 10

BATTLES OF THE INTERTESTAMENTAL AND NEW TESTAMENT PERIODS

"Blessed be the name of God forever and ever, to whom belong wisdom and might. He changes times and seasons; he removes kings and sets up kings; he gives wisdom to the wise and knowledge to those who have understanding."

(Daniel 2:20–21)

INTRODUCTION

The period between the Old and New Testaments, from 430 BC to AD 4, is called the intertestamental period. It is also known as the quiet period, or the "four hundred silent years," because there were no recorded prophets who spoke during this period; it seemed as if God had stopped speaking to His people. Yet this does not mean that God was silent or absent. In fact, the Bible had plenty to say about this period long before it even started.

When Nebuchadnezzar invaded Israel, he took some of the best and brightest young Hebrew men into his palace to be his servants. One such man was the prophet Daniel, who was taken from Jerusalem to Babylon in the first deportation in 605 BC. King Nebuchadnezzar had a terrifying dream one night about a statue, so he searched for someone to interpret it for him. God revealed the king's dream and its meaning to Daniel. Daniel approached the king and told him the dream spoke about four kingdoms that were going to rule: the Babylonians under Nebuchadnezzar, the Persians, the Greeks, and finally the Romans. The dream meant these kingdoms would all replace each other; this was the will of God.

Just as the dream foretold, the Medo-Persians replaced the Babylonians as the dominant power in the ancient Near East, ruling from 539 to 334 BC (running about one hundred years into the intertestamental period). Then Alexander the Great defeated Darius of Persia, establishing Greece as the new ruling superpower (334–166 BC). Under Alexander's leadership, the Greeks controlled a vast empire, one that united most of the known world. Alexander spread the Greek language, establishing a common mode of communication. Greek

Roman road in Jerash, Jordan

culture heavily influenced Alexander's empire as well, leading to a period known as the Hellenistic Age. It was during this intertestamental period in 250 BC that the Hebrew Old Testament, known as the Tanakh, was translated into Greek, becoming the translation known today as the Septuagint.

After Alexander died in 323 BC, a power struggle erupted for control of his empire. Judea was ruled by a series of successors, ending with a wicked man named Antiochus Epiphanes, who refused to grant the Jews any religious freedom. Around 168 BC, he sold the office of the rightful line of the priesthood to someone who did not have priestly ancestry. He defiled the temple by erecting a pagan altar (see Mark 13:14) and sacrificing unclean animals. Years of war and violence followed, leading up to the Maccabean Revolt from 166 to 135 BC.

The Romans eventually conquered the Greeks and dominated the land of Israel beginning in 63 BC. The Romans crushed a Jewish revolt in AD 135, bringing an end to the Jewish state. The Romans ruled a more widely dispersed kingdom; they allowed different kings to rule over separate regions, under the leadership of the emperor of Rome and the senate. This set the Roman Empire apart from all prior kingdoms and tied a bow on the prophecy that Daniel had interpreted for Nebuchadnezzar: each kingdom came to power in the exact order of Nebuchadnezzar's dream.

The kingdoms of Greece and Rome—and the part they played in history as orchestrated by God—were staggering. The emergence of a common trade and a diplomatic language called *koine* or "common" Greek, along with advances in books, set the stage for the writing and collecting of both the Old and New Testaments into a single book. This, combined with efforts to educate the masses,

The Fall of Jerusalem
Francesco Hayez (1791–1882)

allowed more people to read and understand the scriptures. God used this as preparation for Jesus to enter the world and advance His kingdom.

The Romans also unified nations and created an infrastructure through which the news about the Messiah could spread and the church could grow. The Roman system of government offered protection and safe travel, the Roman road system allowed for relatively easy passage from one country to the next, and Roman citizenship allowed missionaries to live in other parts of the empire without conflict. Roman infrastructure was pivotal for the spreading of the news about Jesus, continuing His work of bringing salvation to humanity after His ascension to heaven.

It is profoundly clear this was not a period of silence but of fulfillment. God's plan of redemption was coming to pass. He was paving a way for the Messiah to come and for the spread of the good news of salvation in Him—while at the same time dealing with the Jewish people's ongoing rebellion.

Detail of Alexander the Great, mosaic (c. 100 BC)

Alexander's Conquests, 334–323 BC

LOCATION

Cyrus the Great founded the Persian Empire in the sixth century BC. It was located in western and central Asia, and eventually stretched from the Indus Valley in the east to Thrace and Macedon on the northeastern border of Greece. At the pinnacle of its power, the Persian Empire spread out over three continents: Asia, Africa, and Europe. The Persians also ruled over nations such as Iran, Iraq, Syria, Jordan, Israel, and Lebanon. When Alexander conquered the Persian Empire for Greece, he took over a vast territory.

Issus is close to the present-day Turkish town of Iskenderun. Tyre is an ancient Phoenician city in modern-day Lebanon.

KEY PLAYERS

- Alexander the Great: the son of King Philip II of Macedon; king of Macedon upon his father's death in 336 BC
- Darius III: the last king of the Persian Empire, who ruled from 336 to 330 BC

WEAPONS AND WARRIORS

One of the unique weapons employed by Alexander the Great was the *sarissa*, invented by his father. The sarissa was a long spear with a heavy metal tip. These spears were held by Greek troops while advancing in formation; they protruded out from the formation to deter the enemy from charging.

Alexander the Great

Battle Synopsis

In November of 333 BC, Alexander met Darius in battle at a mountain pass south of Issus. The Persian army outnumbered the Greeks, and they would have had the advantage in an open field. Yet the narrow battlefield on this mountain pass allowed Alexander to defeat the Persians, even though Darius escaped. After the battle, Alexander captured Darius's war chest along with his family in Damascus. After taking the Persian kingdom, Alexander marched down the Phoenician coast with his powerful army, forcing the surrender of all the major cities there—except Tyre, which held out for seven months before conceding defeat in 332 BC. Alexander was far from satisfied, though. He acquired the Holy Land in 332 BC and continued south into Egypt.

OUTCOME

SHORT-TERM

In a very short time, Alexander was able to conquer the land east of the Mediterranean, including Syria, Egypt, Persia, and Babylonia. The Jews did not resist Alexander's advancement, since he allowed them to maintain a level of independence.

LONG-TERM

These conquests encouraged the spread of Greek language and culture, a phenomenon known as Hellenization. This led to the emergence of *koine* Greek as the common language in the civilized world.

GOD'S ROLE

Hundreds of years before Alexander began his conquest, God allowed Daniel to see into the future: The Greeks would someday rule over what at that time was the Babylonian Empire (Daniel 2:39). When it finally came to pass, it may have looked as though Alexander was in charge; but only God has the power to remove kings and set up kings (Daniel 2:21). God had a purpose and a plan for the events at this exact point in history. He used the Greeks to establish a unified language for a large portion of the world, which allowed the Word of God to be recorded so that all people could read it. Missionaries were able to speak to people in diverse parts of the world. Through Alexander, God prepared the way for the message of Jesus to be proclaimed to much of the known world.

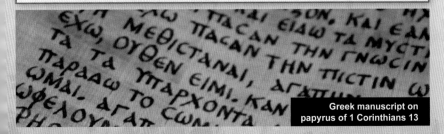

Greek manuscript on papyrus of 1 Corinthians 13

Ptolemaic Domination of Israel, 323–198 BC
DANIEL 8:8, 21-22

LOCATION

After Alexander the Great died, the kingdom was carved up into four regions under four different rulers. Ptolemy I Soter was given control of Egypt, as well as the land of Israel. The Seleucid Empire began with Seleucus I Nicator, who ruled Persia and the nations in that region. The Seleucid dynasty of Syria and the Ptolemaic dynasty of Egypt constantly fought over control of the region from Persia to Egypt. Six major wars were fought in the regions of southern Israel and northern Egypt during their reigns.

KEY PLAYERS

Ptolemaic rulers: members of the Macedonian Greek royal family who ruled the Ptolemaic Empire in Egypt during the Hellenistic period

Seleucid rulers: members of a Greek dynasty founded by Seleucus I Nicator following the division of the empire that had been forged by Alexander the Great

WEAPONS AND WARRIORS

These wars were fought among the divided Greek army. Therefore, the rival groups would have been equally well equipped with horses that were experienced in battle as well as disciplined foot soldiers who knew how to stay in formation during the chaos of battle. The Greek army had developed the use of spies on covert missions to disrupt the enemy from behind enemy lines.

Ancient Greek helmet

BATTLE SYNOPSIS

Alexander's death in 323 BC unleashed a power struggle for control of his empire. Conflict between his four leading generals eventually led to the establishment of two great dynasties: the Ptolemies, centered in Egypt, and the Seleucids, based in Syria. Because Israel was strategically located between Syria and Egypt, the nation was caught in a constant tug-of-war between these two rivals. The Ptolemies gained control of Israel and ruled its people for 125 years; thousands of Jews were deported to Egypt. The two empires fought six major conflicts, which are known as the Syrian Wars.

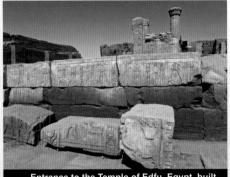

Entrance to the Temple of Edfu, Egypt, built during the Ptolemaic period
© Sphinx Wang / Shutterstock.com

The Jews lived in relative peace and prosperity under Ptolemaic rule. Their overlords allowed them to maintain their religious freedom during this time.

OUTCOME

SHORT-TERM

The city of Alexandria, Egypt, developed into a major center of scholarship and learning. A Greek translation of the Old Testament, the Septuagint, was produced during this period, marking a major achievement in the transmission of God's Word.

LONG-TERM

Centuries later, the Septuagint would provide Christians throughout the Mediterranean world with an understandable translation of the Bible. The early church was able to teach from the Old Testament in a language almost everyone could understand.

GOD'S ROLE

The God of the Bible is a missionary God who is interested in making sure that His glory can be seen by all creation and that His Word can be heard and understood. When Jews were deported to Egypt, they were placed in one of the centers of academic study in the ancient world. Because of this, they were able to translate the scriptures, as well as other writings, into a language that the entire Mediterranean world was able to understand. Even though Israel seemed to be a pawn in a global war for power between two pagan kings, God was at work laying the foundation for the worldwide proclamation of His Word.

Seleucid Domination of Israel, 198–166 BC

LOCATION

A key battle was fought near Paneas, also called Banias (Caesarea Philippi), in 198 BC. Paneas was located in northern Israel, southwest of Mount Hermon and close to the source of the Jordan River. The city was green with lush vegetation. The surrounding region, known as the Paneion, was dotted with shrines dedicated to the Greek god Pan. The name of the city of Paneas was changed to Caesarea Philippi during the period of Roman rule. Today Paneas is known as Banyas.

KEY PLAYERS

Ptolemaic rulers: members of the Macedonian Greek royal family who ruled the Ptolemaic Empire in Egypt during the Hellenistic period

Seleucid rulers: members of a Greek dynasty founded by Seleucus I Nicator following the division of the empire that had been forged by Alexander the Great

Antiochus III: the Seleucid king of the Hellenistic Syrian Empire from 223 to 187 BC

WEAPONS AND WARRIORS

There are few records of this battle, but what ensured the Seleucid army's victory was its use of the *cataphract* in a decisive manner. The cataphract was an armored cavalry of sorts. Both horse and rider were covered with a protective armor made up of small metal rings or plates joined together called chain mail.

Battle Synopsis

There was constant war and strife between the Ptolemies of Egypt and the Seleucids of Syria. The Seleucids failed repeatedly to gain control of Israel until 198 BC, when the Seleucid ruler Antiochus III defeated Egypt at Paneas near the sources of the Jordan. The Egyptian army was attacked from the side with cataphracts. Seleucid cataphracts promptly attacked the Egyptian infantry from the rear, giving victory to the Seleucids. The Seleucids occupied Israel, and Jerusalem evolved into a primarily Greek city. This battle marked the end of Ptolemaic rule in Judea.

Outcome

Short-Term

Some Jews welcomed the encroaching Hellenization of Jerusalem; other more conservative Jewish groups opposed it.

Long-Term

This dark period in Jewish history eventually led to a rebellion against the Seleucids, known as the Maccabean Revolt, followed by a brief period of Jewish independence.

God's Role

God is always involved in world history, and He was no less involved in this takeover of Israel. The resulting Hellenization of the nation propelled the Jews into mainstream Greek culture and language, preparing both the Jewish people and the surrounding nations for the Messiah's arrival and the spread of the gospel.

Spring of Banias River (Caesarea Philippi), northern Israel. Pan's cave is in the background.

The Maccabean Revolt, 166—135 BC

DANIEL 11:21-35

LOCATION

The Maccabean Revolt occurred in Judea. When Antiochus IV Epiphanes (Daniel 11:21) took over Israel, he entered Jerusalem and defiled the temple. A Jewish priest named Mattathias refused to offer pagan sacrifices and fled to the uninhabited Judaean wilderness, an ideal place of refuge. His sons took over the resistance after he died and fought from the wilderness of Judea all the way to Jerusalem to regain control of Israel.

KEY PLAYERS

- Mattathias: a priest who refused to offer sacrifices to Greek gods in the Jewish temple and gathered an army of rebels to fight the Seleucids
- Judas: Mattathias's son who took his father's place leading the revolt after his father's death in 166 or 165 BC
- Simon: one of Judas's brothers, who established a line of priest-kings who would rule Israel until the Roman occupation began in 63 BC
- Antiochus IV Epiphanes: a Greek king of the Seleucid Empire from 175 to 164 BC, who was known for his irrational behavior

WEAPONS AND WARRIORS

The band of Jewish rebels called the Maccabees effectively used guerrilla warfare tactics against the larger, stronger Greek army. Such tactics may have included ambushes, sabotage, raids, petty warfare, and hit-and-run attacks. These fighters possessed extraordinary mobility to wage war against the larger and less mobile Greek army. The name *Maccabees* is derived from the Hebrew word for "hammer." They were appropriately named; when the Maccabees attacked, they came down on the enemy like a hammer.

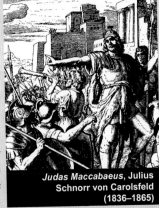

Judas Maccabaeus, Julius Schnorr von Carolsfeld (1836–1865)

BATTLE SYNOPSIS

Antiochus IV Epiphanes, an evil villain and persecutor of the Jews, attempted to impose Greek culture on every aspect of life in Israel. In 168 BC, he ordered the building of an altar to Zeus in the Jewish temple. He banned circumcision. He ordered pigs to be sacrificed on the altar—an outright desecration of God's holy dwelling place. A Jewish priest named Mattathias and his five sons (John, Simon, Eleazar, Jonathan, and Judah) led a revolt against Antiochus. Judah became known as "Judah the Hammer," or Judas Maccabaeus. After Mattathias died, Judah took his father's place as leader; and in 165 BC, the Jews emerged victorious. The temple was cleansed, and a new altar was built in place of the defiled one.

According to Jewish literature, pure olive oil was needed for the temple menorah, which was required to burn constantly. While cleansing the temple, a flask with enough oil for one day was found, yet it miraculously burned for eight days—the exact time needed to prepare a fresh supply of oil. An eight-day festival ("Feast of Dedication," John 10:22), known today as Hanukkah, was declared by Jewish leaders to celebrate and commemorate this miracle.

Tombs of the Maccabees

Judah's brother Simon formed the Hasmonaean dynasty two decades later.

OUTCOME

SHORT-TERM

Antiochus left an infant son named Antiochus V Eupator as his only heir. A series of civil wars erupted between rival claimants to the throne after the death of Antiochus IV, effectively crippling the Seleucid Empire.

LONG-TERM

Five main Jewish sects emerged after the Maccabean revolt: the Pharisees, Sadducees, Essenes, Herodians, and Zealots. Each was based on their own interpretation of scripture, how best to relate to government, and what role tradition played in the life of the community of the faithful.

GOD'S ROLE

Confronted with yet another struggle, the people of Israel faced a crisis of faith. Could God be trusted to protect the nation, and especially the temple, from defilement at the hand of Gentiles? God used the Maccabees, a family who hung on to His promises to the Jewish people, to purge the nation of sin and restore it spiritually. God gave the Maccabees wisdom and strength to fight a battle they should not have been able to win on their own. Even though the Greeks dominated Israel, God was stronger and delivered His people.

Military Heroes and Villains: Antiochus IV Epiphanes

During much of this intertestamental period, the Greeks ruled over Israel. After Alexander the Great died, his kingdom was divided among four leaders. Seleucus, a commander who took control of the Syrian region, established the Seleucid dynasty. Antiochus IV, an evil, arrogant tyrant, was the eighth Seleucid king; he ruled from about 175 to 164 BC. He took on the name Epiphanes, which means "manifest one" or "select of God." The Jewish people hated him and nicknamed him Epimanes, meaning "madman."

When Antiochus IV came to power, he was no friend of the Jews, to say the least. He tried to wipe out all forms of Jewish worship and even tried to annihilate the Jews. Any Jew who refused to worship Greek gods, was put to death. Praying to God or observing the Sabbath was a capital offense. If a male infant was circumcised, he was killed along with his mother. Antiochus IV looted the temple and increased taxes. With no respect for the priesthood, he sold the office of high priest to the highest bidder—first to Jason, the brother of high priest Onias III, and later to a man named Menelaus (who did not even descend from the priestly line). This solidified the full Hellenization, or influence of ancient Greek culture, of Jerusalem.

Bust of Antiochus IV Epiphanes

The most disgraceful thing that Antiochus IV did against the Jews occurred in 168 BC. He entered the temple in Jerusalem, erected an altar to the pagan god Zeus, and sacrificed pigs on it. In Judaism, pigs are considered unclean animals. These acts desecrated the temple and triggered the Maccabean Revolt. The Maccabees' victory over Antiochus IV and their subsequent cleansing of the temple are still commemorated by Jews today with the annual festival of Hanukkah. Antiochus IV's calculated and ruthless attempts to eradicate Judaism were not quickly forgotten by the Jews. The "madman" is remembered in Jewish history as the personification of evil.

Rock carving of the seven-branched menorah, one of the oldest symbols of the Jewish people

Pompey's Capture of Jerusalem, 63 BC

DANIEL 7:7

LOCATION

As Israel's capital, Jerusalem was the most important and influential city in the country. When Pompey set out to conquer the Judaean region, he had to consider taking Jerusalem. First-century historian Josephus recorded in *The Wars of the Jews* (1.14) that the walls of Jerusalem were so firm that it would be hard for anyone to overcome them. He noted that the temple rested behind the city's high and strong walls and the valley surrounding these walls was treacherous. Even if the city was taken, the temple provided a second place of refuge for the Jews living in the city.

KEY PLAYERS

- Pompey the Great: a Roman military general and political leader from about 82 to 48 BC
- Hyrcanus II: a member of the Hasmonaean dynasty who was appointed by the Romans as Jewish high priest and "ethnarch," or minor ruler, of Judea
- Antipater I: Hyrcanus's adviser, who was made governor of Judea by Roman authorities and held the real power behind the throne; Herod the Great's father
- Phasael: Antipater's son who was captured by Antigonus and later committed suicide
- Herod the Great: Antipater's son who appealed to the Romans for help and was subsequently appointed king of Judea

WEAPONS AND WARRIORS

By the time of Pompey, the Roman military was a full-time military force recruited from Roman citizens. These soldiers did more than just fight; they also helped with provincial law enforcement. In addition, they were involved in constructing military and civil infrastructure, including forts and fortified defenses, roads, bridges, ports, public buildings, and entire cities.

Roman soldiers

Battle Synopsis

Pompey the Great seized Jerusalem in 63 BC. Pompey had been asked to intercede in a civil war between Hyrcanus II and Aristobulus II for the Hasmonaean kingdom of Israel. Pompey conquered Jerusalem, bringing an end to Jewish independence; Israel was integrated into the Roman Republic.

The Romans made Hyrcanus II high priest and ruler of the people, but his was only a puppet regime. The real power behind the throne belonged to Hyrcanus's adviser, a man named Antipater, who had captured the attention of Roman authorities. The Romans installed Antipater as governor of Judea and appointed his sons Phasael and Herod as military governors of Jerusalem and Galilee. Antipater was an Edomite, not a Jew, but the Romans didn't differentiate between the two.

Bust of Pompey

Antipater was killed in 43 BC. A power struggle erupted between Antigonus, the son of Aristobulus II, and Antipater's two sons, Herod and Phasael. Phasael committed suicide, but Herod fled to Rome and was appointed king of Judea. He returned to Israel with a Roman army and promptly defeated and executed Antigonus, the last of the Hasmonaean rulers. The Herodian dynasty began.

Outcome

Short-Term

The Jewish nation was weakened by the power struggle between the two Hasmonaeans, allowing Rome to gain power over Jerusalem. As a result, Herod—a Gentile—was appointed king of Judea.

Long-Term

The end of the Hasmonaean dynasty paved the way for the Herodian dynasty, which ruled during Jesus' lifetime.

God's Role

God had already revealed to the prophet Daniel that Rome would dominate Israel one day (Daniel 2:33–40; 7). His plan was to bring about His Messiah not only through the line of Judah and from the house of David, but into a Roman world. Why would God do this? The answer shows His brilliance. The established Roman infrastructure allowed for the message about Jesus to be carried throughout much of the world. The Romans had developed a strong road system, which carried the message of the gospel quickly after Jesus' death and resurrection. Rome's established political system allowed for Roman citizens to travel from country to country without hindrance. Though they may not have known it, kings, leaders, and all peoples of this earth were used by God to achieve His redemptive purposes.

Roman Rule/Pax Romana

The *Pax Romana*, or "the peace of Rome," began with Augustus's accession to power in 31 BC; it lasted until AD 180 when Marcus Aurelius died. During this time, Roman soldiers patrolled borders with success, and the empire was relatively free from major invasion, piracy, and social disorder. Arts and architecture advanced, along with commerce and a strong economy. The Pax Romana marked an age of political and economic stability for the Roman Empire.

Statue of Caesar Augustus, first emperor of the Roman Empire

With this new peace came relative freedom of travel, and the construction of massive Roman road systems opened the door for Christianity to spread within the empire rapidly. The Roman legal system brought a sense of justice to the land, and this afforded early Christians some small measure of legal protection—especially as they traveled from town to town sharing the gospel.

This peace was not birthed from moral or altruistic motives, however. The Pax Romana existed only because the military constantly suppressed revolt. Roman soldiers were ruthless, and they frequently imposed control over people without much legal recourse. Anyone who appeared to be a threat to Roman peace was dealt with severely.

The Romans allowed the Jews to freely dictate their own government, but this freedom was limited to enforcing laws in Israel consistent with Roman law or practice. One way the Roman government maintained control was by taxing the Jews once a year, a tax affirming their allegiance to the Roman emperor as their supreme ruler. This tax infuriated many devout Jews and eventually stirred them to revolt against Rome.

24

Reassembled Altar of Peace, constructed by Caesar Augustus to celebrate his inauguration of the Pax Romana

Roman road through the mountains of Spain

Jewish Revolt, AD 66—73
MATTHEW 24:1-8

LOCATION

Jerusalem found itself again at the center of the military stage. As Rome increased its oppression of Israel, the Jews grew more and more frustrated. Their anger eventually boiled over into revolt against the Roman superpower. Jerusalem rested on a plateau 2,500 feet above sea level between the Mediterranean Sea and the Dead Sea, in the Judaean Mountains. The city was surrounded by the Kidron Valley on the east and the Hinnom Valley on the south and west.

KEY PLAYERS

- Vespasian: a skilled military commander who became the Roman emperor. He gave his son Titus the honor of delivering the final deathblow to the Jews who revolted and to the city of Jerusalem.
- Titus: the son of Vespasian who ended the Jewish rebellion and later succeeded his father as a Roman emperor

WEAPONS AND WARRIORS

Jewish rebels began this war as a protest, attacking Roman citizens but not the entire Roman army. They first employed guerrilla tactics, rather than waging a full-scale offensive. Eventually, the rebels graduated from attacking citizens to assassinating soldiers stationed at the Roman military garrison in Judea.

Marble statue of Emperor Titus

BATTLE SYNOPSIS

The Romans used oppressive force to keep the peace in their empire. The Jews became increasingly frustrated and angry at the burden of heavy taxation and being forced to contribute to Rome's wicked leadership. Their frustration soon escalated into protest.

The Romans quickly suppressed these minor outbreaks of resistance. Soon, however, stronger revolts erupted, leading to a full-scale rebellion in AD 66. Jewish masses wiped out the small Roman militia stationed in Jerusalem. The Roman ruler in neighboring Syria, Cestius Gallus, responded with a larger garrison of soldiers, which the Jewish revolutionaries promptly drove off as well.

It looked like the Jews could possibly defeat Rome. However, when the Romans returned in AD 67, led by General Vespasian, they attacked with sixty thousand heavily armed and highly professional fighters. Later, Vespasian's son Titus took over the assault. In July of AD 70, the Romans burned the city of Jerusalem and left the temple in ruins. The rebellion dragged on for another three years after Jerusalem was destroyed, until the last pockets of resistance were finally extinguished. The last Jewish stronghold to fall was a fortress on a mountaintop at Masada, in the desert near the Dead Sea. When the Romans finally broke through Masada's walls, they found more than nine hundred dead Jewish rebels inside; they had chosen to commit suicide rather than surrender or face a massacre.

OUTCOME

SHORT-TERM

Approximately one million Jews died as a result of the revolt against Rome. Those who survived fled from Jerusalem, utterly demoralized.

LONG-TERM

This Jewish revolt paved the way for the Bar Kokhba revolt some sixty years later. Together these two rebellions contributed to the total loss of Jewish political authority in the land until the modern state of Israel was recognized in 1948.

GOD'S ROLE

Time and time again, the people of Israel demonstrated they wanted to rule the land apart from God. Thus He allowed the rebellion against the Romans and the resulting consequences. Yet what looked like ultimate defeat was actually part of God's promises coming to pass. Back in the time of Abraham, God had promised that Israel would become the vehicle of blessing for the entire world, God's means of salvation for the nations. However, God also knew the hearts of people; He knew the people He chose for this great purpose would rebel against Him. The result of this rebellion left the Jews scattered throughout the world, exactly as God had said (Deuteronomy 28:64). And yet God had promised, "I will bless those who bless you, and him who dishonors you I will curse, and in you *all the families of the earth shall be blessed*" (Genesis 12:3, emphasis added). Even though the people of Israel were dispersed to foreign lands, God did not (and will not) take His eyes off them.

The Fall of Jerusalem, AD 70
MATTHEW 24:1-8; LUKE 19:44; 21:5-6

LOCATION

Jerusalem, as it had so many times in its long history, found itself in the center of a major conflict. The Romans used soldiers who were home from war to fortify major cities in their empire. Because Israel was situated in the center of a major trade route, Jerusalem—Israel's capital—became the focus of Roman attention. Rome strengthened Jerusalem's walls to protect it against invading armies. When the Jews revolted against Rome, the work Rome invested in making the city a secure citadel became an obstacle.

KEY PLAYERS

- Emperor Nero: a Roman emperor who committed suicide rather than face assassination for allegedly burning Rome to make room for construction of the extravagant Domus Aurea villa
- Vespasian: a skilled military commander who became the Roman emperor. He gave his son Titus the honor of delivering the final deathblow to the Jews who revolted and to the city of Jerusalem.
- Titus: the son of Vespasian who ended the Jewish rebellion and later succeeded his father as a Roman emperor

WEAPONS AND WARRIORS

Titus, the Roman commander, surrounded Jerusalem with three squadrons on the western side of the city and one on the Mount of Olives to the east. He deceitfully allowed Jewish pilgrims to enter Jerusalem to celebrate the Feast of Passover but then denied them safe passage out of the city. The sudden increase in population affected food and water supplies, which rapidly deteriorated. Eventually, the Romans breached Jerusalem's walls. Josephus recorded that the Romans torched the city and its temple; these fires were still burning a month after the war was over.

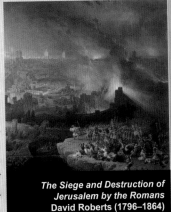

The Siege and Destruction of Jerusalem by the Romans
David Roberts (1796–1864)

Detail on the *Arch of Titus*, showing Roman soldiers carrying away the spoils of the temple, including the menorah

BATTLE SYNOPSIS

Fed up with the corruption of wealthy aristocrats and landowners, severe Roman taxation, the threat of Roman opposition, and an incompetent Roman administration, the Jews rebelled against Rome in AD 66. In response, Emperor Nero sent his army, under the leadership of General Vespasian, to restore order. By the year 68, the rebellion in northern Israel had been squashed, so the Romans turned their attention to Jerusalem. That same year, Emperor Nero committed suicide, creating a power vacuum in Rome. Chaos ensued. Vespasian was eventually declared emperor and took the throne in Rome, leaving his son Titus to lead the final assault on Jerusalem.

The Triumph of Titus, Lawrence Alma-Tadema (1836–1912)

Masada, the fortress where Jewish Zealots held out for several years against Rome

Roman legions surrounded Jerusalem and cut off its food and water supplies. After a nightmarish three-year siege, Roman soldiers breached Jerusalem's outer walls and ransacked the city. The assault culminated in the complete destruction of Herod's magnificent temple, the center of Jewish worship, which was burned to the ground. Many Jews died from starvation. Many thousands more were killed by the Romans, who showed no mercy to their enemies.

Those who escaped death were enslaved and sent to work in Egyptian mines or dispersed throughout the empire to gladiatorial arenas, where they were butchered for public entertainment. Sacred artifacts from the temple were brought to Rome and displayed in glorification of the empire's victory. The remains of the temple burned for close to a month, ensuring its utter destruction.

OUTCOME

SHORT-TERM

Jesus' prediction regarding Herod's temple—namely, that not one stone would be left standing (Matthew 24:1–3)—came true. Judea was reorganized as a Roman province, and a permanent Roman military unit was stationed at Caesarea.

LONG-TERM

The war transformed Judaism. The priestly clan disappeared from history, and synagogue worship replaced the sacrificial system.

GOD'S ROLE

Jesus predicted that Jerusalem would face destruction (Luke 19:41–44) and that the temple would be destroyed (Matthew 24:1–2). The Jewish revolt and the destruction of the temple did not occur outside of God's control. Their survivors' dispersion to the four corners of the earth was evidence of God's faithfulness to His Word. God had told the Israelites thousands of years before the fall of Jerusalem that if they disobeyed Him, He would "scatter [them] among the peoples, and [they would] be left few in number among the nations" (Deuteronomy 4:27; see also Psalm 106:24–27). For the next nineteen hundred years, the Jews would not live in or control the land God had promised their ancestors.

The Jews' dispersion to distant lands was not permanent, and the destruction of Jerusalem was not Israel's final chapter. God promised that after a period of time known only to Him, He would bring His people back into the land. Many believe that the prophet Isaiah spoke of this future for Israel when he said: "In that day the Lord will extend his hand yet a second time to recover the remnant that remains of his people, from Assyria, from Egypt, from Pathros, from Cush, from Elam, from Shinar, from Hamath, and from the coastlands of the sea. He will raise a signal for the nations and will assemble the banished of Israel, and gather the dispersed of Judah from the four corners of the earth" (Isaiah 11:11–12).

Bar Kokhba Revolt, AD 132–135

LOCATION

The final battle of the Bar Kokhba revolt took place seven miles southwest of Jerusalem in Bethar, Bar Kokhba's headquarters, which housed both the Sanhedrin (the Jewish high court) and the nasi (the leader of the Sanhedrin). Bethar was an important military stronghold. Strategically located on a rocky mountain ridge, Bethar looked out on the Jerusalem–Beit Guvrin Road and the Valley of Sorek. The city was bordered by the Valley of Rephaim on the east, north, and west. Jewish refugees escaped to Bethar by the thousands during the Bar Kokhba revolt.

KEY PLAYERS

- Hadrian: a Roman emperor who suppressed the Bar Kokhba revolt in Judea
- Simon bar Kokhba: the charismatic Jewish leader of the Bar Kokhba revolt against the Roman Empire

WEAPONS AND WARRIORS

Simon bar Kokhba mustered an army of four hundred thousand fighters. By the time of the Bar Kokhba revolt, the ballista was a common weapon used by the Romans. The ballista could accurately launch missiles at targets a great distance away.

Copy of an ancient Roman ballista

Battle Synopsis

Another Jewish rebellion broke out when, according to one tradition, Emperor Hadrian banned circumcision and ordered the building of a temple to Jupiter on the Jewish Temple Mount. Initially, the Bar Kokhba revolt was a success. Kokhba created a mini-state within Judea, minted coins, and declared it the "Era of Redemption of Israel." The Romans were taken by surprise but soon amassed an army larger than the one Titus led during the first great revolt. War broke out for three years between Israel and Rome until finally, in 135 BC, the Jewish forces were brutally crushed. Roman losses were heavy, too. After being driven from many of their strongholds, Kokhba and his few remaining soldiers retreated to the fortress of Bethar. Betrayed by insiders who revealed its secret fortifications, Bethar fell to the Romans on Tishah-b'Ab, the ninth day of the month of Ab, in AD 135.

Stone bullets of an early Roman ballista

Outcome

Short-Term

Jewish independence was lost. Surviving Jews were sold into slavery, and many were transported to Egypt. The Romans banned Jews from entering Jerusalem, and Jewish resistance came to an end.

Long-Term

Jerusalem was renamed Aelia Capitolina and it became a pagan city. Herodotus replaced the name *Judea* on maps with the name *Syria Palaestina*. From this point the region became known as Palestine.

God's Role

Centuries before the Bar Kokhba revolt, God had warned His people with the following words:

> "But if you will not listen to me and will not do all these commandments, if you spurn my statutes, and if your soul abhors my rules, so that you will not do all my commandments, but break my covenant, then I will do this to you: I will visit you with panic, with wasting disease and fever that consume the eyes and make the heart ache. And you shall sow your seed in vain, for your enemies shall eat it. I will set my face against you, and you shall be struck down before your enemies. Those who hate you shall rule over you, and you shall flee when none pursues you." (Leviticus 26:14–17)

Military Heroes and Villains: Simon bar Kokhba

One of the great leaders and legends in the history of Judaism is Simon bar Kokhba. Not much has been written about Simon as a leader, except for the iron fist with which he ruled and the large, forbidding army he amassed. Each of his four hundred thousand soldiers was supposedly strong enough to uproot a cedar tree. Kokhba practiced a strict form of Judaism, adhering to Jewish laws that included keeping the Sabbath, paying tithes, and observing the festivals.

Taking Rome by force was Kokhba's intent. Under his leadership, the Jews seized towns throughout Judea and fortified them with walls and underground passages. If a city was under siege, the Jewish people living there used these underground passages to sneak food and water in and out of the city. Kokhba captured about fifty strongholds in Judea and just under one thousand undefended towns and villages, including Jerusalem. Soon Kokhba was able to mint coins; the people believed they were finally going to achieve the deliverance they had fought for.

A famous rabbi of this time, Rabbi Akiva, gave Simon the surname "bar Kokhba," meaning "son of a star" in the Aramaic language. This idea came from a messianic prophecy in Numbers 24:17: "A star shall come out of Jacob." Akiva was crowning Kokhba the Messiah. Kokhba vowed to rebuild the temple in Jerusalem, which was one of the things the promised Messiah was supposed to do, according to the prophets and Jewish tradition. However, Kokhba never rebuilt the temple.

After it was discovered that someone was revealing Kokhba's military secrets to the Romans, Kokhba grew paranoid. He accused a highly respectable rabbi named Elazar of being a traitor and had the rabbi executed, a move that cost him the support of the rabbis. They began calling him "Bar Koziba," or "son of a lie." Their hopes that Kokhba was the promised Messiah were dashed. After three and a half years of revolt, the Romans proved too powerful for the Jews; Kokhba died in battle at Bethar in the Judaean hills.

Iron tips of Roman
catapult missiles

Things to Think About

- During this period there were some Jews who led the nation well, while there were others who did not. What are some of the differences you can spot among the different leaders?

- How does the book of Daniel help us understand the period between the Old and New Testaments?

- What are some of the characteristics you learned about God from this chapter?

- What are some of the characteristics you learned about human beings from this chapter?

- What are some of the lessons you learned about what happens when you do not listen to God?

- What did you learn about God's control over the world from this chapter?

- How did God use this period in history to set the table for the advancement of the church throughout the world?

Close-up of the *Fall of Jerusalem*, Francesco Hayez (1791–1882)

Chapter 11

BATTLES TO COME

"They will make war on the Lamb, and the Lamb will conquer them, for he is Lord of lords and King of kings, and those with him are called and chosen and faithful."

(Revelation 17:14)

INTRODUCTION

According to tradition, one of Jesus' most loyal followers, John, had been taken captive, bound in chains, and thrown in jail because of his devotion to Jesus. He was taken from his cell and severely beaten. When he survived that, he was exiled to a remote island called Patmos to live by himself for the remainder of his life.

But John was not the only one who faced persecution—many others were arrested, beaten, and even killed for their steadfast love for and faith in Jesus, whom they claimed was the long-awaited Jewish Messiah—God incarnate. God, in His omnipotence, knew that members of the early church needed encouragement; they needed to know that evil would not win, that Jesus is not powerless, and that justice will one day come to this earth. Satan will be defeated; those who have acted in horrifying ways toward the church will face God's wrath.

While banished to the island of Patmos, John heard the voice of the risen Christ, from heaven, saying, "Come up here, and I will show you what must take place after this" (Revelation 4:1). In His kindness, Jesus did just that: He revealed to John things to come. Many scholars believe Revelation was written around

AD 95. The visions in John's book affirm other Old Testament writings foretelling future conflict.

The book of Revelation, also known as the Apocalypse, is not simply the record of battles to come; it reveals the future culmination of all of God's promises to humanity. It records the coming victory of Jesus over evil. John's writing tells of the kingdom of God and how it will overcome the kingdoms of this world, and how just and fair punishment will come to those who oppose God and His children. Every follower of Jesus who has faced oppression or persecution will find hope in understanding the battles described in Revelation. Jesus Christ is the supreme Judge and King of the world, and all men and women will one day give an account to Him.

There is debate among scholars of how to understand these wars. The position held by this author is that these passages refer to future, literal conflicts. However, each person must answer for themselves the following questions: Was John describing things that took place in his lifetime, a long progression of events between then and the end of history, or future occasions? Or are they symbolic representations of timeless realities? Should these battles be read as stories, as historical events, or as allegories? While these questions will continue to be debated, the key to understanding Revelation is to remember one simple truth: Jesus is the final Judge of the living and the dead, the righteous and the wicked (see Ecclesiastes 3:17). On that final day, the Lord will judge "the secrets of men by Christ Jesus" (Romans 2:16), and only those whose names are written in the book of life will be allowed to enter His eternal kingdom (Revelation 20:11–15).

A rock on the island of Patmos, Greece

However you interpret the battles in Revelation, the judgment they depict is real. At some point in the future, according to God's calendar, history will culminate in Jesus' rightful reign forever on earth. The apostle Paul reminded the church in Thessalonica that those who persecute the church will someday face God's wrath.

26

[Your suffering] is evidence of the righteous judgment of God, that you may be considered worthy of the kingdom of God, for which you are also suffering—since indeed God considers it just to repay with affliction those who afflict you, and to grant relief to you who are afflicted as well as to us, when the Lord Jesus is revealed from heaven with his mighty angels in flaming fire, inflicting vengeance on those who do not know God and on those who do not obey the gospel of our Lord Jesus. They will suffer the punishment of eternal destruction, away from the presence of the Lord and from the glory of his might, when he comes on that day to be glorified in his saints, and to be marveled at among all who have believed, because our testimony to you was believed. (2 Thessalonians 1:5–10)

John on the Island of Patmos
Jacopo Vignali (1592–1664)

Find comfort and hope in these words. Jesus wins! Justice will come. Evil be done away with once and for all.

Battle of Gog and Magog
EZEKIEL 38-39; REVELATION 20:7-10

LOCATION

In John's vision, the nations of the earth are deceived by Satan and attempt to dethrone Jesus. They surround "the camp of the saints and the beloved city" (Revelation 20:9)—apparently a reference to Jerusalem—to make war against Jesus.

Some see this event as a literal war that will take place in Jerusalem at a future point after the millennium. Others see it as an event that has already taken place in Jerusalem many years ago. Still others see it as an allegory that describes the constant spirit of rebellion that Jesus will put an end to one day. Many believe this battle is the same as the one described as the last battle (see page 272).

KEY PLAYERS

- Gog: the leader of a great army attacking the land of Israel in Ezekiel 38–39. Gog is described as coming from the land of Magog, and as the prince of Meshech and Tubal. He is also described as a military and political leader, as well as a coalition builder.

- Magog: a son of Japheth and grandson of Noah (Genesis 10:2) whose descendants likely settled north of Israel, near the Black Sea. In Ezekiel, Magog may refer to a people (see 39:6), or it could mean the "land of Gog."

WEAPONS AND WARRIORS

In John's vision, nations gather with all their powerless man-made weapons to bring an end to Jesus' rule. In Ezekiel's vision, the land of Israel experiences a great earthquake, and people kill each other out of fear (Ezekiel 38:21); even the animals are distressed. The entire world is overrun by disaster from "divine weapons." Great rain, terrible hail, fire, and burning sulfur pour down on Israel's enemies.

Battle Synopsis

Revelation describes Satan's release from prison after one thousand years; he is set free to deceive the nations and gather them for a climactic battle. There is some debate as to how to understand this war. Some believe it is the same conflict described in Revelation 16:13–16 and 19:17–21. Others see it as a completely different battle occurring at the end of the age. In Revelation 20, Satan's armies are referred to as Gog and Magog—symbolic titles for oppressors who will gather against God and His people to destroy them. However, God is depicted calling down fire from heaven to annihilate His enemies (see also Ezekiel 38:22; 39:6).

Outcome

Short-Term

God protects His people. God's enemies are destroyed in one battle.

Long-Term

Those who have sought to dethrone Jesus as King of kings and Lord of lords are finally destroyed. The people of God are forever secure. Satan is finally done away with. In the end, Satan will be forever defeated and thrown into a lake of fire and sulfur.

God's Role

Since the fall, humankind has stood in opposition to the rule of God on earth. As nations formed and kingdoms emerged, leaders fought not just to advance their personal interests but to confiscate the kingly rule and reign that is reserved for Jesus alone (Psalm 2). One day God will put an end to this by wiping out all vestiges of rebellion and bringing complete justice to the world. "But on that day, the day that Gog shall come against the land of Israel, declares the Lord God, my wrath will be roused in my anger. For in my jealousy and in my blazing wrath I declare, On that day there shall be a great earthquake in the land of Israel" (Ezekiel 38:18–19).

Military Heroes and Villains: Michael

Archangel Michael

THE ILLUSTRATED GUIDE TO BIBLE BATTLES

God has authority over both His physical created world that we can see and a very active spiritual realm. He allows angels to cross the divide into our world to protect His children from the evil of Satan and his forces. Michael is one of these angels.

Michael's name means "who is like God?" This contrasts Satan's rebellious words to Yahweh: "*I will make myself like* the Most High" (Isaiah 14:14, emphasis added). Michael is called an archangel in the Bible and plays a unique and crucial role in heaven and on earth. *Archangel* means "chief angel," indicating that Michael holds a high rank in heaven; he is the only angel in the Bible designated as an archangel.

In the book of Daniel, Michael is identified as Israel's protector, the guardian of God's people. Michael appeared as a great warrior who assisted Gabriel by defeating the demonic "prince of the kingdom of Persia" (Daniel 10:13); this defeat allowed Gabriel to reach Daniel and explain Daniel's visions to him. In a later vision, Daniel was informed that Michael will continue to protect Israel in the end of days. "At that time shall arise Michael, the great prince who has charge of your people. And there shall be a time of trouble, such as never has been since there was a nation till that time" (Daniel 12:1).

In an account found only in Jude 9, Michael has a dispute with Satan over the body of Moses. John, the author of the New Testament book of Revelation, wrote prophetically of the final triumph of Michael and his angelic warriors against the army of the great dragon, Satan (Revelation 12:7–9). Clearly, God has given Michael an important role in protecting the people of Israel and assuring His plan will come to pass.

Over time, Michael took on a prominent role in the life of the church. By the fourth century, entire sanctuaries were dedicated to him. He was first venerated as a great healer but later evolved to a special patron and protector of the church. By the sixth century, devotion to Michael had spread throughout Christendom. Though some have overesteemed him, his role in the preservation of God's people is significant, and it will continue to be as the end of the age draws near.

War in Heaven between Michael and Satan

DANIEL 12:1; REVELATION 12:1-17

LOCATION

Heaven is the name for the realm where God and His angels dwell. They can see us, but humans are not able to move in and out of this dimension. One day, according to Revelation 21, the realms of heaven and earth will be united. Though hard to imagine, the Bible speaks of a war in heaven itself. Job 1 describes God allowing Satan into heaven so he can try to thwart His plans. In Zechariah 3, Satan is again seen in heaven, this time accusing the people of Israel like a prosecutor in a court of law.

KEY PLAYERS

- Michael: perhaps the highest of all angels since he is the only one referred to as "archangel" in the Bible. Michael has charge over the nation of Israel and leads God's armies against Satan's forces.
- The dragon: Satan, who is compared to a fire-breathing monster in the Bible and is known as the age-old accuser of God's people. This dragon is not a literal fiery beast but a creature whose character is murderous and whose power is fierce.

WEAPONS AND WARRIORS

Because the dragon will fight Michael, it appears as if Satan is bent on attacking the Jewish people, given that Michael is identified as Israel's protector (see Daniel 12:1). The dragon continually seeks to tempt God's children into rebellion. This is a spiritual battle, as are the weapons used: truth, deceit, fear, and faith (Ephesians 6:12–18). Though Satan was defeated at the cross (Colossians 2:15), a battle that can only be imagined was (or will be) fought in heaven among the angels.

Battle Synopsis

John saw a vision of the last great angelic war between the archangel Michael and God's angels on the one hand and the dragon (Satan) and his fallen angels or demons on the other.

In this vision, Satan is cast out of heaven forever, ending his mission of deception and accusation against God's children. There is great celebration in heaven. However, because Satan is enraged by the reality that his time is coming to an end, he intensifies his attacks on God's people on earth in the last days. He becomes "furious with the woman" and "makes war on the rest of her offspring" (Revelation 12:17). Some take this as a metaphor for the nation of Israel. Others see it as a reference to the new Israel, composed of both Jewish and Gentile followers of Jesus.

Archangel Michael and War with the Bad Angels
Leopold Kupelwieser (1796–1862)
© Renata Sedmakova / Shutterstock.com

Outcome

Short-Term

Satan's power and freedom will be seriously hindered and his access to heaven denied; during this horrible time the inhabitants of earth will suffer terribly.

Long-Term

God will deal with sin and its source once and for all. Satan will be forever bound, never able to tempt God's people again. This will usher in a new time when the children of God will dwell with Him in peace forever.

God's Role

Those who read Revelation will find great encouragement in the results of this battle. Even though it sometimes looks as though Satan is winning, especially as the book depicts a period of great suffering and tribulation, Satan already lost this battle at the cross. Jesus' death and resurrection defeated Satan and sin forever. Michael the archangel will cast Satan out of heaven to earth. God ultimately has power over Satan and will not allow him to stand in the way of the fulfillment of His redemptive plan.

Military Heroes and Villains: Satan

S atan, whose very name means "adversary," is a created angel who became arrogant in his beauty and high status. He appeared in Job, thought by many to be the oldest book in the Old Testament, presenting himself among the "sons of God," or angels, with devious intentions. Ultimately, Satan wanted to usurp God's throne. Though the context of Isaiah 14 pertains to the king of Babylon, it has traditionally been applied to Satan's rebellion and fall. Notice the number of prideful statements found in the passage:

You said in your heart,
  "*I will ascend* to heaven;
above the stars of God,
  I will set my throne on high;
I will sit on the mount of assembly
  in the far reaches of the north;
I will ascend above the heights of the clouds;
  I will make myself like the Most High." (Isaiah 14:13–14, emphasis added)

In the Old Testament, Satan (appearing in the form of a serpent) tempted Eve to eat from the tree that God said not to eat from (Genesis 3:1–6). Satan prompted David to count his people, violating God's command (1 Chronicles 21:1). He also stood at the right hand of the high priest Joshua "to accuse him" (Zechariah 3:1; Revelation 12:10). In the New Testament, Satan is called the "ruler of this world"

Satan before the Lord, Corrado Giaquinto (1703–1765)

(John 14:30) and the "prince of the power of the air" (Ephesians 2:2). According to Matthew and Luke, at the beginning of Jesus' ministry, Satan tested Him, trying to persuade Him to turn against God's plan (Matthew 4; Luke 4; see also Mark 1:13).

The entire Bible progressively reveals this great conflict between good and evil, of God versus Satan. Satan is the tempter behind every war, every sin, and every act of unrighteousness. Thankfully, the purpose for God making His remarkable and inexplicable entrance into the world in human flesh, as Jesus the Christ, was "to destroy the works of the devil" (1 John 3:8; see also Hebrews 2:14). Jesus defeated Satan with His death and resurrection; as a result, Satan is no longer allowed to reign over the hearts and lives of people who trust Jesus (Colossians 2).

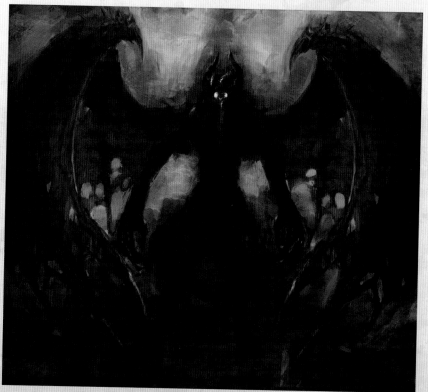

Armageddon
REVELATION 16:1-21

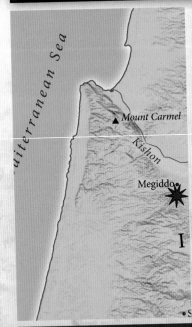

LOCATION

The Hebrew Armageddon (or Har Mageddon, meaning "the mountain of Megiddo") is the site of this battle. However, because there is no mountain called Megiddo in Israel, the exact location is unclear. Since "Har" in Hebrew can mean either mountain or hill, a candidate is the hill country surrounding the plain or valley of Megiddo. More than two hundred battles have been waged in this strategic area located about sixty miles north of Jerusalem. The valley of Megiddo is described in scripture as a place of mourning and despair (Zechariah 12:11). Megiddo was of great importance to the ancient world. It protected the western branch of a narrow pass and trade route that connected Egypt and Assyria.

KEY PLAYERS

- Satan: the anointed angel who desired to be like God and was subsequently cast out of heaven. His mission is to have authority over humans and be worshipped by them. He is also referred to as "the dragon."
- The beast: one who rises to power during the events depicted in Revelation; a liar and a deceiver; the antichrist, who denies both God the Father and God the Son (1 John 2:22)
- False prophet: the third party in an unholy trinity with the antichrist and Satan, who empowers them
- The kings of the whole world: kings and rulers opposed to the Messiah

WEAPONS AND WARRIORS

There are many divine "weapons" God uses to judge the earth. In this battle, one of these weapons is a giant earthquake, which kills a massive number of people and literally rearranges the entire landscape. Other weapons are one-hundred-pound hailstones that pummel the earth and decimate God's enemies.

Battle Synopsis

From the mouths of the dragon, the beast, and the false prophet, demons go out to the kings of the world (Revelation 16:13–14). These demons are spirits that perform miracles to entice God's enemies to gather for war against Him. The nations come against God in this battle (Psalm 2:2). The antichrist is seen leading a worldwide system against a soon-returning Jesus (Revelation 17:12–16; 19:19). Ready for war, an angel (the last of seven angels who pour out bowls of God's wrath) pours his bowl of wrath into the air, perhaps showing pronouncement against the "prince of the power of the air," or Satan (Ephesians 2:2). Simultaneously, a loud voice thunders from heaven, proclaiming, "It is done!" (Revelation 16:17). God will show mercy for as long as possible, but a time is coming when no more will be given.

Dragon rising from the magma

Outcome

Short-Term

At Armageddon, the antichrist and his followers are overthrown and defeated, and the nations' rebellion against God comes to an end.

Long-Term

Some see this battle ushering in a period of time known as the millennium, or the thousand-year reign of Christ, when Satan is bound and imprisoned. Others see it as a time when all rebellion ends and God begins the consummation of the ages.

God's Role

God is the central figure and clear victor in this battle. The fight is called "the great day of God" (Revelation 16:14)—not the great day of humankind, not the great day of the antichrist, and not the great day of the dragon.

Through this battle, God makes His name great and shows He is in control of all creation. He is the cause of the tremendous earthquake and hailstorm. This is in keeping with what God has promised elsewhere: "Once more I will shake not only the earth but also the heavens" (Hebrews 12:26).

However, what cannot be shaken—faith—will remain (1 Corinthians 13:13).

The Last Battle

LOCATION

Jerusalem, the place God chose for the dwelling place for His name (Deuteronomy 12:5; Ezra 6:12), appears to be the location of the last battle depicted in the Bible. The city of Jerusalem, which means "city of peace," is mentioned a thousand times throughout the Bible. Other names for Jerusalem include Ariel, city of God, city of David, Jebus, city of righteousness, city of the great King, holy city, faithful city, Salem, and Zion.

KEY PLAYERS

- Satan: the anointed angel who desired to be like God and was subsequently cast out of heaven. His mission is to have authority over humans and be worshipped by them. He is also referred to as "the dragon."
- Jesus: the commander and prince of the angelic armies, the victorious King of kings and Lord of lords. Jesus is God who became flesh and dwelt among humans, dying for the world's sins, saving people from the righteous judgment of God.

WEAPONS AND WARRIORS

Satan's warriors are the combined armies of the world standing with all the human strength and man-made weaponry they can muster against God.

BATTLE SYNOPSIS

In John's vision, Jesus triumphantly establishes His worldwide kingdom for a thousand years, after which Satan is released to organize people of the earth in another rebellion against God. Satan's army surrounds "the camp of the saints and the beloved city" (Revelation 20:9)—apparently a reference to Jerusalem—with what looks like a goal of laying siege to it and destroying Jesus. Yet a siege does not take place. In one moment, God wipes out His enemies with fire from heaven. Satan is cast into a lake of fire and sulfur, where the beast and the false prophet have been since the beginning of the thousand-year reign (Revelation 19:20).

Four Horsemen of the Apocalypse
Viktor Vasnetsov (1848–1926)

OUTCOME

SHORT-TERM

Satan, the beast, and the false prophet are judged and tormented forever. Everyone who has ever rebelled against God will stand already condemned before Him at the great white throne, where they will be judged and sentenced.

LONG-TERM

The new Jerusalem will descend from heaven. God will dwell with His people forever, and there will be no sorrow, no death or pain, no darkness or sin. The new creation will never be threatened by evil for the rest of eternity.

GOD'S ROLE

For followers of Jesus, this last battle is the culmination of everything promised in the Bible—a picture of ultimate hope. God will fight this decisive battle on behalf of His people, so that the victory may be complete and the glory may be His alone. He will make all things new. When the new heaven and the new earth are consummated, they will be without the presence of evil or even the potential for evil. God's people will live in His kingdom, walking intimately with Him the way Adam and Eve did in the garden. This will happen in the place designated by God: the new Jerusalem. God's promise of redemption, to reverse the curse placed on humanity for its rebellion and to restore perfect relationship with His people, will finally reach its fulfillment. And there will be peace.

"The chariots of God are twice ten thousand, thousands upon thousands; the Lord is among them; Sinai is now in the sanctuary" (Psalm 68:17).

Military Heroes and Villains: Jesus

> Then I saw in the right hand of him who was seated on the throne a scroll written within and on the back, sealed with seven seals. And I saw a mighty angel proclaiming with a loud voice, "Who is worthy to open the scroll and break its seals?" And no one in heaven or on earth or under the earth was able to open the scroll or to look into it, and I began to weep loudly because no one was found worthy to open the scroll or to look into it. And one of the elders said to me, "Weep no more; behold, the Lion of the tribe of Judah, the Root of David, has conquered, so that he can open the scroll and its seven seals."
> (Revelation 5:1–5)

In Revelation, John ascends to heaven, where he receives his vision of things to come, including the consummation of the age. John waits to see who is worthy to open the scroll and break its seals. He knows that Satan needs to be conquered, justice needs to be dispensed, and truth needs to prevail over Satan's accusations and deception. Is there anyone who can bring victory? Who is the one who is powerful enough and righteous enough to bring justice? The answer is *Jesus*.

Jesus is the Lion of the tribe of Judah, the One who has conquered. He is the anointed Messiah, a great political leader who descended from King David (Jeremiah 23:5), and a military leader who with His death and resurrection has already won the greatest battle of all time: the war against sin. Jesus is the Commander of the angelic armies, the "Lord of hosts." He is the only One with the authority to execute judgment on the earth. He will bring final victory over Satan, and His people will spend eternity with Him without ever having to fear evil or separation from God again.

Transfiguration of Christ
Raffaëlli (1850–1924)

BATTLES TO COME

Things to Think About

- If you were facing persecution from a wicked and oppressive government, how might the battles depicted in Revelation encourage you?

- What does it mean that Jesus is the One worthy to open the scroll?

- How does God bring about the final victory over Satan and his followers?

- How does God's future victory give you hope in your life today?

And I saw no temple in the city, for its temple is the Lord God the Almighty and the Lamb. And the city has no need of sun or moon to shine on it, for the glory of God gives it light, and its lamp is the Lamb. By its light will the nations walk, and the kings of the earth will bring their glory into it, and its gates will never be shut by day—and there will be no night there. (Revelation 21:22–25)

INDEX